VOICES OF FREEDOM

A Documentary History

Sixth Edition

Volume 1

VOICES OF FREEDOM

A Documentary History

Sixth Edition

EDITED BY

ERIC FONER

Volume 1

W.W. NORTON & COMPANY · NEW YORK · LONDON

W. W. Norton & Company has been independent since its founding in 1923, when William Warder Norton and Mary D. Herter Norton first published lectures delivered at the People's Institute, the adult education division of New York City's Cooper Union. The firm soon expanded its program beyond the Institute, publishing books by celebrated academics from America and abroad. By midcentury, the two major pillars of Norton's publishing program—trade books and college texts—were firmly established. In the 1950s, the Norton family transferred control of the company to its employees, and today—with a staff of four hundred and a comparable number of trade, college, and professional titles published each year—W. W. Norton & Company stands as the largest and oldest publishing house owned wholly by its employees.

Editor: Steve Forman
Production Manager: Sean Mintus
Composition: Westchester Publishing Services
Manufacturing: Maple Press
Book Design: Antonina Krass

Library of Congress Cataloging-in-Publication Data

Names: Foner, Eric, 1943- editor.
Title: Voices of freedom : a documentary history / edited by Eric Foner.
Description: Sixth edition. | New York : W.W. Norton & Company, [2020]
Identifiers: LCCN 2019021569 | ISBN 9780393696912 (pbk. : v. 1) |
    ISBN 9780393696929 (pbk. : v. 2)
Subjects: LCSH: United States—History—Sources. | United States—Politics
    and government—Sources.
Classification: LCC E173 .V645 2020 | DDC 973.—dc23 LC record available at
    https://lccn.loc.gov/2019021569

ISBN: 978-0-393-69691-2 (pbk.)

W. W. Norton & Company, Inc., 500 Fifth Avenue, New York, NY 10110
    wwnorton.com
W. W. Norton & Company Ltd., 15 Carlisle Street, London W1D 3BS

1 2 3 4 5 6 7 8 9 0

ERIC FONER is DeWitt Clinton Professor Emeritus of History at Columbia University, where he earned his B.A. and Ph.D. In his teaching and scholarship, he focuses on the Civil War and Reconstruction, slavery, and nineteenth-century America. Professor Foner's publications include *Free Soil, Free Labor, Free Men: The Ideology of the Republican Party Before the Civil War*; *Tom Paine and Revolutionary America*; *Politics and Ideology in the Age of the Civil War*; *Nothing but Freedom: Emancipation and Its Legacy*; *Reconstruction: American's Unfinished Revolution, 1863–1877*; *Freedom's Lawmakers: A Directory of Black Officeholders During Reconstruction*; *The Story of American Freedom*; *Who Owns History? Rethinking the Past in a Changing World*; and *Forever Free: The Story of Emancipation and Reconstruction*. His history of Reconstruction won the *Los Angeles Times* Book Award for History, the Bancroft Prize, and the Parkman Prize. He has served as president of the Organization of American Historians and the American Historical Association. In 2006 he received the Presidential Award for Outstanding Teaching from Columbia University. His most recent books are *The Fiery Trial: Abraham Lincoln and American Slavery*, winner of the Bancroft and Lincoln prizes and the Pulitzer Prize for History, *Gateway to Freedom: The Hidden History of the Underground Railroad*, winner of the New York Historical Society Book Prize, and *The Second Founding: How the Civil War and Reconstruction Remade the Constitution*.

Contents

3

Creating Anglo-America, 1660–1750

4

Slavery, Freedom, and the Struggle for Empire, to 1763

5

The American Revolution, 1763–1783

6

The Revolution Within

7

Founding a Nation, 1783–1791

8

Securing the Republic, 1791–1815

9

The Market Revolution, 1800–1840

10

Democracy in America, 1815–1840

11

The Peculiar Institution

12

An Age of Reform, 1820–1840

13

A House Divided, 1840–1861

14

A New Birth of Freedom: The Civil War, 1861–1865

15

"What Is Freedom?": Reconstruction, 1865–1877

Preface

Voices of Freedom is a documentary history of American freedom from the earliest days of European exploration and settlement of the Western Hemisphere to the present. I have prepared it as a companion volume to *Give Me Liberty!*, my survey textbook of the history of the United States centered on the theme of freedom. This sixth edition of *Voices of Freedom* is organized in chapters that correspond to those in the sixth edition of the textbook. But it can also stand independently as a documentary introduction to the history of American freedom. The two volumes include more than twenty documents not available in the fifth edition.

No idea is more fundamental to Americans' sense of themselves as individuals and as a nation than freedom, or liberty, with which it is almost always used interchangeably. The Declaration of Independence lists liberty among mankind's inalienable rights; the Constitution announces as its purpose to secure liberty's blessings. "Every man in the street, white, black, red or yellow," wrote the educator and statesman Ralph Bunche in 1940, "knows that this is 'the land of the free'... 'the cradle of liberty.'"

The very universality of the idea of freedom, however, can be misleading. Freedom is not a fixed, timeless category with a single unchanging definition. Rather, the history of the United States is, in part, a story of debates, disagreements, and struggles over freedom. Crises like the American Revolution, the Civil War, and the Cold

War have permanently transformed the idea of freedom. So too have demands by various groups of Americans for greater freedom as they understood it.

In choosing the documents for *Voices of Freedom*, I have attempted to convey the multifaceted history of this compelling and contested idea. The documents reflect how Americans at different points in our history have defined freedom as an overarching idea, or have understood some of its many dimensions, including political, religious, economic, and personal freedom. For each chapter, I have tried to select documents that highlight the specific discussions of freedom that occurred during that time period, and some of the divergent interpretations of freedom at each point in our history. I hope that students will gain an appreciation of how the idea of freedom has expanded over time, and how it has been extended into more and more areas of Americans' lives. But at the same time, the documents suggest how freedom for some Americans has, at various times in our history, rested on lack of freedom—for example, slavery, indentured servitude, the subordinate position of women—for others.

The documents that follow reflect the kinds of historical developments that have shaped and reshaped the idea of freedom, including war, economic change, territorial expansion, social protest movements, and international involvement. The selections try to convey a sense of the rich cast of characters who have contributed to the history of American freedom. They include presidential proclamations and letters by runaway slaves, famous court cases and obscure manifestos, ideas dominant in a particular era and those of radicals and dissenters. They range from advertisements in colonial newspapers seeking the return of runaway indentured servants and slaves to debates in the early twentieth century over the definition of economic freedom, the controversy over the proposed Equal Rights Amendment for women, and recent Supreme Court decisions dealing with the right of gay Americans to marry one another.

I have been particularly attentive to how battles at the boundaries of freedom—the efforts of racial minorities, women, and others to secure greater freedom—have deepened and transformed the concept and extended it into new realms. In addition, in this sixth edition I have included a number of new documents that illustrate how the very definition of American identity—answers to the question "Who is an American?"—have affected the evolution of the idea of freedom. These include Benjamin Franklin's argument in 1751 for restricting immigration to English men and women; J. Hector St. John de Crèvecoeur's observations at the time of the War of Independence on the emergence of the American, a "new man," from the diverse peoples of European descent in the new nation; Frederick Douglass's remarkable "Composite Nation" speech soon after the Civil War; Randolph Bourne's 1916 essay "Trans-National America"; and historian Oscar Handlin's critique of the law adopted in 1924 that severely restricted immigration from southern and eastern Europe.

All of the documents in this collection are "primary sources"— that is, they were written or spoken by men and women enmeshed in the events of the past, rather than by later historians. They therefore offer students the opportunity to encounter ideas about freedom in the actual words of participants in the drama of American history. Some of the documents are reproduced in their entirety. Most are excerpts from longer interviews, articles, or books. In editing the documents, I have tried to remain faithful to the original purpose of the author, while highlighting the portion of a text that deals directly with one or another aspect of freedom. In most cases, I have reproduced the wording of the original texts exactly. But I have modernized the spelling and punctuation of some early documents to make them more understandable to the modern reader. Each document is preceded by a brief introduction that places it in historical context and is followed by two questions that highlight key elements of the argument and may help to focus students' thinking about the issues raised by the author.

A number of these documents were suggested by students in a U.S. history class at Juniata College in Huntingdon, Pennsylvania, taught by Professor David Hsiung. I am very grateful to these students, who responded enthusiastically to an assignment by Professor Hsiung that asked them to locate documents that might be included in *Voices of Freedom* and to justify their choices with historical arguments. Some of the documents are included in the online exhibition "Preserving American Freedom" created by the Historical Society of Pennsylvania.

Taken together, the documents in these volumes suggest the ways in which American freedom has changed and expanded over time. But they also remind us that American history is not simply a narrative of continual progress toward greater and greater freedom. While freedom can be achieved, it may also be reduced or rescinded. It can never be taken for granted.

Eric Foner

VOICES OF FREEDOM

A Documentary History

Sixth Edition

Volume 1

CHAPTER 1

A New World

1. Adam Smith, The Results of Colonization (1776)

Source: Adam Smith, An Inquiry into the Nature and Causes of the Wealth of Nations *(London, 1776), vol. 2, pp. 190–91, 235–37.*

"The discovery of America," the Scottish writer Adam Smith announced in his celebrated work *The Wealth of Nations*, published in 1776, was one of "the two greatest and most important events recorded in the history of mankind." Smith is regarded as the founder of modern economics. It is not surprising that looking back nearly three centuries after the initial voyage of Christopher Columbus in 1492, Smith focused primarily on the economic results of the conquest and colonization of North and South America. The influx of goods from the New World, he insisted, greatly increased the "enjoyments" of the people of Europe and the market for European goods. Nonetheless, Smith did not fail to note the price paid by the indigenous population of the New World, who suffered a dramatic decline in population due to epidemics, wars of conquest, and the exploitation of their labor. "Benefits" for some, Smith observed, went hand in hand with "dreadful misfortunes" for others—a fitting commentary on the long encounter between the Old and New Worlds.

━━━━━━━

OF THE ADVANTAGES which Europe has derived from the Discovery of America, and from that of a Passage to the East Indies by the Cape of Good Hope

What are [the advantages] which Europe has derived from the discovery and colonization of America?

The general advantages which Europe, considered as one great country, has derived from the discovery and colonization of America, consist, first, in the increase of its enjoyments; and, secondly, in the augmentation of its industry.

The surplus produce of America, imported into Europe, furnishes the inhabitants of this great continent with a variety of commodities which they could not otherwise have possessed; some for conveniency and use, some for pleasure, and some for ornament, and thereby contributes to increase their enjoyments.

The discovery and colonization of America, it will readily be allowed, have contributed to augment the industry, first, of all the countries which trade to it directly, such as Spain, Portugal, France, and England; and, secondly, of all those which, without trading to it directly, send, through the medium of other countries, goods to it of their own produce; such as Austrian Flanders, and some provinces of Germany, which, through the medium of the countries before mentioned, send to it a considerable quantity of linen and other goods. All such countries have evidently gained a more extensive market for their surplus produce, and must consequently have been encouraged to increase its quantity....

• • •

The discovery of America, and that of a passage to the East Indies by the Cape of Good Hope, are the two greatest and most important events recorded in the history of mankind. Their consequences have already been very great; but, in the short period of between two and three centuries which has elapsed since these discoveries were made, it is impossible that the whole extent of their consequences can have been seen. What benefits or what misfortunes to mankind may hereafter result from those great events, no human wisdom can foresee. By uniting, in some measure, the most distant parts of the world, by enabling them to relieve one another's wants, to increase one another's enjoyments, and to encourage one another's industry, their general tendency would seem to be beneficial. To the natives however, both of the East and West Indies, all the commercial benefits which can have resulted from those events have been sunk and lost in the dreadful misfortunes which they have occasioned....

• • •

In the meantime one of the principal effects of those discoveries has been to raise the mercantile system to a degree of splendour and glory which it could never otherwise have attained to. It is the object of that system to enrich a great nation rather by trade and manufactures than by the improvement and cultivation of land, rather by the industry of the towns than by that of the country. But, in consequence of those discoveries, the commercial towns of Europe, instead of being the manufacturers and carriers for but a very small part of the world (that part of Europe which is washed by the Atlantic Ocean, and the countries which lie round the Baltic and Mediterranean seas), have now become the manufacturers for the numerous and thriving cultivators of America, and the carriers and in some respects the manufacturers too, for almost all the different nations of Asia, Africa, and America. Two new worlds have been opened to their industry, each of them much greater and more extensive than the old one, and the market of one of them growing still greater and greater every day.

Questions

1. According to Adam Smith, how did the "discovery and colonization" of America affect the economic development of Europe?

2. Why does Smith believe that the "benefits" of colonization outweigh the "misfortunes"?

2. Giovanni da Verrazano, Encountering Native Americans (1524)

Source: Giovanni da Verrazano, from The Voyages of Giovanni da Verrazano, *1524–1528, Lawrence C. Wroth, ed., Susan Tarrow, trans. (1970), pp. 133–34, 137–38, 140–43. Copyright © 1970 by Yale University Press. Reprinted by permission of Yale University Press.*

One of the first European explorers to encounter the Indians of eastern North America, Giovanni da Verrazano was an Italian-born navigator who sailed in 1524 under the auspices of King Philip I of France. His voyage took him from modern-day Cape Fear, North Carolina, north to the coast of Maine. In the following excerpt from his diary, which he included in a letter to the king, Verrazano tries to describe the appearance, economic life, customs, and beliefs of some of the region's various Native American groups. Some, he reports, were friendly and generous; others warlike and hostile. He is particularly interested in their spiritual beliefs, concluding that they have "no religion." Verrazano found the east coast thickly populated. By the time English settlement began in the early seventeenth century, many of the groups he encountered had been all but destroyed by epidemic diseases.

———

SINCE THE STORM that we encountered in the northern regions, Most Serene King, I have not written to tell your majesty of what happened to the four ships which you sent over the Ocean to explore new lands, as I thought you had already been informed of everything—how we were forced by the fury of the winds to return in distress to Brittany with only the *Normandy* and the *Dauphine*, and that after undergoing repairs there, began our voyage with these two ships, equipped for war, following the coasts of Spain, Your Most Serene Majesty will have heard; and then according to our new plan, we continued the original voyage with only the *Dauphine*; now on our return from this voyage I will tell Your Majesty of what we found....

Seeing that the land continued to the south, we decided to turn and skirt it toward the north, where we found the land we had sighted earlier. So we anchored off the coast and sent the small boat in to land. We had seen many people coming to the seashore, but they fled when they saw us approaching; several times they stopped and turned around to look at us in great wonderment. We reassured them with various signs, and some of them came up, showing great delight at seeing us and marveling at our clothes, appearance, and our whiteness; they showed us by various signs where we could most easily secure the boat, and offered us some of their food. We were on land, and I shall now tell Your Majesty briefly what we were able to learn of their life and customs.

They go completely naked except that around their loins they wear skins of small animals like martens, with a narrow belt of grass around the body, to which they tie various rails of other animals which hang down to the knees; the rest of the body is bare, and so is the head. Some of them wear garlands of birds' feathers. They are dark in color, not unlike the Ethiopians, with thick black hair, not very long, tied back behind the head like a small tail. As for the physique of these men, they are well proportioned, of medium height, a little taller than we are. They have broad chests, strong arms, and the legs and other parts of the body are well composed. There is nothing else, except that they tend to be rather broad in the face; but not all, for we saw many with angular faces. They have big black eyes, and an attentive and open look. They are not very strong, but they have a sharp cunning, and are agile and swift runners. From what we could tell from observation, in the last two respects they resemble the Orientals. . . .

We reached another land 15 leagues from the island, where we found an excellent harbor; before entering it, we saw about 20 boats full of people who came around the ship uttering various cries of wonderment. They did not come nearer than fifty paces, but stopped to look at the structure of our ship, our persons, and our clothes; then all together they raised a loud cry which meant that they were joyful. We reassured them somewhat by imitating their gestures, and they came near enough for us to throw them a few little bells and mirrors and many trinkets, which they took and looked at, laughing, and then they confidently came on board ship. . . . These people are the most beautiful and have the most civil customs that we have found on this voyage. They are taller than we are; they are a bronze color, some tending more toward whiteness, others to a tawny color; the face is clear-cut; the hair is long and black, and they take great pains to decorate it; the eyes are black and alert, and their manner is sweet and gentle, very like the manner of the ancients. . . .

Their women are just as shapely and beautiful; very gracious, of attractive manner and pleasant appearance; their customs and behavior follow womanly custom as far as befits human nature; they go nude except for stag skin embroidered like the men's, and some wear rich lynx skins on their arms; their bare heads are decorated with various ornaments made of braids of their own hair which hang down over their breasts on either side. . . . Both men and women have various trinkets hanging from their ears as the Orientals do; and we saw that many had sheets of worked copper which they prize more than gold. They do not value gold because of its color; they think it the most worthless of all, and rate blue and red above all other colors. The things we gave them that they prized the most were little bells, blue crystals, and other trinkets to put in the ear or around the neck. They did not appreciate cloth of silk and gold, nor even of any other kind, nor did they care to have them; the same was true for metals like steel and iron, for many times when we showed them some of our arms, they did not admire them, nor ask for them, but merely examined the workmanship. They did the same with mirrors; they would look at them quickly, and then refuse them, laughing.

They are very generous and give away all they have. We made great friends with them, and one day before we entered the harbor with the ship, when we were lying at anchor one league out to sea because of unfavorable weather, they came out to the ship with a great number of their boats; they had painted and decorated their faces with various colors, showing us that it was a sign of happiness. They brought us some of their food, and showed us by signs where we should anchor in the port for the ship's safety, and then accompanied us all the way until we dropped anchor. . . .

At a distance of fifty leagues, keeping more to the north, we found high country full of very dense forests, composed of pines, cypresses, and similar trees which grow in cold regions.

The people were quite different from the others, for while the previous ones had been courteous in manner, these were full of crudity and vices, and were so barbarous that we could never make any communication with them, however many signs we made to them. They were clothed in skins of bear, lynx, sea-wolf and other animals. As far as we could judge from several visits to their houses, we think they live on game, fish, and several fruits which are a species of root which the earth produces itself. . . . We saw no sign of cultivation, nor would the land be suitable for producing any fruit or grain on account of its sterility. If we wanted to trade with them for some of their things, they would come to the seashore on some rocks where the breakers were most violent, while we remained in the little boat, and they sent us what they wanted to give on a rope, continually shouting at us not to approach the land; they gave us the barter quickly, and would take in exchange only knives, hooks for fishing and sharp metal. We found no courtesy in them, and when we had nothing more to exchange and left them, the men made all the signs of scorn and shame that any brute creature would make. Against their wishes, we penetrated two or three leagues inland with 25 armed men, and when we disembarked on the shore, they shot at us with their bows and uttered loud cries before fleeing into the woods. . . .

Due to a lack of [a common] language, we were unable to find out by signs or gestures how much religious faith these people we found possess. We think they have neither religion nor laws, that they do not know of a First Cause or Author, that they do not worship the sky, the stars, the sun, the moon, or other planets, nor do they even practice any kind of idolatry; we do not know whether they offer any sacrifices or other prayers, nor are there any temples or churches of prayer among their peoples. We consider that they have no religion and that they live in absolute freedom, and that everything they do proceeds from Ignorance; for they are very easily persuaded, and they imitated everything that they saw us Christians do with regard to divine worship, with the same fervor and enthusiasm that we had.

Questions

1. How much do Verrazano's observations seem to be affected by his own beliefs and experiences?

2. Why does he write that Indians live in "absolute freedom," and why does he consider this a criticism rather than a compliment?

3. Bartolomé de las Casas on Spanish Treatment of the Indians, from *History of the Indies* (1528)

Source: Bartolomé de las Casas, "History of the Indies (1528)," excerpt from History of the Indies, *trans. and ed. Andrée M. Collard (New York: Harper and Row, 1971), pp. 82, 112–15. Copyright © 1971 by Andrée Collard, renewed 1999 by Joyce J. Contrucci. Reprinted by permission of Joyce Contrucci.*

Known as the "Apostle of the Indians," Bartolomé de las Casas, a Catholic priest, was the most eloquent critic of Spanish mistreatment of the New World's native population. Las Casas took part in the exploitation of Indian labor on Hispaniola and Cuba. But in 1514, he freed his Indian slaves and began to preach against the injustices of Spanish rule. In his *History of the Indies*, Las Casas denounced Spain for causing the deaths of millions of innocent people. The excerpt that follows details events on

Hispaniola, the Caribbean island first conquered and settled by Spain. Las Casas called for the Indians to enjoy the rights of other subjects of Spain.

Largely because of Las Casas's efforts, in 1542 Spain promulgated the New Laws, ordering that Indians no longer be enslaved. But Spain's European rivals seized upon Las Casas's criticisms to justify their own ambitions. His writings became the basis for the Black Legend, the image of Spain as a uniquely cruel empire. Other nations would claim that their imperial ventures were inspired by the desire to rescue Indians from Spanish rule.

—————

IN THAT YEAR of 1500, . . . the King determined to send a new governor to Hispaniola, which at the time was the only seat of government in the Indies. The new governor was fray Nicolás de Ovando, Knight of Alcántara, and at that time comendador of Lares.

• • •

At first, the Indians were forced to stay six months away at work; later, the time was extended to eight months and this was called a shift, at the end of which they brought all the gold for minting. The King's part was subtracted and the rest went to individuals, but for years no one kept a single peso because they owed it all to merchants and other creditors, so that the anguish and torments endured by the Indians in mining that infernal gold were consumed entirely by God and no one prospered. During the minting period, the Indians were allowed to go home, a few days' journey on foot. One can imagine their state when they arrived after eight months, and those who found their wives there must have cried, lamenting their condition together. How could they even rest, since they had to provide for the needs of their family when their land had gone to weeds? Of those who had worked in the mines, a bare 10 per cent survived to start the journey home. Many Spaniards had no scruples about making them work on Sundays and holidays, if not in the mines then on minor tasks such as building and repairing houses, carrying firewood, etc. They fed them cassava bread, which is adequate nutrition only when supplemented with meat, fish or other more substantial food. The minero killed a pig once a week but he kept more than half for himself and had the leftover apportioned and cooked daily for thirty or forty Indians, which came to a bite of meat the size of a walnut per individual, and they dipped the cassava in this as well as in the broth.

• • •

The comendador arranged to have wages paid as follows, which I swear is the truth: in exchange for his life of services, an Indian received 3 *maravedís* every two days, less one-half a *maravedí* in order not to exceed the yearly half gold peso, that is, 225 *maravedís*, paid them once a year as pin money or *cacona*, as Indians call it, which means bonus or reward. This sum bought a comb, a small mirror and a string of green or blue glass beads, and many did without that consolation for they were paid much less and had no way of mitigating their misery, although in truth, they offered their labor up for nothing, caring only to fill their stomachs to appease their raging hunger and find ways to escape from their desperate lives. For this loss of body and soul, then, they received less than 3 *maravedís* for two days; many years later their wages were increased to 1 gold peso by the order of King Hernando, and this was no less an affront, as I will show later.

I believe the above clearly demonstrates that the Indians were totally deprived of their freedom and were put in the harshest, fiercest, most horrible servitude and captivity which no one who has not seen it can understand. Even beasts enjoy more freedom when they are allowed to graze in the fields. But our Spaniards gave no such opportunity to Indians and truly considered them perpetual slaves, since the Indians had not the free will to dispose of their persons but instead were disposed of according to Spanish greed and cruelty, not as men in captivity but as beasts tied to a rope to prevent free movement. When they were allowed to go home, they often found it deserted and had no other recourse than to go out into the woods to find food and to die. When they fell ill, which was very frequently because they are a delicate people unaccustomed to such work, the Spaniards did not believe them and pitilessly called them lazy dogs, and kicked and beat them; and when illness was apparent they sent them home as useless, giving them some cassava for the twenty- to eighty-league journey. They would go then, falling into the first stream and dying there in desperation; others would hold on longer but very few ever made it home. I sometimes came upon dead bodies on my way, and upon others who were gasping and moaning in their death agony, repeating "Hungry, hungry." And this was the freedom, the good treatment and the Christianity that Indians received.

• • •

About eight years passed under the comendador's rule and this disorder had time to grow; no one gave it a thought and the multitude of people who originally lived on this island...was consumed at such a rate that in those eight years 90 per cent had perished. From here this sweeping plague went to San Juan, Jamaica, Cuba and the continent, spreading destruction over the whole hemisphere.

• • •

Questions

1. What do you think Las Casas hoped to accomplish by writing so critically about Spanish treatment of the Indians?

2. Why, after describing illness and starvation among the Indians, does Las Casas write, "This was the freedom, the good treatment and the Christianity that Indians received"?

---

4. The Pueblo Revolt (1680)

Source: Charles W. Hackett, "Declarations of Josephe and Pedro Naranjo," in Revolt of the Pueblo Indians of New Mexico and Otermín's Attempted Reconquest 1680–1682, vol. 2, pp. 238–48, 1942. Reprinted with permission of the University of New Mexico Press.

In 1680, the Pueblo Indians of modern-day New Mexico revolted against Spanish rule. During the seventeenth century, governors, settlers, and missionaries had sought to exploit the labor of an Indian population that declined from about 60,000 in 1600 to some 17,000 eighty years later. Franciscan friars worked diligently, often violently, to convert Indians to Catholicism. Some natives accepted baptism. But the friars' efforts to stamp out traditional religious ceremonies in New Mexico—they burned Indian idols, masks, and other sacred objects—alienated far more Indians than they converted. Under the leadership of Popé, a local religious leader, the rebelling Indians killed 400 colonists, including twenty-one Franciscan missionaries. The Pueblo Revolt was the most complete victory for Native Americans over Europeans and the only wholesale expulsion of settlers in the history of North America. The uprising, concluded a royal attorney who interviewed survivors in Mexico City, arose from the "many oppressions" the Indians had suffered. In 1692, the Spanish launched an invasion that reconquered New Mexico.

DECLARATION OF JOSEPHE, SPANISH-SPEAKING INDIAN.
[PLACE OF THE RIO DEL NORTE, DECEMBER 19, 1681.]

Asked what causes or motives the said Indian rebels had for renouncing the law of God and obedience to his Majesty, and for committing so many kinds of crimes, and who were the instigators of the rebellion, and what he had heard while he was among the apostates, he said that the prime movers of the rebellion were two Indians of San Juan, one named El Popé and the other El Taqu, and another from Taos named Saca, and another from San Ildefonso named Francisco. He knows that these were the principals, and the causes they gave were alleged ill treatment and injuries received from the present secretary, Francisco Xavier, and the maestre de campo, Alonso García, and from the sargentos mayores, Luis de Quintana and Diego López, because they beat them, took away what they had, and made them work without pay. Thus he replies.

Asked if he has learned or it has come to his notice during the time that he has been here the reason why the apostates burned the images, churches, and things pertaining to divine worship, making a mockery and a trophy of them, killing the priests and doing the other things they did, he said that he knows and has heard it generally stated that while they were besieging the villa the rebellious traitors burned the church and shouted in loud voices, "Now the God of the Spaniards, who was their father, is dead, and Santa Maria, who was their mother, and the saints, who were pieces of rotten wood," saying that only their own god lived. Thus they ordered all the temples and images, crosses and rosaries burned, and this function being over, they all went to bathe in the rivers, saying that they thereby washed away the water of baptism. For their churches, they placed on the four sides and in the center of the plaza some small circular enclosures of stone where they went to offer flour, feathers, and the seed of maguey, maize, and tobacco, and performed other superstitious rites, giving the children to understand that they must all do this in the future. The captains and chiefs ordered that the names of Jesus and of Mary should nowhere be uttered, and that they should discard their baptismal names, and abandon the wives whom God had given them in matrimony, and take the ones that they pleased. He saw that as soon as the remaining Spaniards had left, they ordered all the estufas erected, which are their houses of idolatry, and danced throughout the kingdom the dance of the cazina, making many masks for it in the image of the devil. Thus he replied to this question....

Asked if he knows, or whether it has come to his notice, that the said apostates have erected houses of idolatry which they call estufas in the pueblos, and have practiced dances and superstitions, he said there is a general report throughout the kingdom that they have done so and he has seen many houses of idolatry which they have built, dancing the dance of the cachina, which this declarant has also danced. Thus he replied to the question.

Declaration of Pedro Naranjo of the Queres Nation.
[Place of the Río del Norte, December 19, 1681.]

Asked for what reason they so blindly burned the images, temples, crosses, and other things of divine worship, he stated that the said

Indian, Popé, came down in person, and with him El Saca and El
Chato from the pueblo of Los Taos, and other captains and leaders
and many people who were in his train, and he ordered in all the
pueblos through which he passed that they instantly break up
and burn the images of the holy Christ, the Virgin Mary and the
other saints, the crosses, and everything pertaining to Christianity, and that they burn the temples, break up the bells, and separate from the wives whom God had given them in marriage and
take those whom they desired. In order to take away their baptismal names, the water, and the holy oils, they were to plunge into
the rivers and wash themselves with amole, which is a root native
to the country, washing even their clothing, with the understanding that there would thus be taken from them the character
of the holy sacraments. They did this, and also many other things
which he does not recall, given to understand that this mandate
had come from the Caydi and the other two who emitted fire from
their extremities in the said estufa of Taos, and that they thereby
returned to the state of their antiquity, as when they came from
the lake of Copala; that this was the better life and the one they
desired, because the God of the Spaniards was worth nothing and
theirs was very strong, the Spaniards' God being rotten wood.
These things were observed and obeyed by all except some who,
moved by the zeal of Christians, opposed it, and such persons the
said Popé caused to be killed immediately. He saw to it that they
at once erected and rebuilt their houses of idolatry which they
call estufas, and made very ugly masks in imitation of the devil
in order to dance the dance of the cacina; and he said likewise
that the devil had given them to understand that living thus in
accordance with the law of their ancestors, they would harvest a
great deal of maize, many beans, a great abundance of cotton, cal-
abashes, and very large watermelons and cantaloupes; and that
they could erect their houses and enjoy abundant health and
leisure.

Questions

1. What actions did Indians take during the Pueblo Revolt to demonstrate their new freedom from Spanish rule?

2. Why do you think religion played such a large role in the Pueblo Revolt?

---

5. Father Jean de Brébeuf on the Customs and Beliefs of the Hurons (1635)

Source: Reuben G. Thwaites, ed., **The Jesuit Relations and Allied Documents: Travels and Explorations of the Jesuit Missionaries in New France, 1610–1791** *(Cleveland, 1896–1901), vol. 12, pp. 117–24.*

The viability of New France, with its small white population and emphasis on the fur trade rather than agricultural settlement, depended on friendly relations with local Indians. The French neither appropriated substantial amounts of Indian land like the English nor conquered native inhabitants militarily and set them to forced labor, as in Spanish America. The Jesuits, a missionary religious order, sought to convert Indians to Catholicism. One of the Jesuit missionaries to the Huron people in modern-day Quebec, Jean de Brébeuf, left a vivid description of the lives and customs of the Indians. In the following excerpt, he dwells upon their religious beliefs, marriage customs, and gender relations—all aspects of Indian life that seemed very alien to Europeans—and describes how he tried to convert them. De Brébeuf was killed after being captured during a war between Hurons and Iroquois in 1649.

It REMAINS NOW to say something of the country, of the manners and customs of the Hurons, of the inclination they have to the Faith, and of our insignificant labors.

As to the first, the little paper and leisure we have compels me to say in a few words what might justly fill a volume. The Huron country is not large, its greatest extent can be traversed in three or four days. Its situation is fine, the greater part of it consisting of plains. It is surrounded and intersected by a number of very beautiful lakes or rather seas, whence it comes that the one to the North and to the Northwest is called "fresh-water sea" [Lake Huron]. . . . There are twenty Towns, which indicate about 30,000 souls speaking the same tongue, which is not difficult to one who has a master. It has distinctions of genders, number, tense, person, moods; and, in short, it is very complete and very regular, contrary to the opinion of many. . . .

It is so evident that there is a Divinity who has made Heaven and earth that our Hurons cannot entirely ignore it. But they misapprehend him grossly. For they have neither Temples, nor Priests, nor Feasts, nor any ceremonies.

They say that a certain woman called *Eataensic* is the one who made earth and man. They give her an assistant, one named *Jouskeha*, whom they declare to be her little son, with whom she governs the world. This *Jouskeha* has care of the living, and of the things that concern life, and consequently they say that he is good. *Eataensic* has care of souls; and, because they believe that she makes men die, they say that she is wicked. And there are among them mysteries so hidden that only the old men, who can speak with authority about them, are believed.

This God and Goddess live like themselves, but without famine; make feasts as they do, are lustful as they are; in short, they imagine them exactly like themselves. And still, though they make them human and corporeal, they seem nevertheless to attribute to them a certain immensity in all places.

They say that this *Eataensic* fell from the Sky, where there are inhabitants as on earth, and when she fell, she was with child. If you ask them who made the sky and its inhabitants, they have no other reply than that they know nothing about it. And when we preach to them of one God, Creator of Heaven and earth, and of all things, and even when we talk to them of Hell and Paradise and of our other mysteries, the headstrong reply that this is good for our Country and not for theirs; that every Country has its own fashions. But having pointed out to them, by means of a little globe that we had brought, that there is only one world, they remain without reply.

I find in their marriage customs two things that greatly please me; the first, that they have only one wife; the second, that they do not marry their relatives in a direct or collateral line, however distant they may be. There is, on the other hand, sufficient to censure, were it only the frequent changes the men make of their wives, and the women of their husbands.

They believe in the immortality of the soul, which they believe to be corporeal. The greatest part of their Religion consists of this point. We have seen several stripped, or almost so, of all their goods, because several of their friends were dead, to whose souls they had made presents. Moreover, dogs, fish, deer, and other animals have, in their opinion, immortal and reasonable souls. In proof of this, the old men relate certain fables, which they represent as true; they make no mention either of punishment or reward, in the place to which souls go after death. And so they do not make any distinction between the good and the bad, the virtuous and the vicious; and they honor equally the interment of both, even as we have seen in the case of a young man who poisoned himself from the grief he felt because his wife had been taken away from him. Their superstitions are infinite, their feast, their medicines, their fishing, their hunting, their wars,—in short almost their whole life turns upon this pivot; dreams, above all have here great credit.

As regards morals, the Hurons are lascivious, although in two leading points less so than many Christians, who will blush some day in their presence. You will see no kissing nor immodest caressing; and in marriage a man will remain two or three years apart from his wife, while she is nursing. They are gluttons, even to disgorging; it is true, that does not happen often, but only in some superstitious feasts,—these, however, they do not attend willingly. Besides they endure hunger much better than we,—so well that after having fasted two or three entire days you will see them still paddling, carrying loads, singing, laughing, bantering, as if they had dined well. They are very lazy, are liars, thieves, pertinacious beggars. Some consider them vindictive; but, in my opinion, this vice is more noticeable elsewhere than here.

We see shining among them some rather noble moral virtues. You note, in the first place, a great love and union, which they are careful to cultivate by means of their marriages, of their presents, of their feasts, and of their frequent visits. On returning from their fishing, their hunting, and their trading, they exchange many gifts; if they have thus obtained something unusually good, even if they have bought it, or if it has been given to them, they make a feast to the whole village with it. Their hospitality towards all sorts of strangers is remarkable; they present to them, in their feasts, the best of what they have prepared, and, as I have already said, I do not know if anything similar, in this regard, is to be found anywhere. They never close the door upon a Stranger, and, once having received him into their houses, they share with him the best they have; they never send him away, and when he goes away of his own accord, he repays them by a simple "thank you."

• • •

About the month of December, the snow began to lie on the ground, and the savages settled down into the village. For, during the whole Summer and Autumn, they are for the most part either in their rural cabins, taking care of their crops, or on the lake fishing, or trading; which makes it not a little inconvenient to instruct them. Seeing them, therefore, thus gathered together at the beginning of this year, we resolved to preach publicly to all, and to acquaint them with the reason of our coming into their Country, which is not for their furs, but to declare to them the true God and his son, Jesus Christ, the universal Saviour of our souls.

The usual method that we follow is this: We call together the people by the help of the Captain of the village, who assembles them all in our house as in Council, or perhaps by the sound of the bell. I use the surplice and the square cap, to give more majesty to my appearance. At the beginning we chant on our knees the *Pater noster*, translated into Huron verse. Father Daniel, as its author, chants a couplet alone, and then we all together chant it again; and those among the Hurons, principally the little ones, who already know it, take pleasure in chanting it with us. That done, when every one is seated, I rise and make the sign of the Cross for all; then, having recapitulated what I said last time, I explain something new. After that we question the young children and the girls, giving a little bead of glass or porcelain to those who deserve it. The parents are very glad to see their children answer well and carry off some little prize, of which they render themselves worthy by the care they take to come privately to get instruction. On our part, to arouse their emulation, we have each lesson retraced by our two little French boys, who question each other,—which transports the Savages with admiration. Finally the whole is concluded by the talk of the Old Men, who propound their difficulties, and sometimes make me listen in my turn to the statement of their belief.

Two things among others have aided us very much in the little we have been able to do here, by the grace of our Lord; the first is, as I have already said, the good health that God has granted us in the midst of sickness so general and so widespread. The second is the temporal assistance we have rendered to the sick. Having brought for ourselves some few delicacies, we shared them with them, giving to one a few prunes, and to another a few raisins, to others something else. The poor people came from great distances to get their share.

Questions

1. Which aspects of Indian practices and beliefs does de Brébeuf find admirable and which does he criticize most strongly?

2. How do Huron gender and family relations seem to differ from those of Europeans?

6. Jewish Petition to the Dutch West India Company (1655)

Source: Samuel Oppenheim, "The Early History of the Jews in New York City, 1654–1664," in Publications of the American Jewish Historical Society *(1909), pp. 9–11.*

Among European colonies in the seventeenth century, New Netherland was noted for religious toleration, although its rulers made a careful distinction between private worship in a home, which was allowed, and public worship, which was confined to the established Dutch Reformed church. In 1655, a group of Jews arrived from Brazil, from which they had been expelled after the Portuguese wrested control of the colony from the Dutch. When Governor Petrus Stuyvesant ordered them to leave, Jews in Amsterdam asked the Dutch West India Company to reverse the decision. The company granted the request, so long as the newcomers did not become a public "charge"—that is, require financial assistance.

—————

To the Honorable Lords, Directors of the Chartered West India Company, Chamber of the City of Amsterdam.

The merchants of the Portuguese Nation residing in this City respectfully remonstrate to your Honors that it has come to their knowledge that your Honors raise obstacles to the giving of permits or passports to the Portuguese Jews to travel and to go to reside in New Netherland, which if persisted in will result to the great disadvantage of the Jewish nation. It also can be of no advantage to the general Company but rather damaging.

There are many of the nation who have lost their possessions at Pernambuco [Brazil] and have arrived from there in great poverty, and part of them have been dispersed here and there. So that your petitioners had to expend large sums of money for their necessaries of life, and through lack of opportunity all cannot remain here to live. And as they cannot go to Spain or Portugal because of the

Inquisition, a great part of the aforesaid people must in time be obliged to depart for other territories of their High Mightinesses the States-General and their Companies, in order there, through their labor and efforts, to be able to exist under the protection of the administrators of your Honorable Directors, observing and obeying your Honors' orders and commands.

It is well known to your Honors that the Jewish nation in Brazil have at all times been faithful and have striven to guard and maintain that place, risking for that purpose their possessions and their blood.

Yonder land is extensive and spacious. The more of loyal people that go to live there, the better it is in regard to the population of the country as in regard to the payment of various excises and taxes which may be imposed there, and in regard to the increase of trade, and also to the importation of all the necessaries that may be sent there.

Your Honors should also consider that the Honorable Lords, the Burgomasters of the City and the Honorable High Illustrious Mighty Lords, the States-General, have in political matters always protected and considered the Jewish nation as upon the same footing as all the inhabitants and burghers. Also it is conditioned in the treaty of perpetual peace with the King of Spain that the Jewish nation shall also enjoy the same liberty as all other inhabitants of these lands.

Your Honors should also please consider that many of the Jewish nation are principal shareholders in the Company. They having always striven their best for the Company, and many of their nation have lost immense and great capital in its shares and obligations.

The Company has by a general resolution consented that those who wish to populate the Colony shall enjoy certain districts of land gratis. Why should now certain subjects of this State not be allowed to travel thither and live there? The French consent that the Portuguese Jews may traffic and live in Martinique, Christopher and others of their territories, whither also some have gone from here, as your

Honors know. The English also consent at the present time that the Portuguese and Jewish nation may go from London and settle at Barbados, whither also some have gone.

As foreign nations consent that the Jewish nation may go to live and trade in their territories, how can your Honors forbid the same and refuse transportation to this Portuguese nation who reside here and have been settled here well on to about sixty years, many also being born here and confirmed burghers, and this to a land that needs people for its increase?

Therefore the petitioners request, for the reasons given above (as also others which they omit to avoid prolixity), that your Honors be pleased not to exclude but to grant the Jewish nation passage to and residence in that country; otherwise this would result in a great prejudice to their reputation. Also that by an Apostille and Act the Jewish nation be permitted, together with other inhabitants, to travel, live and traffic there, and with them enjoy liberty on condition of contributing like others, &c.

Questions

1. What does the petition tell us about the extent of religious toleration in the seventeenth century?

2. How do the petitioners argue that allowing Jews to settle will benefit New Netherland?

CHAPTER 2

Beginnings of English America, 1607–1660

7. Exchange between John Smith and Powhatan (1608)

Source: John Smith, The Generall Historie of Virginia . . . *(London, 1624), pp. 74–76.*

When English colonists arrived in Virginia in 1607, they landed in an area inhabited by more than 15,000 Indians, members of some thirty tribes loosely united in a confederacy whose leader the settlers called Powhatan, the native word for both his tribe and the title of paramount chief. In a history written in 1624, the English leader John Smith recalled his exchange with Powhatan sixteen years earlier. Of course, Powhatan's words are filtered through Smith's memory. But the exchange seems to capture differences in outlook between the two leaders.

───────

THE 12 OF JANUARY we arrived at Werowocomoco.... Quartering in the next houses we found, we sent to Powhatan for provision, who sent us plenty of bread, turkeys, and venison; the next day having feasted us after his ordinary manner, he began to ask us when we would be gone, saying he sent not for us, neither had he any corn; and his people much less, yet for forty swords he would procure us forty baskets.... The King concluded the matter with a merry laughter, asking for our commodities, but none he liked without guns and swords, valuing a basket of corn more precious than a basket of copper, saying he would rate his corn, but not the copper.

Captain Smith seeing the intent of this subtle savage began to deal with him after this manner.

Powhatan, though I had many courses to have made my provision, yet believing your promises to supply my wants, I neglected all to satisfy your desire, and to testify my life, I sent you my men for your building, neglecting my own. What your people had you have engrossed, forbidding them our trade, and now you think by consuming the time, we shall consume for want, not having to fulfill your strange demands. As for swords and guns, I told you long ago I had none to spare, and you must know those I have can keep me from want, yet steal or wrong you I will not, nor dissolve that friendship we have mutually promised, except you constrain me by our bad usage.

The King having attentively listened to this discourse, promised that both he and his country would spare him what he could, which within two days they should receive. Yet Captain Smith, said the King, some doubt I have of your coming hither, that makes me not so kindly seek to relieve you as I would, for many do inform me, your coming hither is not for trade, but to invade my people, and possess my country, who dare not come to bring you corn, seeing you thus armed with your men. To free us of this fear, leave abroad your weapons, for here they are useless, we being all friends, and for ever Powhatan's. . . .

While we expected the coming in of the country, we wrangled out of the King ten quarters of corn for a copper kettle. . . . Wherewith each seemed well contented, and Powhatan began to expostulate the difference of Peace and War after this manner.

Captain Smith, you may understand that I having seen the death of all my people thrice, and not any one living of these three generations but myself, I know the difference of Peace and War better than any in my country. But now I am old and ere long must die, my brethren, namely Opichapam, Opechancanough, and Kekataugh, my two sisters, and their two daughters, are distinctly each others successors. I wish their experience no less than mine, and your love to them no less than mine to you. But this [rumor] that you are come to destroy my country, so much frightens all my people as they dare not visit you. What will it avail you to take that by force you may quickly have by love, or to destroy them that provide you food? What can you get by war, when we can hide our provisions and fly to the woods, whereby you must famish by wronging us your friends. And why are you thus jealous of our loves seeing us unarmed, and both do and are willing still to feed you, with that you cannot get but by our laborers? Think you I am so simple, not to know it is better to eat good meat, lie well, and sleep quietly with my women and children, laugh and be merry with you, have copper, hatchets, or what I want being your friend, than be forced to fly from all, to lie cold in the woods, feed upon acorns, roots, and such trash, and be so hunted by you, that I can neither rest, eat, nor sleep, but my tired men must watch, and if a twig but break, every one cries there comes Captain Smith. Then I must fly I know not where, and thus with miserable fear, end my miserable life, leaving my pleasures to such youths as you. . . . Let this therefore assure you of our love, and every year our friendly trade shall furnish you with corn, and now also, if you would come in friendly manner to see us, and not this with your guns and swords as to invade your foes.

To this subtle discourse, [Smith] replied.

Seeing you will not rightly conceive of our words, we strive to make you know our thoughts by our deeds; the vow I made you of my love, both myself and my men have kept. As for your promise I find it every day violated by some of your subjects, yet we finding your love and kindness, our custom is so far from being ungrateful, that for your sake only we have curbed our thirsting desire of revenge, else had they known as well the cruelty we use to our enemies, as our true love and courtesy to our friends. And I think your judgment suffi- cient to conceive, as well by the adventures we have undertaken, as by the advantage we have (by our arms) of yours, that had we intended you any hurt, long ere this we could have effected it.

Questions

1. What goods does each leader seek from the other?

2. How does the exchange illuminate some of the roots of conflict between settlers and Indians?

---

8. Sending Women to Virginia (1622)

Source: Susan Myra Kingsbury, ed., **The Records of the Virginia Company of London** *(Washington, D.C., 1906–35), vol. 1, pp. 256–57.*

Early Virginia lacked one essential element of English society—stable family life. Given the demand for male servants to work in the tobacco fields, for most of the seventeenth century men in the Chesapeake outnumbered women by four or five to one. The Virginia Company avidly promoted the immigration of women, sending "tobacco brides" to the colony in 1620 and 1621 for arranged marriages (so-called because the husband was ordered to give a payment in tobacco to his wife). The company preferred that the women marry only free, independent colonists. Unlike these women, however, the vast majority of women who emigrated to the region in the seventeenth century came as indentured servants. Since they usually had to complete their terms of service before marrying, they did not begin to form families until their mid-twenties. Virginia remained for many years a society with large numbers of single men, widows, and orphans rather than the family-oriented community the company desired.

WE SEND YOU in this ship one widow and eleven maids for wives for the people in Virginia. There hath been especial care had in the choice of them; for there hath not any one of them been received but upon good commendations, as by a note herewith sent you may perceive. We pray you all therefore in general to take them into your care; and more especially we recommend them to you Master Pountis, that at their first landing they may be housed, lodged and provided for of diet till they be married, for such was the haste of sending them away, as that straitened with time we had no means to put provisions aboard, which defect shall be supplied by the magazine ship. And in case they cannot be presently married, we desire they may be put to several householders that have wives till they can be provided of husbands. There are near fifty more which are shortly to come, are sent by our most honorable Lord and Treasurer the Earl of Southampton and certain worthy gentlemen, who taking into their consideration that the Plantation can never flourish till families be planted and the respect of wives and children fix the people on the soil, therefore have given this fair beginning, for the reimbursing of whose charges it is ordered that every man that marries them give 120 lbs. weight of the best leaf tobacco for each of them, and in case any of them die, that proportion must be advanced to make it up upon those that survive.... And though we are desirous that marriage be free according to the law of nature, yet would we not have these maids deceived and married to servants, but only to freemen or tenants as have means to maintain them. We pray you therefore to be fathers to them in this business, not enforcing them to marry against their wills; neither send we them to be servants, save in case of extremity, for we would have their condition so much bettered as multitudes may be allured thereby to come unto you. And you may assure such men as marry those women that the first servants sent over by the Company shall be consigned to them, it being our intent to preserve families and to prefer married men before single persons.

Questions

1. What advantages does the Virginia Company see in the promotion of family life in the colony?

2. Why does the company prefer that the women marry landowning men rather than servants?

---

9. Henry Care, English Liberties (1680)

Source: Henry Care, English Liberties: Or, The Free-Born Subject's Inheritance *(London, 1680), pp. 1–5.*

The political battles of the seventeenth century ended with England enjoying a "mixed" or "balanced" constitutional system in which the king continued to rule, but his power was restrained by that of Parliament and by the rule of law. In 1680, in his book, *English Liberties: Or, The Free-Born Subject's Inheritance,* the writer Henry Care contrasted the government of England with democracy on the one hand and unrestrained monarchy on the other, as represented by France and other European countries. He described English government as "qualified monarchy," and called it the best political structure in the world.

Care was hardly egalitarian in outlook. He wrote of a society composed of "superior" and "inferior" classes. But he insisted that the essence of English liberty was that all citizens were "guarded in their persons and property by the fence of law," and could not be subjected to imprisonment or loss of property without being tried before a jury of their peers. By the 1680s, it had become a commonplace that England was the freest nation on earth. Care claimed that the English were freer and happier than any other people. The belief in freedom as the common heritage of all Englishmen and their empire as the world's guardian of liberty would help to legitimize English colonization in the Western Hemisphere and to cast its imperial wars against Catholic France and Spain as struggles between freedom and tyranny.

THE CONSTITUTION OF our English government (the best in the world) is no arbitrary tyranny like the Turkish Grand Seignior's, or the French King's, whose wills (or rather lusts) dispose of the lives and fortunes of their unhappy subjects; nor an Oligarchy where the great men (like fish in the ocean) prey upon, and live by devouring the lesser at their pleasure. Nor yet a Democracy or popular state, much less an Anarchy, where all confusedly are hail fellows well met. But a most excellently mixed or qualified Monarchy, where the King is vested with large prerogatives sufficient to support majesty; and restrained only from power of doing himself and his people harm, which would be contrary to the end of all government ... the nobility adorned with privileges to be a screen to majesty, and a refreshing shade to their inferiors, and the commonality, too, so guarded in their persons and properties by the fence of law, [which] renders them Freemen, not Slaves.

In France and other nations the mere will of the prince is law, his word takes off any man's head, imposes taxes, or seizes any man's estate, when, how, and as often as he [wishes], and if one be accused or but so much suspected of any crime, he may either presently execute him, or banish or imprison him at pleasure.... Nay if there be no witnesses, yet he may be put to the rack, the tortures thereof make an innocent person confess himself guilty....

But in England, the law is both the measure and the bond of every subject's duty and allegiance, each man having a fixed fundamental right born with him as to the freedom of his person and property in his estate, which he cannot be deprived of, but either by his consent, or some crime for which the law has imposed such a penalty as forfeiture....

This original happy frame of government is truly and properly called an Englishman's liberty, a privilege not to [be] exempt from the law, but to be freed in person and estate, from arbitrary violence and oppression.... And this birthright of Englishmen shines most conspicuously in two things: Parliaments [and] juries.

By the first, the subject has a share by his chosen representatives in the legislative (or law-making) power, for no new laws bind the people of England, but such as are by common consent agreed on in that great council.

By the second, he has a share in the executive part of the law, no causes being tried, nor any man adjudged to lose life ... or estate but upon the verdict of his peers (or equals).... These two grand pillars of English liberty, are the fundamental vital privileges, whereby we have been and are preserved more free and happy than any other people in the world.

Questions

1. Why does Henry Care consider the English system of government "the best in the world"?

2. How does Care define "an Englishman's liberty"?

10. John Winthrop, Speech to the Massachusetts General Court (1645)

Source: John Winthrop, Speech to the General Court of Massachusetts, July 3, 1645, in James Savage, The History of New England from 1630 to 1649 by John Winthrop *(Boston, 1825–26), vol. 2, pp. 279–82.*

The early settlers of New England were mainly Puritans, English Protestants who believed that the Church of England in the early seventeenth century retained too many elements of Catholicism. Like other emigrants to America, Puritans came in search of liberty, especially the right to worship and govern themselves in what they deemed a Christian manner. Freedom for Puritans had nothing to do with either religious toleration or unrestrained individual behavior. In a 1645 speech to the Massachusetts legislature explaining the Puritan conception of freedom, Governor John

Winthrop distinguished sharply between two kinds of liberty. "Natural" liberty, or acting without restraint, suggested "a liberty to [do] evil." "Moral" liberty meant "a liberty to [do] that only which is good." It meant obedience to religious and governmental authority—following God's law and the law of rulers like Winthrop himself.

Winthrop's distinction between "moral" and "natural" liberty has been invoked many times by religious groups who feared that Americans were becoming selfish and immoral and who tried to impose their moral standards on society as a whole.

• • •

THE GREAT QUESTIONS that have troubled the country, are about the authority of the magistrates and the liberty of the people. It is yourselves who have called us to this office, and being called by you, we have our authority from God, in way of an ordinance, such as hath the image of God eminently stamped upon it, the contempt and violation whereof hath been vindicated with examples of divine vengeance. I entreat you to consider, that when you choose magistrates, you take them from among yourselves, men subject to like passions as you are. Therefore when you see infirmities in us, you should reflect upon your own, and that would make you bear the more with us, and not be severe censurers of the failings of your magistrates, when you have continual experience of the like infirmities in yourselves and others. We account him a good servant, who breaks not his covenant. The covenant between you and us is the oath you have taken of us, which is to this purpose, that we shall govern you and judge your causes by the rules of God's laws and our own, according to our best skill. When you agree with a workman to build you a ship or house, etc., he undertakes as well for his skill as for his faithfulness, for it is his profession, and you pay him for both. But when you call one to be a magistrate, he doth not profess nor undertake to have sufficient skill for that office, nor can you furnish him with gifts, etc., therefore you must run the hazard of his skill and ability. But if he fail in faithfulness, which by his oath he is bound unto, that he must answer for. If it fall out that the case be clear to common apprehension, and the rule clear also, if he transgress here, the error is not in the skill, but in the evil of the will: it must be required of him. But if the case be doubtful, or the rule doubtful, to men of such understanding and parts as your magistrates are, if your magistrates should err here, yourselves must bear it.

For the other point concerning liberty, I observe a great mistake in the country about that. There is a twofold liberty, natural (I mean as our nature is now corrupt) and civil or federal. The first is common to man with beasts and other creatures. By this, man, as he stands in relation to man simply, hath liberty to do what he lists; it is a liberty to evil as well as to good. This liberty is incompatible and inconsistent with authority, and cannot endure the least restraint of the most just authority. The exercise and maintaining of this liberty makes men grow more evil, and in time to be worse than brute beasts.... This is that great enemy of truth and peace, that wild beast, which all the ordinances of God are bent against, to restrain and subdue it. The other kind of liberty I call civil or federal, it may also be termed moral, in reference to the covenant between God and man, in the moral law, and the politic covenants and constitutions, amongst men themselves. This liberty is the proper end and object of authority, and cannot subsist without it; and it is a liberty to that only which is good, just, and honest. This liberty you are to stand for, with the hazard (not only of your goods, but) of your lives, if need be. Whatsoever crosseth this, is not authority, but a distemper thereof. This liberty is maintained and exercised in a way of subjection to authority; it is of the same kind of liberty wherewith Christ hath made us free. The woman's own choice makes such a man her husband; yet being so chosen, he is her lord, and she is to be subject to him, yet in a way of liberty, not of bondage; and a true wife accounts her subjection her honor and freedom, and would not think her condition safe and free, but in her subjection to her husband's authority. Such is the liberty of the church under the authority of Christ, her king and husband; his yoke is so easy and sweet to her as a bride's ornaments; and if through forwardness or wantonness, etc., she shake it off, at any time, she is at no rest in her spirit, until she take it up again; and whether her lord smiles upon her, and embraceth her in his arms, or whether he frowns, or rebukes, or smites her, she apprehends the sweetness of his love in all, and is refreshed, supported, and instructed by every such dispensation of his authority over her. On the other side, ye know who they are that complain of this yoke and say, let us break their bands, etc., we will not have this man to rule over us. Even so, brethren, it will be between you and your magistrates. If you stand for your natural corrupt liberties, and will do what is good in your own eyes, you will not endure the least weight of authority, but will murmur, and oppose, and be always striving to shake off that yoke; but if you will be satisfied to enjoy such civil and lawful liberties, such as Christ allows you, then will you quietly and cheerfully submit unto that authority which is set over you, in all the administrations of it, for your good. Wherein, if we fail at anytime, we hope we shall be willing (by God's assistance) to hearken to good advice from any of you, or in any other way of God; so shall your liberties be preserved, in upholding the honor and power of authority amongst you.

Questions

1. Why does Winthrop use an analogy to the status of women within the family to explain his understanding of liberty?

2. Why does Winthrop consider "natural" liberty dangerous?

---

11. The Trial of Anne Hutchinson (1637)

Source: Thomas Hutchinson, The History of the Colony and Province of Massachusetts-Bay: Volume II, *edited by Lawrence Shaw Mayo, Cambridge, Mass.: Harvard University Press, Copyright © 1936 by the President and*

A midwife and the daughter of a clergyman, Anne Hutchinson arrived in Massachusetts with her husband in 1634. She began holding meetings in her home where she led discussions of religious issues. Hutchinson charged that most of the ministers in Massachusetts were guilty of faulty preaching by distinguishing "saints" predestined to go to Heaven from the damned through activities such as church attendance and moral behavior rather than by an inner state of grace.

In 1637, Hutchinson was placed on trial before a civil court for sedition (expressing opinions dangerous to authority). Hutchinson's examination by John Winthrop and deputy governor Thomas Dudley, excerpted below, is a classic example of the collision between established power and individual conscience. For a time, Hutchinson more than held her own. But when she spoke of divine revelations, of God speaking to her directly rather than through ministers or the Bible, she violated Puritan doctrine and sealed her own fate. Hutchinson and a number of her followers were banished.

Trial at the Court at Newton. 1637

GOV. JOHN WINTHROP: Mrs. Hutchinson, you are called here as one of those that have troubled the peace of the commonwealth and the churches here; you are known to be a woman that hath had a great share in the promoting and divulging of those opinions that are the cause of this trouble, and to be nearly joined not only in affinity and affection with some of those the court had taken notice of and passed censure upon, but you have spoken divers things, as we have been informed, very prejudicial to the honour of the churches and ministers thereof, and you have maintained a meeting and an assembly in your house that hath been condemned by the general assembly as a thing not tolerable nor comely in the sight of God nor fitting for your sex, and notwithstanding that was cried down you have continued the same. Therefore we have thought good to send for you to understand how things are, that if you be in an erroneous way we may reduce you that so you may become a profitable member here among us. Otherwise if you be obstinate in your course that then the court may take such course that you may trouble us no further. Therefore I would intreat you to express whether you do assent and hold in practice to those opinions and factions that have been handled in court already, that is to say, whether you do not justify Mr. Wheelwright's sermon and the petition.

MRS. ANNE HUTCHINSON: I am called here to answer before you but I hear no things laid to my charge.

GOV. JOHN WINTHROP: I have told you some already and more I can tell you.

MRS. ANNE HUTCHINSON: Name one, Sir.

GOV. JOHN WINTHROP: Have I not named some already?

MRS. ANNE HUTCHINSON: What have I said or done?

GOV. JOHN WINTHROP: Why for your doings, this you did harbor and countenance those that are parties in this faction that you have heard of.

MRS. ANNE HUTCHINSON: That's matter of conscience, Sir.

GOV. JOHN WINTHROP: Your conscience you must keep, or it must be kept for you.

MRS. ANNE HUTCHINSON: Must not I then entertain the saints because I must keep my conscience.

GOV. JOHN WINTHROP: Say that one brother should commit felony or treason and come to his brother's house, if he knows him guilty and conceals him he is guilty of the same. It is his conscience to entertain him, but if his conscience comes into act in giving countenance and entertainment to him that hath broken the law he is guilty too. So if you do countenance those that are transgressors of the law you are in the same fact.

MRS. ANNE HUTCHINSON: What law do they transgress?

GOV. JOHN WINTHROP: The law of God and of the state.

MRS. ANNE HUTCHINSON: In what particular?

GOV. JOHN WINTHROP: Why in this among the rest, whereas the Lord doth say honour thy father and thy mother.

MRS. ANNE HUTCHINSON: Ey Sir in the Lord.

GOV. JOHN WINTHROP: This honour you have broke in giving countenance to them.

MRS. ANNE HUTCHINSON: In entertaining those did I entertain them against any act (for there is the thing) or what God has appointed?

GOV. JOHN WINTHROP: You knew that Mr. Wheelwright did preach this sermon and those that countenance him in this do break a law.

MRS. ANNE HUTCHINSON: What law have I broken?

GOV. JOHN WINTHROP: Why the fifth commandment.

MRS. ANNE HUTCHINSON: I deny that for he (Mr. Wheelwright) saith in the Lord.

GOV. JOHN WINTHROP: You have joined with them in the faction.

MRS. ANNE HUTCHINSON: In what faction have I joined with them?

GOV. JOHN WINTHROP: In presenting the petition.

MRS. ANNE HUTCHINSON: Suppose I had set my hand to the petition. What then?

GOV. JOHN WINTHROP: You saw that case tried before.

MRS. ANNE HUTCHINSON: But I had not my hand to (not signed) the petition.

GOV. JOHN WINTHROP: You have councelled them.

MRS. ANNE HUTCHINSON: Wherein?

GOV. JOHN WINTHROP: Why in entertaining them.

MRS. ANNE HUTCHINSON: What breach of law is that, Sir?

GOV. JOHN WINTHROP: Why dishonouring the commonwealth, Mrs. Hutchinson.

MRS. ANNE HUTCHINSON: But put the case, Sir, that I do fear the Lord and my parents. May not I entertain them that fear the Lord because my parents will not give me leave?

GOV. JOHN WINTHROP: If they be the fathers of the commonwealth, and they of another religion, if you entertain them then you dishonour your parents and are justly punishable.

MRS. ANNE HUTCHINSON: If I entertain them, as they have dishonoured their parents I do.

GOV. JOHN WINTHROP: No but you by countenancing them above others put honor upon them.

MRS. ANNE HUTCHINSON: I may put honor upon them as the children of God and as they do honor the Lord.

GOV. JOHN WINTHROP: We do not mean to discourse with those of your sex but only this: you so adhere unto them and do endeavor to set forward this faction and so you do dishonour us.

MRS. ANNE HUTCHINSON: I do acknowledge no such thing. Neither do I think that I ever put any dishonour upon you.

• • •

GOV. JOHN WINTHROP: Your course is not to be suffered for. Besides that we find such a course as this to be greatly prejudicial to the state. Besides the occasion that it is to seduce many honest persons that are called to those meetings and your opinions being known to be different from the word of God may seduce many simple souls that resort unto you. Besides that the occasion which hath come of late hath come from none but such as have frequented your meetings, so that now they are flown off from magistrates and ministers and since they have come to you. And besides that it will not well stand with the commonwealth that families should be neglected for so many neighbors and dames and so much time spent. We see no rule of God for this. We see not that any should have authority to set up any other exercises besides what authority hath already set up and so what hurt comes of this you will be guilty of and we for suffering you.

MRS. ANNE HUTCHINSON: Sir, I do not believe that to be so.

GOV. JOHN WINTHROP: Well, we see how it is. We must therefore put it away from you or restrain you from maintaining this course.

MRS. ANNE HUTCHINSON: If you have a rule for it from God's word you may.

GOV. JOHN WINTHROP: We are your judges, and not you ours and we must compel you to it.

MRS. ANNE HUTCHINSON: If it please you by authority to put it down I will freely let you for I am subject to your authority. . . .

• • •

DEPUTY GOV. THOMAS DUDLEY: I would go a little higher with Mrs. Hutchinson. About three years ago we were all in peace. Mrs. Hutchinson, from that time she came hath made a disturbance, and some that came over with her in the ship did inform me what she was as soon as she was landed. I being then in place dealt with the pastor and teacher of Boston and desired them to enquire of her, and then I was satisfied that she held nothing different from us. But within half a year after, she had vented divers of her strange opinions and had made parties in the country, and at length it comes that Mr. Cotton and Mr. Vane were of her judgment, but Mr. Cotton had cleared himself that he was not of that mind.

• • •

But now it appears by this woman's meeting that Mrs. Hutchinson hath so forestalled the minds of many by their resort to her meeting that now she hath a potent party in the country. Now if all these things have endangered us as from that foundation and if she in particular hath disparaged all our ministers in the land that they have preached a covenant of works, and only Mr. Cotton a covenant of grace, why this is not to be suffered, and therefore being driven to the foundation and it being found that Mrs. Hutchinson is she that hath depraved all the ministers and hath been the cause of what is fallen out, why we must take away the foundation and the building will fall.

MRS. ANNE HUTCHINSON: I pray, Sir, prove it that I said they preached nothing but a covenant of works.

DEP. GOV. THOMAS DUDLEY: Nothing but a covenant of works. Why a Jesuit may preach truth sometimes.

MRS. ANNE HUTCHINSON: Did I ever say they preached a covenant of works then?

DEP. GOV. THOMAS DUDLEY: If they do not preach a covenant of grace clearly, then they preach a covenant of works.

MRS. ANNE HUTCHINSON: No, Sir. One may preach a covenant of grace more clearly than another, so I said....

DEP. GOV. THOMAS DUDLEY: When they do preach a covenant of works do they preach truth?

MRS. ANNE HUTCHINSON: Yes, Sir. But when they preach a covenant of works for salvation, that is not truth.

DEP. GOV. THOMAS DUDLEY: Ask you this: when the ministers do preach a covenant of works do they preach a way of salvation?

MRS. ANNE HUTCHINSON: I did not come hither to answer questions of that sort.

DEP. GOV. THOMAS DUDLEY: Because you will deny the thing.

MRS. ANNE HUTCHINSON: Ey, but that is to be proved first.

DEP. GOV. THOMAS DUDLEY: I will make it plain that you did say that the ministers did preach a covenant of works.

MRS. ANNE HUTCHINSON: I deny that.

DEP. GOV. THOMAS DUDLEY: And that you said they were not able ministers of the New Testament, but Mr. Cotton only.

MRS. ANNE HUTCHINSON: If ever I spake that I proved it by God's word.

• • •

MRS. ANNE HUTCHINSON: If you please to give me leave I shall give round of what I know to be true. Being much troubled to see the falseness of the constitution of the Church of England, I had like to have turned Separatist. Whereupon I kept a day of solemn humiliation and pondering of the thing; this scripture was brought unto me—he that denies Jesus Christ to be come in the flesh is antichrist. This I considered of and in considering found that the papists did not deny him to be come in the flesh, nor we did not deny him— who then was antichrist? Was the Turk antichrist only? The Lord knows that I could not open scripture; he must by his prophetical office open it unto me. So after that being unsatisfied in the thing, the Lord was pleased to bring this scripture out of the Hebrews.

He that denies the testament denies the testator, and in this did open unto me and give me to see that those which did not teach the new covenant had the spirit of antichrist, and upon this he did discover the ministry unto me; and ever since, I bless the Lord, he hath let me see which was the clear ministry and which the wrong.

Since that time I confess I have been more choice and he hath left me to distinguish between the voice of my beloved and the voice of Moses, the voice of John the Baptist and the voice of antichrist, for all those voices are spoken of in scripture. Now if you do condemn me for speaking what in my conscience I know to be truth I must commit myself unto the Lord.

MR. NOWEL (ASSISTANT TO THE COURT): How do you know that was the spirit?

MRS. ANNE HUTCHINSON: How did Abraham know that it was God that bid him offer his son, being a breach of the sixth commandment?

DEP. GOV. THOMAS DUDLEY: By an immediate voice.

MRS. ANNE HUTCHINSON: So to me by an immediate revelation.

DEP. GOV. THOMAS DUDLEY: How! an immediate revelation.

• • •

GOV. JOHN WINTHROP: Mrs. Hutchinson, the sentence of the court you hear is that you are banished from out of our jurisdiction as being a woman not fit for our society, and are to be imprisoned till the court shall send you away.

Questions

1. What seem to be the major charges against Anne Hutchinson?

2. What does the Hutchinson case tell us about how Puritan authorities understood the idea of religious freedom?

12. Roger Williams, Letter to the Town of Providence (1655)

Source: Perry Miller and Thomas H. Johnson, eds., The Puritans *(2 vols.: New York, 1963), vol. 1, p. 225.*

Roger Williams, the son of a London merchant, studied at Cambridge University and emigrated to New England in 1631. He is considered one of the founders of the principle of religious toleration. Williams was banished from the Massachusetts Bay Colony after preaching that the colonists must not occupy Indian land without first purchasing it, and that the government had no right to punish individuals for their religious beliefs. He went on to found the community of Providence, Rhode Island. After traveling to England and returning to Providence in 1654, he found it torn by dissension, with some settlers refusing to accept civil authority at all. Williams published the following letter, explaining his view of the extent and limits of liberty. He made it clear that while no one should be forced to follow any particular religious belief, this did not lessen the requirement that all members of a community must obey the "masters and officers" in charge of civil matters.

THAT EVER I SHOULD SPEAK or write a tittle, that tends to ... an infinite liberty of conscience, is a mistake, and which I have ever disclaimed and abhorred. To prevent such mistakes, I shall at present only propose this case: There goes many a ship to sea, with many hundred souls in one ship, whose weal or woe is common, and is a true picture of a commonwealth, or a human combination or society. It hath fallen out sometimes, that both papists and Protestants, Jews and Turks [Muslims], may be embarked in one ship; upon which supposal I affirm, that all the liberty of conscience, that ever I pleaded for, turns upon these two hinges—that none of the papists, Protestants, Jews, or Turks, be forced to come to the ship's prayers or worship, nor compelled from their own particular prayers or worship, if they practice any. I further add, that I never denied, that notwithstanding this liberty, the commander of this ship ought to command the ship's course, yea, and also command that justice, peace and sobriety, be kept and practiced, both among the seamen and all the passengers. If any of the seamen refuse to perform their services, or passengers to pay their freight; if any refuse to help, in person or purse, towards the common charges or defense; if any refuse to obey the common laws and orders of the ship, concerning their common peace or preservation; if any shall mutiny and rise up against their commanders and officers; if any should preach or write that there ought to be no commanders or officers, because all are equal in Christ, therefore no masters nor officers, no laws nor orders, nor corrections nor punishments;—I say, I never denied, but in such cases, whatever is pretended, the commander or commanders may judge, resist, compel and punish such transgressors, according to their deserts and merits. This if seriously and honestly minded, may, if it so please the Father of lights, let in some light to such as willingly shut not their eyes.

ROGER WILLIAMS

Questions

1. In what ways does Williams place limits on liberty?

2. What are the strengths and weaknesses of Williams's analogy between civil society and a group of people aboard a ship?

---

13. The Levellers, The Agreement of the People Presented to the Council of the Army (1647)

Source: **The Agreement of the People Presented to the Council of the Army** *(London, 1647).*

During the 1640s, the battle for political supremacy in England between the Stuart monarchs James I and Charles I and Parliament culminated in civil war, the temporary overthrow of the monarchy, and, in 1649, the execution of Charles I. This struggle produced an intense public debate over the concept of English freedom. In 1647, the Levellers, history's first democratic political movement, proposed a written constitution, the Agreement of the People, which began by proclaiming "at how high a rate we value our just freedom." At a time when "democracy" was still widely seen as the equivalent of anarchy and disorder, the document proposed to abolish the monarchy and House of Lords and greatly expand the right to vote. It called for religious freedom and equality before the law for all Englishmen.

The Levellers were soon suppressed. But the Agreement of the People offered a glimpse of the modern, democratic definition of freedom as a universal entitlement in a society based on equal rights, rather than the traditional idea of "liberties" as a collection of limited rights defined by social class, with some groups enjoying far more than others.

———

AN AGREEMENT OF the People for a firm and present peace upon grounds of common right.

Having by our late labors and hazards made it appear to the world at how high a rate we value our just freedom, and God having so far owned our cause as to deliver the enemies thereof into our hands, we do now hold ourselves bound in mutual duty to each other to take the best care we can for the future to avoid both the danger of returning into a slavish condition and the chargeable remedy of another war; for, as it cannot be imagined that so many of our countrymen would have opposed us in this quarrel if they had understood their own good, so may we safely promise to ourselves that, when our common rights and liberties shall be cleared, their endeavors will be disappointed that seek to make themselves our masters. Since, therefore, our former oppressions and scarce-yet-ended troubles have been occasioned, either by want of frequent national meetings in Council, or by rendering those meetings ineffectual, we are fully agreed and resolved to provide that hereafter our representatives be neither left to an uncertainty for the time nor made useless to the ends for which they are intended. In order whereunto we declare:

I

That the people of England, being at this day very unequally distributed by Counties, Cities and Boroughs for the election of their deputies
in Parliament, ought to be more indifferently proportioned, according to the number of the inhabitants; the circumstances whereof for
number, place, and manner are to be set down before the end of this
present Parliament.

II

That, to prevent the many inconveniences apparently arising from
the long continuance of the same persons in authority, this present
Parliament be dissolved upon the last day of September which shall
be in the year of our Lord 1648.

III

That the people do, of course, choose themselves a Parliament once
in two years, viz. upon the first Thursday in every second March,
after the manner as shall be prescribed before the end of this Parliament, to begin to sit upon the first Thursday in April following, at
Westminster or such other place as shall be appointed from time to
time by the preceding Representatives, and to continue till the last
day of September then next ensuing, and no longer.

IV

That the power of this, and all future Representatives of this Nation,
is inferior only to theirs who choose them, and doth extend, without the consent or concurrence of any other person or persons, to the
enacting, altering, and repealing of laws; to the erecting and abolishing of offices and courts; to the appointing, removing, and calling to account magistrates and officers of all degrees; to the making

war and peace; to the treating with foreign states; and, generally, to whatsoever is not expressly or impliedly reserved by the represented to themselves:

Which are as followeth,

1. That matters of religion and the ways of God's worship are not at all entrusted by us to any human power, because therein we cannot remit or exceed a title of what our consciences dictate to be the mind of God, without wilful sin; nevertheless the public way of instructing the nation (so it be not compulsive) is referred to their discretion.

2. That the matter of impressing and constraining any of us to serve in the wars is against our freedom; and therefore we do not allow it in our Representatives; the rather, because money (the sinews of war), being always at their disposal, they can never want numbers of men apt enough to engage in any just cause.

3. That after the dissolution of this present Parliament, no person be at any time questioned for anything said or done in reference to the late public differences, otherwise than in execution of the judgments of the present Representatives, or House of Commons.

4. That in all laws made or to be made every person may be bound alike, and that no tenure, estate, charter, degree, birth, or place do confer any exemption from the ordinary course of legal proceedings whereunto others are subjected.

5. That as the laws ought to be equal, so they must be good, and not evidently destructive to the safety and well-being of the people.

These things we declare to be our native rights, and therefore are agreed and resolved to maintain them with our utmost possibilities against all opposition whatsoever; being compelled thereunto not only by the examples of our ancestors, whose blood was often spent in vain for the recovery of their freedoms, suffering themselves through fraudulent accommodations to be still deluded of the fruit of their victories, but also by our own woeful experience, who, having long expected and dearly earned the establishment of these certain rules of government, are yet made to depend for the settlement of our peace and freedom upon him that intended our bondage and brought a cruel war upon us.

Questions

1. What are the Levellers criticizing when they propose that "in all laws made or to be made every person may be bound alike"?

2. What are the main rights that the Levellers are aiming to protect?

CHAPTER 3

Creating Anglo-America, 1660–1750

14. William Penn, Pennsylvania Charter of Privileges and Liberties (1701)

Source: Francis N. Thorpe, **The Federal and State Constitutions, Colonial Charters, and Other Organic Laws** *... (7 vols.: Washington, D.C., 1909), vol. 5, pp. 3076–81.*

The last English colony to be established in the seventeenth century was Pennsylvania, founded in 1680 by William Penn. A devout member of the Society of Friends, or Quakers, Penn envisioned the colony as a place where those facing religious persecution in Europe could enjoy spiritual freedom. Quakers held that the spirit of God dwelled within all people, not just the elect, and that this "inner light," rather than the Bible or teachings of the clergy, offered the surest guidance in spiritual matters. Thus, the government had no right to enforce any particular form of religious worship.

Penn drew up a Frame of Government in 1682 but it proved unworkable and in 1701 was replaced with a Charter of Liberties that established a political system that lasted until the American Revolution. Its first clause restated Penn's cherished principle of religious toleration, although it limited officeholding to Christians. It also established an elected legislature and promised that colonists would enjoy the same rights as "free-born subjects of England."

KNOW YE ... That for the further Well-being and good Government of the said Province, and Territories; ... I the said William Penn do declare, grant and confirm, unto all the Freemen, Planters and Adventurers, and other Inhabitants of this Province and Territories, these following Liberties, Franchises and Privileges ...

Because no People can be truly happy, though under the greatest enjoyment of civil liberties, if abridged of the freedom of their consciences, as to their religious profession and worship: And Almighty God being the only Lord of Conscience, Father of Lights and Spirits; and the Author as well as object of all divine knowledge, faith and worship, who only doth enlighten the Minds, and persuade and convince the understandings of people, I do hereby grant and declare, that no person or persons, inhabiting in this Province or Territories, who shall confess and acknowledge One almighty God, the Creator, Upholder and Ruler of the World; and profess him or themselves obliged to live quietly under the Civil Government, shall be in any case molested or prejudiced, in his or their person or estate, because of his or their conscientious persuasion or practice, nor be compelled to frequent or maintain any religious worship, place or ministry, contrary to his or their mind, or to do or suffer any other act or thing, contrary to their religious persuasion.

And that all persons who also profess to believe in Jesus Christ, the Savior of the World, shall be capable (notwithstanding their other persuasions and practices in point of conscience and religion) to serve this Government in any capacity, both legislatively and executively....

For the well governing of this Province and Territories, there shall be an Assembly yearly chosen, by the freemen thereof, to consist of four persons out of each county, of most note for virtue, wisdom and ability, ... which Assembly shall have power to choose a Speaker and other officers; ... prepare Bills in order to pass into Laws; impeach criminals, and redress grievances; and shall have all other powers and privileges of an Assembly, according to the rights of the free-born subjects of England.

Questions

1. What are Penn's arguments in favor of religious liberty?

2. Why does the document refer to "the rights of the free-born subjects of England"?

---

15. Nathaniel Bacon on Bacon's Rebellion (1676)

Source: **Virginia Magazine of History and Biography,** *vol. 1 (1894),* *pp. 55–61.*

The largest popular revolt in the early English colonies was Bacon's Rebellion, which occurred in Virginia in 1676. For thirty years, Governor William Berkeley had run a corrupt regime in alliance with an inner circle of tobacco planters, while heavy taxes reduced the prospects of small farmers. His refusal to allow white settlement in areas reserved for Indians angered colonists who saw landownership as central to freedom.

After a minor confrontation between Indians and settlers on Virginia's western frontier, settlers demanded that the governor authorize the extermination or removal of the colony's Indians to open more land for whites. Berkeley refused. An uprising began that quickly grew into a full-fledged rebellion. The leader, Nathaniel Bacon, was himself a wealthy and ambitious planter. But his call for the removal of all Indians from the colony, a reduction of taxes, and an end to rule by "grandees" rapidly gained support from small farmers, landless men, indentured servants, and even some slaves. Bacon's "manifesto," which follows, outlined the rebels' complaints against the governor and the colony's "protected and darling Indians." The uprising failed. But the frightened authorities reduced taxes and adopted a more aggressive Indian policy, opening western areas to small farmers. They also accelerated the shift from indentured white labor to African slaves.

IF VIRTUE BE a sin, if piety be guilt, all the principles of morality, goodness and justice be perverted, we must confess that those who are now called rebels may be in danger of those high imputations. Those loud and several bulls would affright innocents and render the defence of our brethren and the inquiry into our sad and heavy oppressions, treason. But if there be, as sure there is, a just God to appeal to; if religion and justice be a sanctuary here; if to plead the cause of the oppressed; if sincerely to aim at his Majesty's honour and the public good without any reservation or by interest; if to stand in the gap after so much blood of our dear brethren bought and sold; if after the loss of a great part of his Majesty's colony deserted and dispeopled, freely with our lives and estates to endeavour to save the remainders be treason; God Almighty judge and let guilty die. But since we cannot in our hearts find one single spot of rebellion or treason, or that we have in any manner aimed at subverting the settled government or attempting of the person of any either magistrate or private man, notwithstanding the several reproaches and threats of some who for sinister ends were disaffected to us and censured our innocent and honest designs, and since all people in all places where we have yet been can attest our civil, quiet, peaceable behaviour far different from that of rebellion and tumultuous persons, let truth be bold and all the world know the real foundations of pretended guilt.

We appeal to the country itself what and of what nature their oppressions have been, or by what cabal and mystery the designs of many of those whom we call great men have been transacted and carried on; but let us trace these men in authority and favour to whose hands the dispensation of the country's wealth has been committed. Let us observe the sudden rise of their estates [compared] with the quality in which they first entered this country, or the reputation they have held here amongst wise and discerning men. And let us see whether their extractions and education have not been vile, and by what pretence of learning and virtue they could so soon [come] into employments of so great trust and consequence. Let us consider their sudden advancement and let us also consider whether any public work for our safety and defence or for the advancement and propagation of trade, liberal arts, or sciences is here extant in any way adequate to our vast charge. Now let us compare these things together and see what sponges have sucked up the public treasure, and whether it has not been privately contrived away by unworthy favourites and juggling parasites whose tottering fortunes have been repaired and supported at the public charge. Now if it be so, judge what greater guilt can be than to offer to pry into these and to unriddle the mysterious wiles of a powerful cabal; let all people judge what can be of more dangerous import than to suspect the so long safe proceedings of some of our grandees, and whether people may with safety open their eyes in so nice a concern.

Another main article of our guilt is our open and manifest aversion of all, not only the foreign but the protected and darling Indians. This, we are informed, is rebellion of a deep dye for that both the governor and council are . . . bound to defend the queen and the Appamatocks with their blood. Now, whereas we do declare and can prove that they have been for these many years enemies to the king and country, robbers and thieves and invaders of his Majesty's right and our interest and estates, but yet have by persons in authority been defended and protected even against his Majesty's loyal subjects, and that in so high a nature that even the complaints and oaths of his Majesty's most loyal subjects in a lawful manner proffered by them against those barbarous outlaws, have been by the right honourable governor rejected and the delinquents from his presence dismissed, not only with pardon and indemnity, but with all encouragement and favour; their firearms so destructful to us and by our laws prohibited, commanded to be restored them, and open declaration before witness made that they must have ammunition, although directly contrary to our law. Now what greater guilt can be than to oppose and endeavour the destruction of these honest, quiet neighbours of ours?

Another main article of our guilt is our design not only to ruin and extirpate all Indians in general, but all manner of trade and commerce with them. Judge who can be innocent that strike at this tender eye of interest: since the right honourable the governor hath been pleased by his commission to warrant this trade, who dare oppose it, or opposing it can be innocent? Although plantations be deserted, the blood of our dear brethren spilled; on all sides our complaints; continually murder upon murder renewed upon us; who may or dare think of the general subversion of all manner of trade and commerce with our enemies who can or dare impeach any of . . . traders at the heads of the rivers, if contrary to the wholesome provision made by laws for the country's safety; they dare continue their illegal practises and dare asperse the right honourable governor's wisdom and justice so highly to pretend to have his warrant to break that law which himself made; who dare say that these men at the heads of the rivers buy and sell our blood, and do still, notwithstanding the late act made to the contrary, admit Indians painted and continue to commerce; although these things can be proved, yet who dare be so guilty as to do it? . . .

• • •

THE DECLARATION OF THE PEOPLE

For having upon specious pretences of public works, raised unjust taxes upon the commonalty for the advancement of private favourites and other sinister ends, but no visible effects in any measure adequate.

For not having during the long time of his government in any measure advanced this hopeful colony, either by fortification, towns or trade.

For having abused and rendered contemptible the majesty of justice, of advancing to places of judicature scandalous and ignorant favourites.

For having wronged his Majesty's prerogative and interest by assuming the monopoly of the beaver trade.

By having in that unjust gain bartered and sold his Majesty's country and the lives of his loyal subjects to the barbarous heathen.

For having protected, favoured and emboldened the Indians against his Majesty's most loyal subjects, never contriving, requiring, or appointing any due or proper means of satisfaction for their many invasions, murders, and robberies committed upon us.

• • •

For having the second time attempted the same thereby calling down our forces from the defence of the frontiers, and most weak exposed places, for the prevention of civil mischief and ruin amongst ourselves, whilst the barbarous enemy in all places did invade, murder, and spoil us, his Majesty's most faithful subjects.

Of these, the aforesaid articles, we accuse Sir William Berkeley, as guilty of each and every one of the same, and as one who has traitorously attempted, violated and injured his Majesty's interest here, by the loss of a great part of his colony, and many of his faithful and loyal subjects by him betrayed, and in a barbarous and shameful manner exposed to the incursions and murders of the heathen.

And we do further demand, that the said Sir William Berkeley ... be forthwith delivered up ... within four days after the notice hereof, or otherwise we declare as followeth: that in whatsoever house, place, or ship [he] shall reside, be hid, or protected, we do declare that the owners, masters, or inhabitants of the said places, to be confederates and traitors to the people, and the estates of them, as also of all the aforesaid persons, to be confiscated. This we, the commons of Virginia, do declare desiring a prime union amongst ourselves, that we may jointly, and with one accord defend ourselves against the common enemy.

NATH BACON, Gen'l.
By the Consent of the People.

Questions

1. What are the rebels' main complaints against the government of Virginia?

2. Do Bacon and his followers envision any place for Indians in Virginia society?

16. Letter by an Immigrant to Pennsylvania (1769)

Source: Johannes Hänner, "Letter by an Immigrant to Pennsylvania, 1769," Unpublished Documents on Emigration from the Archives of Switzerland, *Albert B. Faust,* Deutsch-Amerikanische Geschichtsblätter, *vols. 18–19, pp. 37–39, trans. Volker Berghahn. Reprinted by permission of Volker Berghahn.*

Germans, 110,000 in all, formed the largest group of newcomers to the British colonies in the eighteenth century. The desire for religious freedom inspired many migrants, but the primary motivation for emigration was economic. German areas of Europe were plagued by persistent agricultural crises. Families found it increasingly difficult to acquire land.

Most German newcomers settled in frontier areas—rural New York, western Pennsylvania, and the southern backcountry—where they formed tightly knit farming communities in which German for many years remained the dominant language. The letter below, by a German-speaking emigrant from Switzerland to Pennsylvania, illustrates the response of many immigrants to life in America. "We have a free country," he wrote to his relatives at home, singling out ample employment opportunities, low taxes, plentiful food, and abundant land as reasons for coming to America.

Dearest Father, Brother, and Sister and Brother-in-law, . . .

To begin with, we are all, thank God, fresh and healthy as long as the Lord wills, and if at last you are also in good health, this would delight my heart. What I must tell you first of all is that I have been dreaming one day after Johannis and that it seemed to me that my beloved brother-in-law in Bubendorff had died. This would pain me a lot, and the Lord will protect him of this.

I have told you quite fully about the trip, and I will tell you what will not surprise you—that we have a free country. Of the sundry craftsmen, one may do whatever one wants. Nor does the land require payment of tithes [taxes requiring payment of a portion of a farmer's produce to a local landlord, typical in Europe]. . . . By the way, wheat is grown most frequently, rye, oats, . . . apples are plentiful. . . . The land is very big from Canada to the east of us to Carolina in the south and to the Spanish border in the west. . . . Except for Carolina [there are] many large and small rivers. One can settle wherever one wants without asking anyone when he buys or leases something. . . .

I have always enough to do and we have no shortage of food. Bread is plentiful. If I work for two days I earn more bread than in eight days [at home]. . . . Also I can buy many things so reasonably [for example] a pair of shoes for [roughly] seven Pennsylvania shillings. . . . I think that with God's help I will obtain land. I am not pushing for it until I am in a better position. I would like for my brother to come . . . and it will then be even nicer in the country. . . . I assume that the land has been described to you sufficiently by various people and it is not surprising that the immigrant agents [demand payment]. For the journey is long and it costs much to stay away for one year. . . . And at this point I finally greet you all with all good friends and acquaintances very cordially, and I command all of you to the care of the Lord so that you may be well in soul and body.

JOHANNES HÄNNER

Questions

1. What does Johannes Hänner seem to mean when he calls America a "free country"?

2. How does it appear that people in Europe learn about conditions in America?

---

17. An Act Concerning Negroes and Other Slaves (1664)

Source: **Proceedings and Acts of the General Assembly of Maryland** *(Baltimore, 1883), pp. 533–34.*

Both Virginia and Maryland in the 1660s enacted laws to clarify questions arising from the growing importance of slavery and tightened the legal code relating to blacks. These laws drew a sharp distinction between the status of white indentured servants and black slaves and sought to prevent intimate relations between persons of different races. The measure below made all blacks in Maryland, as well as those henceforth imported into the colony, slaves for life (some had previously been treated as indentured servants, required to labor only for a fixed number of years before becoming free), and decreed that a white woman who married a slave must serve her husband's owner until her partner's death.

BE IT ENACTED by the Right Honorable the Lord Proprietary by the advice and consent of the upper and lower house of this present General Assembly, that all Negroes or other slaves already within the province, and all Negroes and other slaves to be hereafter imported into the province, shall serve durante vita [for life]. And all children born of any Negro or other slave shall be slaves as their fathers were, for the term of their lives.

And forasmuch as divers freeborn English women, forgetful of their free condition and to the disgrace of our nation, marry Negro slaves, by which also divers suits may arise touching the issue [children] of such women, and a great damage befalls the masters of such Negroes for prevention whereof, for deterring such freeborn women from such shameful matches. Be it further enacted by the authority, advice, and consent aforesaid, that whatsoever freeborn woman shall marry any slave from and after the last day of this present Assembly shall serve the master of such slave during the life of her husband. And that all the issue of such freeborn women so married shall be slaves as their fathers were. And be it further enacted, that all the issues of English or other freeborn women that have already married Negroes shall serve the masters of their parents till they be thirty years of age and no longer.

Questions

1. What does the Maryland law tell us about how the consolidation of slavery affected ideas about racial difference?

2. What does the document suggest about the limits of freedom in early colonial America?

---

18. Benjamin Franklin, "Observations Concerning the Increase of Mankind" (1751)

Source: [William Clarke], **Observations on the Late and Present Conduct of the French, with Regard to Their Encroachments upon the British Colonies in North America** *(Boston, 1755), pp. 53–54.*

Only a minority of immigrants from Europe to British North America in the eighteenth century came from the British Isles. Some prominent colonists found the growing diversity of the population quite disturbing.

Benjamin Franklin was particularly troubled by the large influx of new-comers from Germany into Pennsylvania in the mid-eighteenth century. In 1751 he wrote an essay, which he circulated to friends in manuscript form, warning against the long-term effects of German immigration on the English culture of the American colonies. He advocated increasing the number of English immigrants and expanding the colonies' control over land to the west to accommodate them (a recipe for continuing conflict with Native Americans). The essay was published four years later as an appendix to a pamphlet on a different subject. Reprinted numerous times, it was widely circulated in the colonies and Great Britain, and was quoted by Adam Smith, David Hume, and other prominent writers of the period on economics and politics.

———

A nation well regulated is like a polypus [octopus]; take away a limb, its place is soon supplied; cut it in two, and each deficient part shall speedily grow out of the part remaining. Thus if you have room and subsistence enough, as you may by dividing, make ten polypes out of one, you may of one make ten nations, equally populous and power-ful; or rather, increase a nation ten fold in numbers and strength.

And since detachments of English from Britain sent to America, will have their places at home so soon supplied and increase so largely here, why should the Palatine [German] boors be suffered to swarm into our settlements, and by herding together establish their language and manners to the exclusion of ours? Why should Penn-sylvania, founded by the English, become a Colony of *Aliens*, who will shortly be so numerous as to Germanize us instead of our Angli-fying them, and will never adopt our language or customs, any more than they can acquire our complexion.

Which leads me to add one remark: That the number of purely white people in the world is proportionably very small. All Africa is black or tawny. Asia chiefly tawny. America (exclusive of the new-comers) wholly so. And in Europe, the Spaniards, Italians, French, Russians and Swedes, are generally of what we call a swarthy com-plexion; as are the Germans also, the Saxons only excepted, who with the English, make the principal body of white people on the face of the earth. I could wish their numbers were increased. And while we are, as I may call it, *scouring* our planet, by clearing America of woods, and so making this side of our globe reflect a brighter light to the eyes of inhabitants in Mars or Venus, why should we ... darken its people? Why increase the sons of Africa, by planting them in America, where we have so fair an opportunity, by excluding all Blacks and Tawneys, of increasing the lovely White and Red? But perhaps I am partial to the complexion of my country, for such kind of partiality is natural to mankind.

Questions

1. What is Franklin's objection to the growing German presence?

2. What does Franklin's characterization of the complexions of various groups suggest about the reliability of his perceptions of non-English peoples?

19. Complaint of an Indentured Servant (1756)

Source: Elizabeth Sprigs to John Spyer, September 22, 1756, in Isabel M. Calder, Colonial Captivities, Marches and Journeys *(New York, 1935), pp. 151–52.*

Throughout the colonial era, only a minority of emigrants from Europe to Britain's North American colonies were fully free. Settlers who could pay for their own passage and arrived ready to take advantage of the opportunities offered by the New World—government officials, clergymen, merchants, artisans, landowning farmers, and members of the lesser nobility—were considerably outnumbered by indentured servants. These men and women voluntarily surrendered their freedom for a specified time (usually five to seven years) in exchange for passage to America. Like slaves, servants could be bought and sold, could not marry without the permission of their owner, were subject to physical punishment, and saw their obligation to labor enforced by the courts. To ensure uninterrupted work by female servants, the law lengthened the term of their indenture if they became pregnant.

The letter below was written to her father in England by Elizabeth Sprigs, an indentured servant in mid-eighteenth-century Maryland. It expressed complaints voiced by many servants from the beginning of settlement. Sprigs, who had clearly had some kind of falling out with her father, described constant labor, poor food and living conditions, and physical abuse. "Many Negroes are better used," she added.

MARYLAND, SEPTEMBER 22, 1756

Honored Father,

My being forever banished from your sight, will I hope pardon the boldness I now take of troubling you with these. My long silence has been purely owing to my undutifulness to you, and well knowing I had offended in the highest degree, put a tie to my tongue and pen, for fear I should be extinct from your good graces and add a further trouble to you. But too well knowing your care and tenderness for me so long as I retained my duty to you, induced me once again to endeavor, if possible, to kindle up that flame again.

O Dear father, believe what I am going to relate the words of truth and sincerity, and balance my former bad conduct [to] my sufferings here, and then I am sure you'll pity your distressed daughter. What we unfortunate English people suffer here is beyond the probability of you in England to conceive. Let it suffice that I am one of the unhappy number, am toiling almost day and night, and very often in the horse's drudgery, with only this comfort that you bitch you do not half enough, and then tied up and whipped to that degree that you'd not serve an animal. Scarce any thing but Indian corn and salt to eat and that even begrudged nay many Negroes are better used, almost naked no shoes nor stockings to wear, and the comfort after slaving during master's pleasure, what rest we can get is to wrap ourselves up in a blanket and lie upon the ground. This is the deplorable condition your poor Betty endures, and now I beg if you have any bowels of compassion left show it by sending me some relief. Clothing is the principal thing wanting, which if you should condescend to, may easily send them to me by any of the ships bound to Baltimore town, Patapsco River, Maryland. And give me leave to conclude in duty to you and uncles and aunts, and respect to all friends.

    Honored Father

    Your undutiful and disobedient child

    Elizabeth Sprigs

Questions

1. What are Elizabeth Sprigs's main complaints about her treatment?

2. Why does she compare her condition unfavorably to that of blacks?

---

20. Women in the Household Economy (1709)

Source: John Lawson, A New Voyage to Carolina *(London, 1709), pp. 84–85.*

In the household economy of eighteenth-century America, the family was the center of economic life. Most work revolved around the home, and all members—men, women, and children—contributed to the family's livelihood. John Lawson, an English naturalist, came to Carolina in 1700 and traveled over a thousand miles, studying the natural environment and trading with Indians. His *A New Voyage to Carolina* offered a very favorable description of life in the colony. Lawson's account vividly described the lives of free Carolina women and the numerous kinds of labor they performed. The work of farmers' wives and daughters often spelled the difference between a family's self-sufficiency and poverty. Lawson was captured and killed during an Indian uprising in 1711.

THE WOMEN ARE the most industrious sex in that place, and, by their good houswifery, make a great deal of cloth of their own cotton, wool and flax; some of them keeping their families (though large) very decently appareled, both with linens and woolens, so that they have no occasion to run into the merchant's debt, or lay their money out on stores for clothing. . . .

They marry very young; some at thirteen or fourteen; and she that stays till twenty, is reckoned a stale maid; which is a very indifferent character in that warm country. The women are very fruitful; most houses being full of little ones. It has been observed, that women long married, and without children, in other places, have removed to Carolina, and become joyful mothers. They have very easy travail in their child-bearing, in which they are so happy, as seldom to miscarry. . . .

Many of the women are very handy in canoes, and will manage them with great dexterity and skill, which they become accustomed to in this watery country. They are ready to help their husbands in any servile work, as planting, when the season of the weather requires expedition; pride seldom banishing good houswifery. The girls are not bred up to the [spinning] wheel and sewing only; but the dairy and affairs of the house they are very well acquainted withal; so that you shall see them, whilst very young, manage their business with a great deal of conduct and alacrity. The children of both sexes are very docile, and learn any thing with a great deal of Ease and Method; and those that have the advantages of education, write good hands, and prove good accountants, which is most coveted, and indeed most necessary in these parts.

Questions

1. What are the most important kinds of work done by Carolina women, according to Lawson?

2. How strict do gender roles appear to have been in early Carolina?

CHAPTER 4

Slavery, Freedom, and the Struggle for Empire, to 1763

21. An Act for the Encouragement of the Importation of White Servants (1698)

Source: Thomas Cooper, ed., **The Statutes at Large of South Carolina** *(Columbia, 1837), vol. 2, pp. 153–56.*

From the outset, South Carolina relied heavily on African slave labor. In 1698, the colonial legislature sought to increase the white population by enacting a law paying the owners of ships that brought young white men to the colony, and requiring slaveowners to accept them as indentured servants. Two years later, the governor announced that the law had fulfilled its purpose and that there were now around 4,000 whites and 4,000 blacks in the colony. The legislature then repealed the law. But very quickly, as rice and indigo cultivation on slave plantations expanded, the population imbalance reappeared. By the time of the American Revolution, slaves represented well over half of South Carolina's population. This law is an early example of the ideas, which recurred in later years, both that a white majority is desirable and that some whites are more desirable than others.

━━━━━━

WHEREAS, THE GREAT number of Negroes which of late have been imported into this colony may endanger the safety thereof if speedy care be not taken and encouragement given for the importation of white servants.

Be it enacted ... that every merchant, owner or master of any ship or vessel, or any other person not intending to settle and plant here, which shall bring any white male servants, Irish only excepted, into Ashley river, above sixteen years of age and under forty, and the same shall deliver to the Receiver General, shall receive and be paid by the said Receiver ... the sum of thirteen pounds for every servant so delivered ... to the Receiver as aforesaid. Provided, that every servant ... hath not less than four years to serve from and after the day of his arrival in Ashley River, and every boy aforesaid, not less than seven years. And if any person shall deliver to the Receiver aforesaid, any, any servant or boy ... which hath less time to serve than the respective times before appointed, the Receiver shall pay such person proportionably to the rates and times aforesaid, for so long time as such servant or boy hath to serve ...

... Every owner of every plantation to which doth belong six men Negro slaves above sixteen years old, shall take from the Receiver one servant, when it shall happen to be his lot to have one, and shall within three months pay the said Receiver so much money for the said servant as the Receiver gave to the person from whom he received the same; and the owner of every plantation to which doth belong twelve Negro men, ... shall when it shall be his lot, take two servants ... and every master of every plantation proportionably.

Questions

1. Why do the lawmakers believe this law is necessary?

2. Why do you think Irish servants are exempted from its provisions?

22. Olaudah Equiano on Slavery (1789)

Source: The Interesting Narrative of the Life of Olaudah Equiano, or Gustavus Vassa, the African, Written by Himself *(London, 1789), vol. 1, pp. 46–49, 69–72, 83–88.*

Of the estimated 7.7 million Africans transported to the New World between 1492 and 1820, over half arrived between 1700 and 1800. Every European empire utilized slave labor and battled for control of this profitable trade. A series of triangular trading routes crisscrossed the Atlantic, carrying British goods to Africa and the colonies, colonial slave-grown products like tobacco, sugar, and rice to Europe, and slaves from Africa to the New World.

The era's most popular account of the slave experience was written by Olaudah Equiano, the son of a West African village chief, kidnapped by slave traders in the 1750s. In the passages that follow, Equiano describes his capture, encounter with other African peoples with whom he had no previous contact, passage to the New World, and sale in the West Indies. Equiano went on to purchase his freedom. His life underscored the greatest contradiction in the history of the eighteenth century—the simultaneous expansion of freedom and slavery.

<hr>

MY FATHER, BESIDES many slaves, had a numerous family, of which seven lived to grow up, including myself and a sister, who was the only daughter. As I was the youngest of the sons, I became, of course, the greatest favourite with my mother, and was always with her; and she used to take particular pains to form my mind. I was trained up from my earliest years in the arts of agriculture and war: my daily exercise was shooting and throwing javelins; and my mother adorned me with emblems, after the manner of our greatest warriors. In this way I grew up till I was turned the age of eleven, when an end was put to my happiness in the following manner:—
Generally, when the grown people in the neighbourhood were gone far in the fields to labour, the children assembled together in some

of the neighbours' premises to play; and commonly some of us used to get up a tree to look out for any assailant, or kidnapper, that might come upon us; for they sometimes took those opportunities of our parents' absence, to attack and carry off as many as they could seize. One day, as I was watching at the top of a tree in our yard, I saw one of those people come into the yard of our next neighbour but one, to kidnap, there being many stout young people in it. Immediately, on this, I gave the alarm of the rogue, and he was surrounded by the stoutest of them, who entangled him with cords, so that he could not escape till some of the grown people came and secured him. But, alas! ere long it was my fate to be thus attacked, and to be carried off, when none of the grown people were nigh. One day, when all our people were gone out to their works as usual, and only I and my dear sister were left to mind the house, two men and a woman got over our walls, and in a moment seized us both; and, without giving us time to cry out, or make resistance, they stopped our mouths, tied our hands, and ran off with us into the nearest wood: and continued to carry us as far as they could, till night came on, when we reached a small house, where the robbers halted for refreshment, and spent the night. We were then unbound, but were unable to take any food; and, being quite overpowered by fatigue and grief, our only relief was some sleep, which allayed our misfortune for a short time. The next morning we left the house, and continued travelling all the day....

• • •

I continued to travel, sometimes by land, sometimes by water, through different countries, and various nations, till, at the end of six or seven months after I had been kidnapped, I arrived at the sea coast. It would be tedious and uninteresting to relate all the incidents which befel me during this journey, and which I have not yet forgotten, of the various hands I passed through, and the manners and customs of all the different people among whom I lived: I shall therefore only observe, that, in all the places where I was, the soil was exceedingly rich; the pomkins, eadas, plantains, yams, &c. &c. were

in great abundance, and of incredible size. There were also vast quan-
tities of different gums, though not used for any purpose; and every
where a great deal of tobacco. The cotton even grew quite wild; and
there was plenty of red wood. I saw no mechanics whatever in all
the way, except such as I have mentioned. The chief employment in
all these countries was agriculture, and both the males and females,
as with us, were brought up to it, and trained in the arts of war.

The first object which saluted my eyes when I arrived on the coast
was the sea, and a slave-ship, which was then riding at anchor, and
waiting for its cargo. These filled me with astonishment, which was
soon converted into terror, which I am yet at a loss to describe, nor
the then feelings of my mind. When I was carried on board I was
immediately handled, and tossed up, to see if I were sound, by some
of the crew; and I was now persuaded that I had gotten into a world of
bad spirits, and that they were going to kill me. Their complexions
too differing so much from ours, their long hair, and the language
they spoke, which was very different from any I had ever heard,
united to confirm me in this belief. Indeed, such were the horrors of
my views and fears at the moment, that, if ten thousand worlds had
been my own, I would have freely parted with them all to have
exchanged my condition with that of the meanest slave in my own
country. When I looked round the ship too, and saw a large furnace
of copper boiling, and a multitude of black people of every description chained together, every one of their countenances expressing
dejection and sorrow, I no longer doubted of my fate, and, quite overpowered with horror and anguish, I fell motionless on the deck and
fainted. When I recovered a little, I found some black people about
me, who I believed were some of those who brought me on board,
and had been receiving their pay; they talked to me in order to cheer
me, but all in vain. I asked them if we were not to be eaten by those
white men with horrible looks, red faces, and long hair? They told
me I was not; and one of the crew brought me a small portion of
spirituous liquor in a wine glass; but, being afraid of him, I would
not take it out of his hand....

• • •

At last we came in sight of the island of Barbadoes, at which the whites on board gave a great shout, and made many signs of joy to us. We did not know what to think of this; but as the vessel drew nearer we plainly saw the harbour, and other ships of different kinds and sizes: and we soon anchored amongst them off Bridge Town. Many merchants and planters now came on board, though it was in the evening. They put us in separate parcels, and examined us attentively. They also made us jump, and pointed to the land, signifying we were to go there. We thought by this we should be eaten by these ugly men, as they appeared to us; and, when soon after we were all put down under the deck again, there was much dread and trembling among us, and nothing but bitter cries to be heard all the night from these apprehensions, insomuch that at last the white people got some old slaves from the land to pacify us. They told us we were not to be eaten, but to work, and were soon to go on land, where we should see many of our country people. This report eased us much; and sure enough, soon after we were landed, there came to us Africans of all languages. We were conducted immediately to the merchant's yard, where we were all pent up together like so many sheep in a fold, without regard to sex or age. As every object was new to me, every thing I saw filled me with surprise. What struck me first was, that the houses were built with bricks, in stories, and in every other respect different from those I have seen in Africa: but I was still more astonished on seeing people on horseback. I did not know what this could mean; and indeed I thought these people were full of nothing but magical arts....

• • •

We were not many days in the merchant's custody before we were sold after their usual manner, which is this:—On a signal given, (as the beat of a drum), the buyers rush at once into the yard where the slaves are confined, and make choice of that parcel they like best. The noise and clamour with which this is attended, and the eagerness visible in the countenances of the buyers, serve not a little to increase the apprehensions of the terrified Africans, who may well be supposed to consider them as the ministers of that destruction to which they think themselves devoted. In this manner, without scruple, are relations and friends separated, most of them never to see each other again. I remember in the vessel in which I was brought over, in the men's apartment, there were several brothers, who, in the sale, were sold in different lots; and it was very moving on this occasion to see and hear their cries at parting. O, ye nominal Christians! might not an African ask you, learned you this from your God? who says unto you, Do unto all men as you would men should do unto you? Is it not enough that we are torn from our country and friends to toil for your luxury and lust of gain? Must every tender feeling be likewise sacrificed to your avarice? Are the dearest friends and relations, now rendered more dear by their separation from their kindred, still to be parted from each other, and thus prevented from cheering the gloom of slavery with the small comfort of being together and mingling their sufferings and sorrows? Why are parents to lose their children, brothers their sisters, or husbands their wives? Surely this is a new refinement in cruelty, which, while it has no advantage to atone for it, thus aggravates distress, and adds fresh horrors even to the wretchedness of slavery.

Questions

1. What picture of life in Africa does Equiano present?

2. What elements of slavery does he seem to think will most outrage his readers?

23. Advertisements for Runaway Slaves and Servants (1738)

Source: **Pennsylvania Gazette,** *July 1738.*

As advertisements in colonial newspapers demonstrated, slaves and indentured servants frequently expressed their desire for freedom by running away. Sometimes they escaped together, despite racial differences between them and the fact that slaves served for life while servants would gain their liberty after a number of years. Pennsylvania was a frequent refuge for fugitives from neighboring Maryland, where slavery and servitude were more deeply entrenched.

RUN AWAY ON the 23d of March last, from the Subscribers, in St. Mary's County, Maryland, the following Servants, and a Negroe, viz.

George Humphrey, an Englishman, aged about 19 Years, fair complexion'd, talks slow, with light brown Hair: Had on a light Cotton Jacket lined with yellow Linnen, a homespun Jacket and Breeches, coarse Shirt and an old Felt Hat.

Barnaby Higgins, an Irishman, aged about 25 Years, Low of Stature, much pockfretten, by Trade a Joyner or Carpenter: Had on a yellow Jacket and Breeches.

Michael Mara, an Irishman, aged about 25 Years, Low of Stature, swarthy Complexion, by Trade a Turner: Had on a yellow Kersey Jacket and grey Breeches. Both the Irishmen had the two first Letters of their Name marked on the Arm.

John Maine, an Englishman, bred to the Sea, middle aged, well set, much disfigured on the Face and Throat from the King's Evil.

John More, an Irishman, had a Blemish on one Eye, middle aged, high Stature, well set, a Labourer and very dextrous at the Spade: Had on a Cinnamon colored Cloth Coat, a good Jacket and Breeches.

And a Negroe Man named Peter, about 25 Years old, Country born, of a middle Stature, well set, talks notably: Had on a brownish Cloth

Coat, a Country Cloth Jacket and Breeches, and a Felt Hat pretty much worn.

They all made off in a Boat on Potomack River, 15 Feet in the Keel, with two Masts and rigged after the Bermudian Manner.

Whoever secures the said Servants and Negroe, so that their Masters may have them again, shall have Thirty Pounds Reward. Maryland Currency; and a proportionable Sum for any one or more of them, and all necessary Charges paid by

Philad. July   John Heard,   Abraham Barns.

10. 1738   Thomas Brook,   Robert Ford.

Run away this Morning from Edward Farmer of Whitemarsh, a stout lusty Mollatto, known in Philadelphia by the Name of Mollatto Memm alias James Earl, has a Scar on his Temple, a wide Mouth and thick Lips, speaks good English. He was Cloathed when he went away, with a new Duroy Jacket of a dirty colour, lined with a dark blue-grey clour'd Shalloon, trim'd with dark collour'd Mohair and Buttons, a fine Shirt, a new fine Hat, a Silk Handkerchief, a speckled Pair of Trowsers, worsted Stockings, and new Shoes and Buckles in them.

Whoever takes up and secures the said Mollatto, or brings him home to his Master, or puts him in the Workhouse of Philadelphia, shall have Five Pounds Reward, paid by

Edward Farmer

Run away on Sunday last, from Henry Sparks, of Glocester Township, West-New-Jersey, an Irish Servant Man, named James Mordox, about 60 Years of Age, of a dark Complexion, grey Hair but cut off, by Trade a Smith. Had on a Suit of brown Cloaths, new Shoes and new Stockings.

Whoever secures the said Servant so that his Master may have him again shall have Forty Shillings Reward, and reasonable Charges paid by Henry Sparks. Philad. July 6. 1738.

Run away on the 20th Inst, from Joseph James of Cohensey, a Servant Man named Lazarus Kenny, is a swarthy Fellow, his Father being a

Molatto and his Mother a white Woman, he is pretty tall and well
set, his Hair cut off: Had on a Felt Hat, grey Kersey Coat and Vest, old
Leather Breeches, an old homespun Shirt, yarn Stockings, round toe'd
Shoes and brass Buckles. He took a large white Stallion that trots altogether, with an old black Saddle and good Snaffel Bridle.

Whoever secures the said Servant and Horse so that they are had
again, shall have Forty Shillings Reward and reasonable Charges,
paid by Joseph James.

Philad. June 29. 1738.

Questions

1. How do owners hope their fugitives will be identified?

2. What do these advertisements tell us about relations between slaves
and servants?

---

24. *The Independent Reflector* on Limited Monarchy and Liberty (1752)

Source: **The Independent Reflector** *(New York), December 21, 1752.*

During the eighteenth century, the idea of the "freeborn Englishman"
became powerfully entrenched in the outlook of both colonists and Brit-
ons. More than any other principle, liberty was seen as what made the
British empire distinct. The passage that follows, from the New York
monthly magazine *The Independent Reflector,* founded in 1752, offers an
example of the era's many paeans to the "inexpressible charm" of liberty
and England's role as liberty's "defender." The author, probably the magazine's editor, Edward Livingston, contrasts the national prosperity and
personal happiness enjoyed by citizens of a "free state" (defined as a limited
monarchy in which freedom of speech and religion were protected) with
the sorry condition of subjects of absolute monarchies. Until the 1770s,

most colonists believed themselves to be part of the freest political system humankind had ever known.

———

WHEN ONE CONSIDERS the Difference between an absolute, and a limited Monarchy, it seems unaccountable, that any Person in his Senses, should prefer the former to the later. . . .

In *limited* Monarchies, the Pride and Ambition of Princes, and their natural Lust for Dominion, are check'd and restrained. . . .

Liberty gives an inexpressible Charm to all our Enjoyments. It imparts a Relish to the most indifferent Pleasure, and renders the highest Gratification the more consummately delightful. It is the Refinement of Life; it sooths and alleviates our Toils; smooths the rugged Brow of Adversity, and endears and enhances every Acquisition. The Subjects of a free State, have something open and generous in their Carriage; something of Grandeur and Sublimity in their Appearance, resulting from their Freedom and Independence, that is never to be met with in those dreary Abodes, where the embittering Circumstance of a precarious Property, mars the Relish of every Gratification, and damps the most magnanimous Spirits. They can think for themselves; publish their Sentiments, and animadvert on Religion and Government, secure and unmolested.

• • •

But in *absolute* Monarchies, the whole Country is overspread with a dismal Gloom. *Slavery* is stamp'd on the Looks of the Inhabitants; and *Penury* engraved on their Visages, in strong and legible Characters. To prevent Complaints, the PRESS is prohibited; and a Vindication of the natural Rights of Mankind, is Treason. Every generous Spirit is broke and depressed: Human Nature is degraded, insulted, spurn'd, and outrag'd: The lovely Image of GOD, is defaced and disfigur'd, and the Lord of the Creation treated like the bestial Herd. The liberal Sciences languish: The politer Arts droop their Heads: Merit is banished to Cells and Deserts; and Virtue frowned into Dungeons, or dispatched to the Gallies: Iniquity is exalted: Goodness trod under Foot: Truth perverted; and the barbarous Outrages of Tyranny, sanctified and adored. The Fields lie waste and uncultivated: Commerce is incumbered with supernumerary Duties: The Tyrant riots in the Spoils of his People; and drains their Purses, to replenish his insatiate Treasury. He wages War against his own Subjects. . . .

Does any one think the above Representation, the Result of a roving Fancy, or figur'd beyond the Life; let him take a Survey of *Rome*; e'er-while the Nurse of Heroes, and the Terror of the World; but now the obscene Haunt of sequestred Bigots, and effeminate Slaves. Where are now her *Scipios*, and *Tullys*, her *Brutuses*, and her *Catos*, with other Names of equal Lustre, who plann'd her Laws, and fought her Battles, during her Freedom and Independence? Alas! they are succeeded by cloistered Monks and castrated Musicians, in Subjection to a filthy old Harlot, that pretends to a Power of devouring her Mediator, and claims a Right to eat up her People. Let him survey all *Italy*, once the Seat of Arts and Arms, and every Thing great and valuable; now the joyless Theatre of Oppression and Tyranny, Superstition and Ignorance. Let him behold all this; and when he has finished his Survey, then let him *believe and tremble.*

But far otherwise, is the Condition of a free People. Under the mild and gentle Administration of a *limited* Prince, every Thing looks cheerful and happy, smiling and serene. Agriculture is encouraged, and proves the annual Source of immense Riches to the Kingdom: The Earth opens her fertile Bosom to the Plough-share, and luxuriant Harvests diffuse Wealth and Plenty thro' the Land: The Fields stand thick with Corn: The Pastures smile with Herbage: The Hills and Vallies are cover'd with Flocks and Herds: Manufacturies flourish; and unprecarious Plenty recompenses the Artificer's Toil: In a Word, Nothing is seen but universal Joy and Festivity. Such is the Happiness of the People, under the blissful Reign of a good King. But do they get a Prince, whose Heart is poison'd with Regard to regal Authority, and who vainly imagines; that the Grandeur of Princes consists in making themselves feared; and accordingly plays the Devil in the Name of the Lord: They boldly assert their Rights, and call aloud for Justice; They cannot, they will not be enslaved. Sooner shall the royal Sinner have the Honour of Martyrdom, and the *Lord's Anointed* perish for his Iniquity, than the whole Frame of the Government be unhinged and dissolved....

• • •

How signal is our Happiness, in being blessed with a Prince, form'd for the Friend of the Nation, and the Defender of the Liberties of *Europe!* A Prince, who despises the Thought of placing his Grandeur in the Violation of the Laws; but is nobly ambitious of reigning in the Hearts of his People: A Prince, who invariably exerts his native Greatness of Soul, and all his inherent and hereditary Virtues, in the Support of Truth, Religion and Liberty: A Prince, in fine, unemulous of arbitrary Sway; but ardently aspiring after those brighter Trophies, that are earn'd in the Paths of Virtue and heroic Deeds; in relieving the Injured, protecting the Oppressed, and by a diffusive Benevolence, promoting the Happiness of Mankind. Long, oh long may he still adorn the Throne of his Ancestors! and when the Sovereign Disposer of Events, shall at last, to the keen and universal Affliction of his People, translate him to the Possession of a Crown, eternal and incorruptible; we may presage, (which will be the only Consideration capable of alleviating our Sorrow,) the greatest Glory, and the brightest Triumphs, from his Royal Highness's eminent Virtues; whose future Reign promises the most distinguished Prosperity to the Nation; and will exhibit to *Britain,* a Monarch, from his benevolent Disposition, and princely Education, the Father of his People, as well as a shining Ornament to that illustrious Family, of which we have already seen two Heroes on the *British Throne;* the Scourges of Tyrants, and the Assertors of Liberty.

Questions

1. What does the author mean by a "free state"?

2. Does the author think that the institution of monarchy is incompatible with freedom?

25. The Trial of John Peter Zenger (1735)

Source: The Trial of John Peter Zenger *(London, 1765), pp. 19–46.*

Under British and colonial law, the government could not censor newspapers, books, and pamphlets before they appeared in print, but authors and publishers could be prosecuted for "seditious libel"—a crime that included defaming government officials—or punished for contempt of public authority. In colonial America, dozens of publishers were hauled before assemblies and forced to apologize for comments regarding one or another member. If they refused, they were jailed.

The most famous colonial court case involving freedom of the press occurred in 1735. This was the trial of John Peter Zenger, a German-born printer, whose newspaper, the *Weekly Journal*, lambasted New York's governor for corruption and "tyranny." Zenger was arrested and put on trial for seditious libel. The judge instructed the jurors to consider only whether Zenger had in fact published the offending words. But Zenger's attorney, Andrew Hamilton, told the jury that the "cause of liberty" itself was at stake. If Zenger's charges were correct, he went on, they should acquit him and "every man who prefers freedom to a life of slavery will bless you." Zenger was found not guilty. The outcome demonstrated that the idea of free expression was becoming ingrained in the popular imagination.

━━━━━━

MR. ATTORNEY. The case before the court is whether Mr. Zenger is guilty of libeling His Excellency the Governor of New York, and indeed the whole administration of the government. Mr. Hamilton has confessed the printing and publishing, and I think nothing is plainer than that the words in the information [indictment] are scandalous, and tend to sedition, and to disquiet the minds of the people of this province. And if such papers are not libels, I think it may be said there can be no such thing as a libel.

MR. HAMILTON. May it please Your Honor, I cannot agree with Mr. Attorney. For though I freely acknowledge that there are such things as libels, yet I must insist, at the same time, that what my client is charged with is not a libel. And I observed just now that Mr. Attorney, in defining a libel, made use of the words "scandalous, seditious, and tend to disquiet the people." But (whether with design or not I will not say) he omitted the word "false."

MR. ATTORNEY. I think I did not omit the word "false." But it has been said already that it may be a libel, notwithstanding it may be true.

MR. HAMILTON. In this I must still differ with Mr. Attorney; for I depend upon it, we are to be tried upon this information now before the court and jury, and to which we have pleaded not guilty, and by it we are charged with printing and publishing a certain false, malicious, seditious, and scandalous libel. This word "false" must have some meaning, or else how came it there? . . .

• • •

MR. CHIEF JUSTICE. You cannot be admitted, Mr. Hamilton, to give the truth of a libel in evidence. A libel is not to be justified; for it is nevertheless a libel that it is true. . . .

MR. HAMILTON. I thank Your Honor. Then, gentlemen of the jury, it is to you we must now appeal, for witnesses, to the truth of the facts we have offered, and are denied the liberty to prove. And let it not seem strange that I apply myself to you in this manner. I am warranted so to do both by law and reason.

The law supposes you to be summoned out of the neighborhood where the fact [crime] is alleged to be committed; and the reason of your being taken out of the neighborhood is because you are supposed to have the best knowledge of the fact that is to be tried. And were you to find a verdict against my client, you must take upon you to say the papers referred to in the information, and which we acknowledge we printed and published, are false, scandalous, and seditious. But of this I can have no apprehension. You are citizens of New York; you are really what the law supposes you to be, honest and lawful men. And, according to my brief, the facts which we offer to prove were not committed in a corner; they are notoriously known to be true; and therefore in your justice lies our safety. And as we are denied the liberty of giving evidence to prove the truth of what we have published, I will beg leave to lay it down, as a standing rule in such cases, that the suppressing of evidence ought always to be taken for the strongest evidence; and I hope it will have weight with you....

• • •

I hope to be pardoned, sir, for my zeal upon this occasion. It is an old and wise caution that when our neighbor's house is on fire, we ought to take care of our own. For though, blessed be God, I live in a government [Pennsylvania] where liberty is well understood, and freely enjoyed, yet experience has shown us all (I'm sure it has to me) that a bad precedent in one government is soon set up for an authority in another. And therefore I cannot but think it mine, and every honest man's duty; that (while we pay all due obedience to men in authority) we ought at the same time to be upon our guard against power, wherever we apprehend that it may affect ourselves or our fellow subjects.

I am truly very unequal to such an undertaking on many accounts. And you see I labor under the weight of many years, and am borne down with great infirmities of body. Yet old and weak as I am, I should think it my duty, if required, to go to the utmost part of the land, where my service could be of any use, in assist—to quench the flame of prosecutions upon informations, set on foot by the government, to deprive a people of the right of remonstrating (and complaining too) of the arbitrary attempts of men in power. Men who injure and oppress the people under their administration provoke them to cry out and complain; and then make that very complaint the foundation for new oppressions and prosecutions. I wish I could say there were no instances of this kind.

But to conclude. The question before the court and you, gentlemen of the jury, is not of small nor private concern. It is not the cause of a poor printer, nor of New York alone, which you are now trying. No! It may, in its consequence, affect every freeman that lives under a British government on the main [land] of America. It is the best cause. It is the cause of liberty. And I make no doubt but your upright conduct, this day, will not only entitle you to the love and esteem of your fellow citizens; but every man who prefers freedom to a life of slavery will bless and honor you, as men who have baffled the attempt of tyranny, and, by an impartial and uncorrupt verdict, have laid a noble foundation for securing to ourselves, our posterity, and our neighbors, that to which nature and the laws of our country have given us a right—the liberty both of exposing and opposing arbitrary power (in these parts of the world, at least) by speaking and writing truth.

• • •

Questions

1. Why does Hamilton equate Zenger's defense with "the cause of liberty"?

2. What does Hamilton seem to think is the greatest threat to liberty?

---

26. The Great Awakening Comes to Connecticut (1740)

Source: George Leon Walker, Some Aspects of the Religious Life of New England *(New York, 1897), pp. 89–92.*

A series of religious revivals known as the Great Awakening swept through the colonies beginning in the 1730s. The revivals were united by a commitment to a "religion of the heart," a more emotional and personal Christianity than that offered by existing churches. The Awakening was a transatlantic movement. More than any other individual, the English minister George Whitefield, who declared "the whole world his parish," sparked the Great Awakening. For two years after his arrival in America in 1739, Whitefield brought his highly emotional brand of preaching to colonies from Georgia to New England.

A Connecticut farmer, Nathan Cole, in a 200-page autobiographical manuscript, offered a vivid account of the impact of Whitefield's preaching and how ordinary colonists responded to its spiritual message. People, Cole wrote, traveled from far and wide to hear Whitefield because of "a concern for their soul." When he heard that Whitefield was nearby, Cole stopped his work, ran to get his wife, and immediately took off on horseback. Cole would later go on to form his own church, illustrating how the Great Awakening inspired ordinary people to think for themselves in religious matters.

NOW IT PLEASED GOD to send Mr. Whitefield into this land; and my hearing of his preaching at Philadelphia, like one of the Old apostles, and many thousands flocking to hear him preach the Gospel, and great numbers were converted to Christ; I felt the Spirit of God drawing me by conviction, longed to see and hear him, and wished he would come this way. And I soon heard he was come to New York and the Jerseys and great multitudes flocking after him under great concern for their Souls and many converted which brought on my concern more and more hoping soon to see him but next I heard he was at Long Island, then at Boston, and next at Northampton.

Then one morning all on a Sudden, about 8 or 9 o'clock there came a messenger and said Mr. Whitefield preached at Hartford and Weathersfield yesterday and is to preach at Middletown this morning [October 23, 1740] at ten of the Clock. I was in my field at work. I dropped my tool that I had in my hand and ran home and run through my house and bade my wife get ready quick to go and hear Mr. Whitefield preach at Middletown, and run to my pasture for my horse with all my might fearing that I should be too late to hear him. I brought my horse home and soon mounted and took my wife up and went forward as fast as I thought the horse could bear, and when my horse began to be out of breath, I would get down and put my wife on the saddle and bid her ride as fast as she could and not stop or slack for me except I bade her, and so I would run until I was much out of breath, and then mount my horse again, and so I did several times to favor my horse, we improved every moment to get along as if we were fleeing for our lives, all the while fearing we should be too late to hear the Sermon, for we had twelve miles to ride double in little more than an hour....

And when we came within about half a mile of the road that comes down from Hartford, Weathersfield, and Stepney to Middletown; on high land I saw before me a cloud or fog rising. I first thought it came from the great river [Connecticut River], but as I came nearer the road, I heard a noise something like a low rumbling thunder and presently found it was the noise of horses' feet coming down the road and this cloud was a cloud of dust made by the horses' feet.... As I drew nearer it seemed like a steady stream of horses and their riders, scarcely a horse more than his length behind another, all of a lather and foam with sweat, their breath rolling out of their nostrils in the cloud of dust every jump; every horse seemed to go with all his might to carry his rider to hear news from heaven for the saving of Souls. It made me tremble to see the sight, how the world was in a struggle, I found a [space] between two horses to slip in my horse; and my wife said ... our clothes will be all spoiled see how they look, for they were so covered with dust, that they looked almost all of a color coats, hats, and shirts and horses.

We went down in the stream; I heard no man speak a word all the way three miles but every one pressing forward in great haste and when we got to the old meeting house there was a great multitude; it was said to be 3 or 4,000 of people assembled together, we got off from our horses and shook off the dust, and the ministers were then coming to the meeting house. I turned and looked towards the great river and saw the ferry boats running swift forward ... bringing over loads of people; the oars rowed nimble and quick, every thing men horses and boats seemed to be struggling for life; the land and banks over the river looked black with people and horses all along the 12 miles. I saw no man at work in his field, but all seemed to be gone.

When I saw Mr. Whitefield come upon the scaffold he looked almost angelical, a young, slim slender youth before some thousands of people with a bold undaunted countenance, and my hearing how God was with him everywhere as he came along it solemnized my mind, and put me into a trembling fear before he began to preach; for he looked as if he was clothed with authority from the Great God, and a sweet solemn solemnity sat upon his brow. And my hearing him preach gave me a heart wound; by God's blessing my old foundation was broken up, and I saw that my righteousness would not save me; then I was convinced of the doctrine of Election and went right to quarreling with God about it, because all that I could do would not save me; and he had decreed from Eternity who should be saved and who not.

Questions

1. What religious doctrine does Whitefield preach?

2. How does Cole's account help us to understand why many established religious leaders were alarmed by Whitefield's appearance in the American colonies?

---

27. Pontiac, Two Speeches (1762 and 1763)

Source: Alexander Henry, Travels and Adventures in Canada and the Indian Territories between the Years 1760 and 1776 [1809] (Toronto, 1901), p. 44; and Francis Parkman, The Conspiracy of Pontiac and the Indian Wars after the Conquest of Canada, *6th ed. (Boston, 1874), vol. 1, pp. 204–7.*

Victory in the Seven Years' War, confirmed in the Treaty of Paris of 1763, established British preeminence in North America east of the Mississippi River. To Indians, it was clear that the abrupt departure of the French from Canada and the Mississippi and Ohio valleys, and the continued expansion of the British settler population, posed a dire threat.

In 1763, Indians of the Ohio Valley and Great Lakes launched a revolt against British rule. Although known as Pontiac's Rebellion, after an Ottawa war leader, the rebellion owed much to the teachings of Neolin, a Delaware religious prophet. Neolin and Pontiac promoted a pan-Indian identity among members of different tribes, urging all Indians to fight to regain their lost independence. In 1763, Indians seized several British forts and killed hundreds of white settlers who had intruded onto Indian lands. British forces soon launched a counterattack, and one by one the tribes made peace. But the uprising laid the groundwork for future resistance.

ENGLISHMAN, ALTHOUGH YOU have conquered the French, you have not yet conquered us! We are not your slaves. These lakes, these woods and mountains, were left to us by our ancestors. They are our inheritance; and we will part with them to none. Your nation supposes that we, like the white people, cannot live without bread—and pork—and beef! But, you ought to know, that He, the Great Spirit and Master of Life, has provided food for us, in these spacious lakes, and on these woody mountains. . . .

• • •

"A Delaware Indian [Neolin]," said Pontiac, "conceived an eager desire to learn wisdom from the Master of Life; but, being ignorant where to find him, he had recourse to fasting, dreaming, and magical incantations. By these means it was revealed to him, that, by moving forward in a straight, undeviating course, he would reach the abode of the Great Spirit. He told his purpose to no one, and having provided the equipments of a hunter,—gun, powder-horn, ammunition, and a kettle for preparing his food,—he set out on his errand. For some time he journeyed on in high hope and confidence. On the evening of the eighth day, he stopped by the side of a brook at the edge of a meadow, where he began to make ready his evening meal, when, looking up, he saw three large openings in the woods before him, and three well-beaten paths which entered them. He was much surprised; but his wonder increased, when, after it had grown dark, the three paths were more clearly visible than ever. Remembering the important object of his journey, he could neither rest nor sleep; and, leaving his fire, he crossed the meadow, and entered the largest of the three openings. He had advanced but a short distance into the forest, when a bright flame sprang out of the ground before him, and arrested his steps. In great amazement, he turned back, and entered the second path, where the same wonderful phenomenon again encountered him; and now, in terror and bewilderment, yet still resolved to persevere, he took the last of the three paths. On this he journeyed a whole day without interruption, when at length, emerging from the forest, he saw before him a vast mountain, of dazzling whiteness. So precipitous was the ascent, that the Indian thought it hopeless to go farther, and looked around him in despair: at that moment, he saw, seated at some distance above, the figure of a beautiful woman arrayed in white, who arose as he looked upon her, and thus accosted him: 'How can you hope, encumbered as you are, to succeed in your design? Go down to the foot of the mountain, throw away your gun, your ammunition, your provisions, and your clothing; wash yourself in the stream which flows there, and you will then be prepared to stand before the Master of Life.' The Indian obeyed, and again began to ascend among the rocks, while the woman, seeing him still discouraged, laughed at his faintness of heart, and told him that, if he wished for success, he must climb by the aid of one hand and one foot only. After great toil and suffering, he at length found himself at the summit. The woman had disappeared, and he was left alone. A rich and beautiful plain lay before him, and at a little distance he saw three great villages, far superior to the squalid wigwams of the Delawares. As he approached the largest, and stood hesitating whether he should enter, a man gorgeously attired stepped forth, and, taking him by the hand, welcomed him to the celestial abode. He then conducted him into the presence of the Great Spirit, where the Indian stood confounded at the unspeakable splendor which surrounded him. The Great Spirit bade him be seated, and thus addressed him:—

"'I am the Maker of heaven and earth, the trees, lakes, rivers, and all things else. I am the Maker of mankind; and because I love you, you must do my will. The land on which you live I have made for you, and not for others. Why do you suffer the white men to dwell among you? My children, you have forgotten the customs and traditions of your forefathers. Why do you not clothe yourselves in skins, as they did, and use the bows and arrows, and the stonepointed lances, which they used? You have bought guns, knives, kettles, and blankets, from the white men, until you can no longer do without them; and, what is worse, you have drunk the poison fire-water, which turns you into fools. Fling all these things away; live as your wise forefathers lived before you. And as for these English,—these dogs dressed in red, who have come to rob you of your hunting-grounds, and drive away the game,—you must lift the hatchet against them. Wipe them from the face of the earth, and then you will win my favor back again, and once more be happy and prosperous.'"

Questions

1. How does Pontiac understand the meaning of freedom?

2. What elements of Indian life does Neolin criticize most strongly?

CHAPTER 5

The American Revolution, 1763–1783

28. Virginia Resolutions on the Stamp Act (1765)

Source: John Pendleton Kennedy, ed., Journals of the House of Burgesses of Virginia *1761–1765 (Richmond, 1907), pp. lxvi–lxvii, 360.*

The passage of the Stamp Act by Parliament in 1765 inspired the first major split between colonists and Great Britain. Pressed for funds because of the enormous expense it had incurred in fighting the Seven Years' War, Parliament for the first time attempted to raise money from direct taxes in the colonies rather than through the regulation of trade. The act required that all sorts of printed material produced in the colonies carry a stamp purchased from authorities.

By imposing the stamp tax without colonial consent, Parliament directly challenged the authority of local elites who, through the assemblies they controlled, had established their power over the raising and spending of money. They were ready to defend this authority in the name of liberty. Virginia's House of Burgesses approved four resolutions offered by the fiery orator Patrick Henry. The Burgesses rejected as too radical the last three resolutions that follow, including one calling for outright resistance to unlawful taxation.

WHEREAS, THE HONOURABLE House of Commons in England, have of late draw[n] into question how far the General Assembly of this colony hath power to enact laws for laying of taxes and imposing duties payable by the people of this, his Majesty's most ancient colony; for settling and ascertaining the same to all future times, the House of Burgesses of this present General Assembly have come to the following resolves.

Resolved, that the first adventurers, settlers of this his Majesty's colony and dominion of Virginia, brought with them and transmitted to their posterity, and all other his Majesty's subjects since inhabiting in this his Majesty's colony, all the privileges and immunities that have at any time been held, enjoyed, and possessed by the people of Great Britain.

Resolved, that by two royal charters granted by King James the first, the colonists aforesaid are declared and entitled to all privileges and immunities of natural born subjects, to all intents and purposes as if they had been abiding and born within the realm of England.

Resolved, that the taxation of the people by themselves, or by persons chosen by themselves to represent them, who can only know what taxes the people are able to bear, or the easiest method of raising them, and must themselves be affected by every tax laid on the people, is the only security against a burdensome taxation, and the distinguishing characteristic of British freedom, without which the ancient constitution cannot exist.

Resolved, that his Majesty's liege people of this ancient colony have enjoyed the right of being thus governed by their own Assembly in the article of taxes and internal police, and that the same have never been forfeited, or any other way yielded up, but have been constantly recognized by the king and people of Great Britain.

Resolved, therefore, that the General Assembly of this colony, together with his Majesty or his substitutes, have in their representatives capacity, the only exclusive right and power to lay taxes and imposts upon the inhabitants of this colony; and that every attempt to vest such power in any other person or persons whatever than the General Assembly aforesaid, is illegal, unconstitutional, and unjust, and has a manifest tendency to destroy British as well as American liberty.

Resolved, that his Majesty's liege people, the inhabitants of this colony, are not bound to yield obedience to any law or ordinance whatever, designed to impose any taxation whatsoever upon them, other than the laws or ordinances of the General Assembly aforesaid.

Resolved, that any person who shall, by speaking or writing, assert or maintain that any person or persons other than the General Assembly of this colony, have any right or power to impose or lay any taxation on the people here, shall be deemed an enemy to his Majesty's colony.

Questions

1. Why do you think the Virginia House of Burgesses adopted the first four resolutions but rejected the final three?

2. What would be the difference between resting the resolutions' arguments on "British freedom" and appealing to a more universal concept of liberty?

29. New York Workingmen Demand a Voice in the Revolutionary Struggle (1770)

Source: Brutus, To the Free and Loyal Inhabitants of the City and Colony of New-York . . . (New York, 1774).

The struggle against British taxation measures of the 1760s greatly expanded the boundaries of colonial politics. The following document illustrates how ordinary workingmen in New York City claimed the right to challenge the city's prominent merchants in determining how far resistance should go. In the aftermath of the Townshend Acts, a series of taxes

imposed by Parliament on the American colonies, leaders in several colonies announced a boycott of British goods. They hoped to pressure British
merchants to persuade their government to repeal the measures. By 1770,
however, colonial merchants, as well as many Americans who did not
want to do without British goods, decided to resume trade. In response, a
New Yorker calling himself Brutus published a call for a continuation of
the policy of nonimportation. He castigated the merchants as "mercantile
Dons" ("Don" being a Spanish word derived from "lord" and suggesting
gentry status). Mechanics (craftsmen), he insisted, had a right to a voice in
public policy. The letter illustrates how the struggle for colonial rights led
to a democratization of politics.

FRIENDS, FELLOW CITIZENS, fellow Countrymen, and fellow
Freeman,

Nothing can be more flagrantly wrong than the assertion of some
of our mercantile Dons, that the mechanics have no right to give
their sentiments about the importation of British commodities. For
who, I would ask, is the member of community, that is absolutely
independent of the rest? Or what particular class among us, has an
exclusive right to decide a question of general concern? When the
Non-Importation Agreement took place, what end was it designed
to answer? Not surely the private emolument of merchants, but the
universal weal of the continent. It was to redeem from perdition,
from total perdition, that stock of English Liberty, to which every
subject, whatever may be his rank, is equally entitled. Amidst all
the disparity of fortune and honors, there is one lot as common to
all Englishmen, as death. It is, that we are all equally free. Sufficient
is it therefore, to show the matchless absurdity of the exclusive claim,
of which a few interested merchants have lately attempted, in a most
assuming manner, to avail themselves, in determining on the question, whether the Non-Importation Agreement shall be rescinded, to
observe, that it was not solemnly entered into for the good of the merchants alone, but for the salvation of the Liberties of us all.

Of this the trading interest of this City were convinced, when, after forming themselves into a Society for executing that Agreement, they not only requested a similar Association of the Mechanics, but by frequent meetings, conspired with them in support of the important Company. When the parties engaged in it, none doubted the necessity of so salutary a measure: every man saw, that between an importation of goods, which stern virtue ought ever to despise as a means to encourage luxury, and the sacrifice of our inestimable Rights as Englishmen, there was no medium. This view of the subject begat and brought to perfection, the important resolution, which has inspired the enemies of our Liberty on the other side of the Atlantic, with fear and astonishment.... Has not our Mother Country, by solemn Act of Legislation, declared that she has a right to impose internal Taxes on us? And is not such an imposition incompatible with our Liberty? But this law is a mere dead letter, unless it be carried into exercise by some future Act. For this Purpose was the Law devised, imposing a Duty upon Tea, Paper, Glass, Painters Colors, etc. the very articles which our Egyptian task-masters thought were most essential to us, as being not hitherto the produce of this country. And shall we not, for our own sakes, show that we can live without them? What are all the riches, the luxuries, and even the conveniences of life, compared with that liberty wherewith God and Nature have set us free, with that inestimable jewel which is the basis of all other enjoyments?... Rouse then my fellow citizen, fellow countrymen, and fellow Freemen, of all ranks, from the man of wealth, to the man whose only portion is Liberty.

Questions

1. What social divisions in the colonies are apparent in this broadside?

2. In what respect does the author believe that all colonists are equal?

30. Association of the New York Sons of Liberty (1773)

Source: Hezekiah Niles, **Principles and Acts of the Revolution in America** *(Baltimore, 1822), pp. 169–70.*

The Sons of Liberty of New York City was one of many such groups that sprang up during the Stamp Act crisis of 1765. It was led by talented and ambitious lesser merchants who enjoyed no standing among the colony's wealthy but commanded a broad following among the city's craftsmen, laborers, and sailors. The Sons took the lead in enforcing the boycott of British imports that led to Parliament's repeal of the act and a second boycott directed against the Townshend Duties of 1767.

In 1773, when Parliament passed the Tea Act, another taxation measure, the Sons again organized resistance. On December 15, the Sons of Liberty announced an agreement or association to resist the Tea Act. Signed by "a great number of the principal gentlemen of the city, merchants, lawyers, and other inhabitants of all ranks," the agreement forthrightly accused Britain of trampling on the freedom of the colonists and threatening to reduce them to "slavery."

━━━━━━━

THE FOLLOWING ASSOCIATION is signed by a great number of the principal gentlemen of the city, merchants, lawyers, and other inhabitants of all ranks, and it is still carried about the city to give an opportunity to those who have not yet signed, to unite with their fellow citizens, to testify their abhorrence to the diabolical project of enslaving America.

THE ASSOCIATION OF THE SONS OF LIBERTY OF NEW YORK

It is essential to the freedom and security of a free people, that no taxes be imposed upon them but by their own consent, or their representatives. For "What property have they in that which another may, by right, take when he pleases to himself?" The former is the undoubted right of Englishmen, to secure which they expended millions and sacrificed the lives of thousands. And yet, to the astonishment of all the world, and the grief of America, the Commons of Great Britain, after the repeal of the memorable and detestable Stamp Act, reassumed the power of imposing taxes on the American colonies; and insisting on it as a necessary badge of parliamentary supremacy, passed a bill, in the seventh year of his present Majesty's reign, imposing duties on all glass, painters' colours, paper, and teas, that should, after the 20th of November, 1767, be "imported from Great Britain into any colony or plantation in America." This bill, after the concurrence of the Lords, obtained the royal assent. And thus they who, from time immemorial, have exercised the right of giving to, or withholding from the crown, their aids and subsidies, according to their *own free will and pleasure*, signified by their representatives in Parliament, do, by the Act in question, deny us, their brethren in America, the enjoyment of the same right. As this denial, and the execution of that Act, involves our slavery, and would sap the foundation of our freedom, whereby we should become slaves to our brethren and fellow subjects, born to no greater stock of freedom than the Americans—the merchants and inhabitants of this city, in conjunction with the merchants and inhabitants of the ancient American colonies, entered into an agreement to decline a part of their commerce with Great Britain, until the above mentioned Act should be totally repealed.

This agreement operated so powerfully to the disadvantage of the manufacturers of England that many of them were unemployed. To appease their clamours, and to provide the subsistence for them, which the non-importation had deprived them of, the Parliament, in 1770, repealed so much of the Revenue Act as imposed a duty on glass, painters' colours, and paper, and left the duty on tea, as *a test of the parliamentary right to tax us*. The merchants of the cities of New York and Philadelphia, having strictly adhered to the agreement, so far as it is related to the importation of articles subject to an American duty, have convinced the ministry, that some other measures must be adopted to execute parliamentary supremacy over this country, and to remove the distress brought on the East India Company, by the ill policy of that Act. Accordingly, to increase the temptation to the shippers of tea from England, an Act of Parliament passed the last session, which gives the whole duty on tea, the company were subject to pay, upon the importation of it into England, to the purchasers and exporters; and when the company have ten millions of pounds of tea in their warehouses exclusive of the quantity they may want to ship, they are allowed to export tea, discharged from the payment of that duty with which they were before chargeable.

In hopes of aid in the execution of this project, by the influence of the owners of the American ships, application was made by the company to the captains of those ships to take the tea on freight; but they virtuously rejected it. Still determined on the scheme, they have chartered ships to bring the tea to this country, which may be hourly expected, to make an important trial of our virtue. If they succeed in the sale of that tea, we shall have no property that we can call our own, and then we may bid adieu to American liberty. Therefore, to prevent a calamity which, of all others, is the most to be dreaded— slavery and its terrible concomitants—we, the subscribers, being influenced from a regard to liberty, and disposed to use all lawful endeavours in our power, to defeat the pernicious project, and to transmit to our posterity those blessings of freedom which our ancestors have handed down to us; and to contribute to the support of the common liberties of America, which are in danger to be subverted, *do*, for those important purposes, agree to associate together, under the name and style of the *sons of New York*, and engage our honour to, and with each other faithfully to observe and perform the following resolutions, viz.

1st. Resolved, that whoever shall aid or abet, or in any manner assist, in the introduction of tea from any place whatsoever, into this colony, while it is subject, by a British Act of Parliament, to the payment of a duty, for the purpose of raising a revenue in America, he shall be deemed an enemy to the liberties of America.

2d. Resolved, that whoever shall be aiding, or assisting, in the landing, or carting of such tea, from any ship, or vessel, or shall hire any house, storehouse, or cellar or any place whatsoever, to deposit the tea, subject to a duty as aforesaid, he shall be deemed an enemy to the liberties of America.

3d. Resolved, that whoever shall sell, or buy, or in any manner contribute to the sale, or purchase of tea, subject to a duty as aforesaid, or shall aid, or abet, in transporting such tea, by land or water, from this city, until the 7th George III, chap. 46, commonly called the Revenue Act, shall be totally and clearly repealed, he shall be deemed an enemy to the liberties of America.

4th. Resolved, that whether the duties on tea, imposed by this Act, be paid in Great Britain or in America, our liberties are equally affected.

5th. Resolved, that whoever shall transgress any of these resolutions, we will not deal with, or employ, or have any connection with him.

Questions

1. How do the Sons of Liberty explain Britain's motivations for passing the Tea Act?

2. What do they consider the relationship between property and liberty?

---

31. Farmington, Connecticut, Resolutions on the Intolerable Acts (1774)

Source: Peter Force, **American Archives** *(Washington, D.C., 1837–53), ser. 4, vol. 1, p. 336.*

Parliament responded to the Boston Tea Party by passing a series of coercive laws. These closed the port of Boston to all trade until the tea had been paid for, radically altered the Massachusetts Charter of 1691 by curtailing town meetings and authorizing the governor to appoint previously elected members of the council, and empowered military commanders to lodge soldiers in private homes. These measures, which Americans called the Intolerable Acts, destroyed the legitimacy of the imperial government in the eyes of many colonists. Opposition now spread to small towns and rural areas that had not participated actively in previous resistance. A gathering of 1,000 residents of Farmington, Connecticut, in May 1774 erected a liberty pole and adopted resolutions proclaiming that they were "the sons of freedom" who "scorn the chains of slavery" Britain had fashioned for America. The Farmington resolutions accused the British ministry of being "instigated by the devil." Especially in New England, the cause of liberty had become the cause of God.

PROCEEDINGS OF FARMINGTON, Connecticut, on the Boston Port Act, May 19, 1774.

Early in the morning was found the following handbill, posted up in various parts of the town, viz:

> To pass through the fire at six o'clock this evening, in honour to the immortal goddess of Liberty, the late infamous Act of the British Parliament for farther distressing the American Colonies; the place of execution will be the public parade, where all Sons of Liberty are desired to attend.

Accordingly, a very numerous and respectable body were assembled of near one thousand people, when a huge pole, just forty-five feet high, was erected and consecrated to the shrine of liberty; after which the Act of Parliament for blocking up the Boston harbour was read aloud, sentenced to the flames and executed by the hands of the common hangman; then the following resolves were passed, *nem.con.*:

1st. That it is the greatest dignity, interest and happiness of every American to be united with our parent State, while our liberties are duly secured, maintained and supported by our rightful Sovereign, whose person we greatly revere; whose government, while duly administered, we are ready with our lives and properties to support.

2d. That the present ministry, being instigated by the devil and led on by their wicked and corrupt hearts, have a design to take away our liberties and properties and to enslave us *forever.*

3d. That the late Act which their malice hath caused to be passed in Parliament, for blocking up the port of Boston, is unjust, illegal and oppressive; and that we and every American are sharers in the insults offered to the town of Boston.

4th. That those pimps and parasites who dared to advise their master to such detestable measures be held in utter abhorrence by us and every American, and their names loaded with the curses of all succeeding generations.

5th. That we scorn the chains of slavery; we despise every attempt to rivet them upon us; we are the sons of freedom and resolved that, till time shall be no more, godlike virtue shall blazon our hemisphere.

Questions

1. How does the language of the resolutions suggest that feelings toward Great Britain have hardened in the colonies?

2. How do the resolutions qualify or limit Americans' sense of loyalty to the British government?

---

32. Thomas Paine, *Common Sense* (1776)

Source: Thomas Paine, Common Sense, *2nd ed. (Philadelphia, 1776), pp. 1, 6–12, 15–30.*

Ironically, a recent emigrant from England offered the most persuasive argument for American independence. Thomas Paine arrived in Philadelphia late in 1774 and quickly became associated with a group of advocates of the American cause. His pamphlet, *Common Sense*, appeared in January

1776. It began not with a recital of colonial grievances but with an attack on the principles of hereditary rule and monarchial government. Paine then drew on the colonists' experiences to make his case for independence. Within the British empire, America's prospects were limited; trading freely with the entire world, its future prosperity was certain. With independence, moreover, the colonies could for the first time insulate themselves from involvement in the endless imperial wars of Europe. But more than such practical considerations, Paine outlined a stirring vision of the historical importance of the American Revolution. The new nation would become the home of freedom, "an asylum for mankind."

Previous political writings had generally been directed toward the educated elite. Paine pioneered a new style of political writing, one designed to expand dramatically the public sphere where political discussion took place. *Common Sense* quickly became one of the most successful and influential pamphlets in the history of political writing.

INTRODUCTION

Perhaps the sentiments contained in the following pages, are not *yet* sufficiently fashionable to procure them general Favor; a long Habit of not thinking a Thing *wrong*, gives it a superficial appearance of being *right*, and raises at first a formidable outcry in defence of Custom. But the Tumult soon subsides. Time makes more Converts than Reason.

As a long and violent abuse of power is generally the means of calling the right of it in question, (and in matters too which might never have been thought of, had not the sufferers been aggravated into the inquiry,) and as the King of England hath undertaken in his *own right*, to support the Parliament in what he calls *Theirs*, and as the good People of this Country are grievously oppressed by the Combination, they have an undoubted privilege to enquire into the Pretensions of both, and equally to reject the Usurpation of *either*.

In the following Sheets, the Author hath studiously avoided every thing which is personal among ourselves. Compliments as well as censure to individuals make no part thereof. The wise and the worthy need not the triumph of a Pamphlet; and those whose sentiments are injudicious or unfriendly will cease of themselves, unless too much pain is bestowed upon their conversions.

The cause of America is in a great measure the cause of all mankind. Many circumstances have, and will arise, which are not local, but universal, and through which the principles of all lovers of mankind are affected, and in the event of which their affections are interested. The laying a country desolate with fire and sword, declaring war against the natural rights of all mankind, and extirpating the defenders thereof from the face of the earth, is the concern of every man to whom nature hath given the power of feeling.

• • •

OF MONARCHY AND HEREDITARY SUCCESSION

Mankind being originally equals in the order of creation, the equality could only be destroyed by some subsequent circumstance; the distinctions of rich, and poor, may in a great measure be accounted for, and that without having recourse to the harsh ill sounding names of oppression and avarice. Oppression is often the *consequence*, but seldom or never the *means* of riches; and though avarice will preserve a man from being necessitously poor, it generally makes him too timorous to be wealthy.

But there is another and greater distinction for which no truly natural or religious reason can be assigned, and that is, the distinction of men into KINGS and SUBJECTS. Male and female are the distinctions of nature, good and bad the distinctions of heaven; but how a race of men came into the world so exalted above the rest, and distinguished like some new species, is worth enquiring into, and whether they are the means of happiness or of misery to mankind.

• • •

All men being originally equals, no *one* by *birth* could have a right to set up his own family in perpetual preference to all others for ever, and though himself might deserve *some* decent degree of honors of his contemporaries, yet his descendants might be far too unworthy to inherit them. One of the strongest *natural* proofs of the folly of hereditary right in kings, is, that nature disapproves it, otherwise she would not so frequently turn it into ridicule by giving mankind an *ass for a lion*.

As to usurpation, no man will be so hardy as to defend it; and that William the Conqueror was an usurper is a fact not to be contradicted. The plain truth is, that the antiquity of English monarchy will not bear looking into.

• • •

Thoughts on the Present State of American Affairs

In the following pages I offer nothing more than simple facts, plain arguments, and common sense: and have no other preliminaries to settle with the reader, than that he will divest himself of prejudice and prepossession, and suffer his reason and his feelings to determine for themselves: that he will put on, or rather that he will not put off, the true character of a man, and generously enlarge his views beyond the present day.

Volumes have been written on the subject of the struggle between England and America. Men of all ranks have embarked in the controversy, from different motives, and with various designs; but all have been ineffectual, and the period of debate is closed. Arms as the last resource decide the contest; the appeal was the choice of the King, and the Continent has accepted the challenge.

• • •

The Sun never shined on a cause of greater worth. 'Tis not the affair of a City, a County, a Province, or a Kingdom; but of a Continent—of at least one eighth part of the habitable Globe. 'Tis not the concern of a day, a year, or an age; posterity are virtually involved in the contest, and will be more or less affected even to the end of time, by the proceedings now. Now is the seed-time of Continental union, faith and honour. The least fracture now will be like a name engraved with the point of a pin on the tender rind of a young oak; the wound would enlarge with the tree, and posterity read it in full grown character.

• • •

As much hath been said of the advantages of reconciliation, which, like an agreeable dream, hath passed away and left us as we were, it is but right that we should examine the contrary side of the argument, and enquire into some of the many material injuries which these Colonies sustain, and always will sustain, by being connected with and dependent on Great-Britain. To examine that connection and dependence, on the principles of nature and common sense, to see what we have to trust to, if separated, and what we are to expect, if dependant.

I have heard it asserted by some, that as America has flourished under her former connection with Great-Britain, the same connection is necessary towards her future happiness, and will always have the same effect. Nothing can be more fallacious than this kind of argument. We may as well assert that because a child has thrived upon milk, that it is never to have meat, or that the first twenty years of our lives is to become a precedent for the next twenty. But even this is admitting more than is true; for I answer roundly, that America would have flourished as much, and probably much more, had no European power taken any notice of her. The commerce by which she hath enriched herself are the necessaries of life, and will always have a market while eating is the custom of Europe.

But she has protected us, say some. That she hath engrossed us is true, and defended the Continent at our expense as well as her own, is admitted; and she would have defended Turkey from the same motive, *viz.* for the sake of trade and dominion.

Alas! we have been long led away by ancient prejudices and made large sacrifices to superstition. We have boasted the protection of Great Britain, without considering, that her motive was *interest* not *attachment*; and that she did not protect us from *our enemies* on *our account*; but from *her enemies* on *her own account*, from those who had no quarrel with us on any *other account*, and who will always be our enemies on the *same account*. Let Britain waive her pretensions to the

Continent, or the Continent throw off the dependence, and we should be at peace with France and Spain, were they at war with Britain.

• • •

But Britain is the parent country, say some. Then the more shame upon her conduct. Even brutes do not devour their young, nor savages make war upon their families; Wherefore, the assertion, if true, turns to her reproach; but it happens not to be true, or only partly so, and the phrase *parent* or *mother country* hath been jesuitically adopted by the King and his parasites, with a low papistical design of gaining an unfair bias on the credulous weakness of our minds. Europe, and not England, is the parent country of America. This new World hath been the asylum for the persecuted lovers of civil and religious liberty from *every part* of Europe. Hither have they fled, not from the tender embraces of the mother, but from the cruelty of the monster; and it is so far true of England, that the same tyranny which drove the first emigrants from home, pursues their descendants still.

• • •

Our plan is commerce, and that, well attended to, will secure us the peace and friendship of all Europe; because it is the interest of all Europe to have America a free port. Her trade will always be a protection, and her barrenness of gold and silver secure her from invaders.

I challenge the warmest advocate for reconciliation to show a single advantage that this continent can reap by being connected with Great Britain. I repeat the challenge; not a single advantage is derived. Our corn will fetch its price in any market in Europe, and our imported goods must be paid for by them where we will.

But the injuries and disadvantages which we sustain by that connection, are without number; and our duty to mankind at large, as well as to ourselves, instruct us to renounce the alliance: because, any submission to, or dependence on, Great Britain, tends directly to involve this Continent in European wars and quarrels, and set us at variance with nations who would otherwise seek our friendship, and against whom we have neither anger nor complaint. As Europe is our market for trade, we ought to form no partial connection with any part of it. It is the true interest of America to steer clear of European contentions, which she never can do, while, by her dependence on Britain, she is made the makeweight in the scale of British politics.

• • •

'Tis repugnant to reason, to the universal order of things, to all examples from former ages, to suppose that this Continent can long remain subject to any external power. The most sanguine in Britain doth not think so. The utmost stretch of human wisdom cannot, at this time, compass a plan, short of separation, which can promise the continent even a year's security. Reconciliation is *now* a fallacious dream. Nature hath deserted the connection, and art cannot supply her place. For, as Milton wisely expresses, "never can true reconcilement grow where wounds of deadly hate have pierced so deep."

A government of our own is our natural right: and when a man seriously reflects on the precariousness of human affairs, he will become convinced, that it is infinitely wiser and safer, to form a constitution of our own in a cool deliberate manner, while we have it in our power, than to trust such an interesting event to time and chance.

• • •

O! ye that love mankind! Ye that dare oppose not only the tyranny but the tyrant, stand forth! Every spot of the old world is overrun with oppression. Freedom hath been hunted round the Globe. Asia and Africa have long expelled her. Europe regards her like a stranger, and England hath given her warning to depart. O! receive the fugitive, and prepare in time an asylum for mankind.

Questions

1. Why does Paine begin his argument for independence with an attack on the principle of monarchy and hereditary succession?

2. What passages illustrate Paine's effort to write in language ordinary readers can understand?

33. Samuel Seabury's Argument against Independence (1775)

Source: *Samuel Seabury*, An Alarm to the Legislature of the Province of
New York *(New York, 1775), pp. 2–5.*

A native of Connecticut, graduate of Yale College, and Anglican minister,
Samuel Seabury was a devoted Loyalist who in 1774 and 1775 published
several pamphlets opposing the revolutionary movement. After being
briefly jailed for his views, he took refuge in New York City when it was
under British occupation during the War of Independence. Unlike many
Loyalists, Seabury remained in the United States after the war and
became the new nation's first Episcopal bishop.

━━━━━━━

WHEN YOU REFLECT upon the present confused and distressed
state of this, and the other colonies, I am persuaded, that you will
think no apology necessary for the liberty I have taken, of addressing you on that subject. The unhappy contention we have entered
into with our parent state, would inevitably be attended with many
disagreeable circumstances, with many and great inconveniences to
us, even were it conducted on our part, with propriety and moderation. What then must be the case, when all proper and moderate
measures are rejected? When not even the appearance of decency is
regarded? When nothing seems to be consulted, but how to perplex,
irritate, and affront, the British Ministry, Parliament, Nation and
King? When every scheme that tends to peace, is branded with igno-
miny; as being the machination of slavery! When nothing is called
FREEDOM but SEDITION! Nothing LIBERTY but REBELLION!

I will not presume to encroach so far upon your time, as to attempt
to point out the causes of our unnatural contention with Great Britain. You are well acquainted with them.—Nor will I attempt to trace
out the progress of that infatuation, which hath so deeply, so miser-
ably, infected the Colonies. You must have observed its rise, and noted

its rapid growth. But I intreat your patience and candour, while I make some observations on the conduct of the Colonies in general, and of this Colony in particular, in the present dispute with our mother country: By which it will appear, that most, if not all the measures that have been adopted, have been illegal in their beginning, tyrannical in their operation,—and that they must be ineffectual in the event.

It is the happiness of the British Government, and of all the British Colonies, that the people have a right to share in the legislature. This right they exercise by choosing representatives; and thereby constituting one branch of the legislative authority. But when they have chosen their representatives, that right, which was before diffused through the whole people, centers in their Representatives alone; and can legally be exercised by none but them. They become the guardians of the lives, the liberties, the rights and properties, of the people: And as they are under the most sacred obligations to discharge their trust with prudence and fidelity, so the people are under the strongest obligations to treat them with honour and respect; and to look to them for redress of all those grievances that they can justly complain of.

But in the present dispute with Great Britain, the representatives of the people have not only been utterly disregarded, but their dignity has been trampled upon, and their authority contravened. A Committee, chosen in a tumultuous, illegal manner, usurped the most despotic authority over the province. They entered into contracts, compacts, combinations, treaties of alliance, with the other colonies, without any power from the legislature of the province. They agreed with the other Colonies to send Delegates to meet in convention at Philadelphia, to determine upon the rights and liberties of the good people of this province, unsupported by any Law. . . .

The state to which the Grand Congress, and the subordinate Committees, have reduced the colonies, is really deplorable. They have introduced a system of the most oppressive tyranny that can possibly be imagined;—a tyranny, not only over the actions, but over the words, thoughts, and minds, of the good people of this province.

People have been threatened with the vengeance of a mob, for speaking in support of order and good government. Every method has been used to intimidate the printers from publishing any thing, which tended to peace, or seemed in favour of government; while the most detestable libels against the King, the British parliament, and Ministry, have been eagerly read, and extravagantly commended, as the matchless productions of some heaven-born genius, glowing with the pure flame of civil liberty....

Behold, Gentlemen, behold the wretched state to which we are reduced! A foreign power is brought in to govern this province. Laws made at Philadelphia, by factious men from New-England, New-Jersey, Pennsylvania, Maryland, Virginia, and the Carolinas, are imposed upon us by the most imperious menaces. Money is levied upon us without the consent of our representatives: which very money, under color of relieving the poor people of Boston, it is too probable will be employed to raise an army against the King. Mobs and riots are encouraged, in order to force submission to the tyranny of the Congress.

Questions

1. Why does Seabury believe the Continental Congress and local committees are undermining Americans' liberties?

2. How does Seabury differ from advocates of independence in his understanding of freedom?

CHAPTER 6

The Revolution Within

34. Abigail and John Adams on Women and the American Revolution (1776)

Source: Charles F. Adams, ed., Familiar Letters of John Adams and His Wife Abigail Adams during the Revolution *(New York: Hurd and Houghton, 1876), pp. 148–50, 155.*

Abigail Adams was one of the revolutionary era's most important women. During the War of Independence, she peppered her husband, John Adams, with questions about the progress of the struggle, kept him informed of events in Massachusetts, and offered opinions on political matters. When Adams served as president during the 1790s he relied on her advice more than on members of his cabinet. In March 1776, Abigail Adams wrote her best-known letter to her husband. She urged Congress, when it drew up a new "Code of Laws," to "remember the ladies." All men, she warned, "would be tyrants if they could."

At a time when many Americans—slaves, servants, women, Indians, apprentices, propertyless men—were denied full freedom, the struggle against Britain inspired challenges to all sorts of inequalities. As John Adams's reply demonstrates, not all American leaders welcomed this upheaval. To him, it was an affront to the natural order of things. To others, it formed the essence of the American Revolution.

Abigail Adams to John Adams

BRAINTREE [MASS.], MARCH 31, 1776

I wish you would ever write me a letter half as long as I write you, and tell me if you may where your fleet are gone? What sort of defense Virginia can make against our common enemy? Whether it is so situated as to make an able defense? Are not the gentry lords and the common people vassals, are they not like the uncivilized natives Britain represents us to be? I hope their riflemen who have shown themselves very savage and even blood-thirsty, are not a specimen of the generality of the people....

I have sometimes been ready to think that the passion for Liberty cannot be equally strong in the breasts of those who have been accustomed to deprive their fellow creatures of theirs. Of this I am certain, that it is not founded upon that generous and Christian principle of doing to others as we would that others should do unto us....

I feel very differently at the approach of spring to what I did a month ago. We knew not then whether we could plant or sow with safety, whether when we had toiled we could reap the fruits of our own industry, whether we could rest in our own cottages, or whether we should not be driven from the sea coasts to seek shelter in the wilderness. But now we feel as if we might sit under our own vine and eat the good of the land.... I think the sun looks brighter, the birds sing more melodiously, and nature puts on a more cheerful countenance. We feel a temporary peace, and the poor fugitives are returning to their deserted habitations.

Though we felicitate ourselves, we sympathize with those who are trembling lest the lot of Boston should be theirs. But they cannot be in similar circumstances unless ... cowardice should take possession of them. They have time and warning given them to see the evil and shun it.

I long to hear that you have declared an independency, and by the way in the new Code of Laws which I suppose it will be necessary for you to make I desire you would Remember the Ladies, and be more generous and favorable to them than your ancestors. Do not put such unlimited power into the hands of the husbands. Remember all men would be tyrants if they could. If particular care and attention is not paid to the Ladies we are determined to foment a Rebellion, and will not hold ourselves bound by any laws in which we have no voice, or representation.

That your sex are naturally tyrannical is a truth so thoroughly established as to admit of no dispute, but such of you as wish to be happy willingly give up the harsh title of Master for the more tender and endearing one of Friend. Why then, not put it out of the power of the vicious and the lawless to use us with cruelty and indignity with impunity? Men of sense in all ages abhor those customs which treat us only as the vassals of your sex. Regard us then as beings placed by providence under your protection and in imitation of the Supreme Being make use of that power only for our happiness.

John Adams to Abigail Adams

PHILADELPHIA, APRIL 14, 1776

As to Declarations of Independency, be patient.... As to your extraordinary Code of Laws, I cannot but laugh. We have been told that our struggle has loosened the bands of government everywhere. That children and apprentices were disobedient, that schools and colleges were grown turbulent, that Indians slighted their guardians and Negroes grew insolent to their masters. But your letter was the first intimation that another tribe more numerous and powerful than all the rest were grown discontented. This is rather too coarse a compliment but you are so saucy, I won't blot it out.

Depend on it. We know better than to repeal our masculine systems. Although they are in full force, you know they are little more than theory. We dare not exert our power in its full latitude. We are obligated to go fair, and softly, and in practice you knew we are the subjects. We have only the names of Masters, and rather than give this up, which would completely subject us to the despotism of the petticoat, I hope General Washington, and all our brave heroes, would fight. I am sure every good politician would plot, as long as he would against despotism, empire, monarchy, aristocracy, oligarchy, or ochlocracy [mob rule]. A fine story indeed.

Questions:

1. What do you think Abigail Adams has in mind when she writes of the "unlimited power" husbands exercise over their wives?

2. Why did the struggle for independence "loosen the bands of government everywhere," as John Adams remarks?

35. Jefferson's Bill for Establishing Religious Freedom (1779)

Source: Paul L. Ford, ed., The Works of Thomas Jefferson *(12 vols.: New York, 1904–5), vol. 2, pp. 438–41.*

A strong advocate of the separation of church and state, Thomas Jefferson drafted a bill to that end in 1779. In Virginia before independence, all persons, regardless of religious persuasion, were taxed to support the Anglican church. The struggle for independence led Baptists, Methodists, and members of nonestablished churches to demand that each religion support itself, without governmental assistance. Jefferson's bill was opposed by a group including Patrick Henry, who favored offering governmental support to a variety of churches. It took until 1786 for Jefferson's measure to become law; at the time he was in Paris, serving as American ambassador to France, and James Madison shepherded it through the legislature.

SECTION I.   Well aware that the opinions and belief of men depend not on their own will, but follow involuntarily the evidence proposed to their minds; that Almighty God hath created the mind free, and manifested his supreme will that free it shall remain by making it altogether insusceptible of restraint; that all attempts to influence it by temporal punishments, or burthens, or by civil incapacitations, tend only to beget habits of hypocrisy and meanness, and are a departure from the plan of the holy author of our religion, who being lord both of body and mind, yet choose not to propagate it by coercions on either, as was in his Almighty power to do, but to exalt it by its influence on reason alone; that the impious presumption of legislature and ruler, civil as well as ecclesiastical, who, being themselves but fallible and uninspired men, have assumed dominion over the faith of others, setting up their own opinions and modes of thinking as the only true and infallible, and as such endeavoring to impose them on others, hath established and maintained false religions over the greatest part of the world and through all time: That to compel a man to furnish contributions of money for the propagation of opinions which he disbelieves and abhors, is sinful and tyrannical; that even the forcing him to support this or that teacher of his own religious persuasion, is depriving him of the comfortable liberty of giving his contributions to the particular pastor whose morals he would make his pattern, and whose powers he feels most persuasive to righteousness; and is withdrawing from the ministry those temporary rewards, which proceeding from an approbation of their personal conduct, are an additional incitement to earnest and unremitting labours for the instruction of mankind; that our civil rights have no dependance on our religious opinions, any more than our opinions in physics or geometry; and therefore the proscribing any citizen as unworthy the public confidence by laying upon him an incapacity of being called to offices of trust or emolument, unless he profess or renounce this or that religious opinion, is depriving him injudiciously of those privileges and advantages to which, in common with his fellow-citizens, he has a natural right; that it tends also to corrupt the principles of that very religion it is meant to encourage, by bribing with a monopoly of worldly honours and emoluments, those who will externally profess and conform to it; that though indeed these are criminals who do not withstand such temptation, yet neither are those innocent who lay the bait in their way; that the opinions of men are not the object of civil government, nor under its jurisdiction; that to suffer the civil magistrate to intrude his powers into the field of opinion and to restrain the profession or propagation of principles on supposition of their ill tendency is a dangerous falacy, which at once destroys all religious liberty, because he being of course judge of that tendency will make his opinions the rule of judgment, and approve or condemn the sentiments of others only as they shall square with or suffer from his own; that it is time enough for the rightful purposes of civil government for its officers to interfere when principles break out into overt acts against peace and good order; and finally, that truth is great and will prevail if left to herself; that she is the proper and sufficient antagonist to error, and has nothing to fear from the conflict unless by human interposition disarmed of her natural weapons, free argument and debate; errors ceasing to be dangerous when it is permitted freely to contradict them.

SECT. II.   We the General Assembly of Virginia do enact that no man shall be compelled to frequent or support any religious worship, place, or ministry whatsoever, nor shall be enforced, restrained, molested, or burthened in his body or goods, or shall otherwise suffer, on account of his religious opinions or belief; but that all men shall be free to profess, and by argument to maintain, their opinions in matters of religion, and that the same shall in no wise diminish, enlarge, or affect their civil capacities.

SECT. III.   And though we well know that this Assembly, elected by the people for their ordinary purposes of legislation only, have no power to restrain the acts of succeeding Assemblies, constituted with powers equal to our own, and that therefore to declare this act to be irrevocable would be of no effect in law; yet we are free to declare, and do declare, that the rights hereby asserted are of the natural rights of mankind, and that if any act shall be hereafter passed to repeal the present or to narrow its operations, such act will be an infringement of natural right.

Questions

1. Why does Jefferson declare that religious freedom is a "natural right"?

2. Does Jefferson seek to weaken or strengthen religion by prohibiting governmental enforcement of religious belief?

---

36. John Adams on the American Revolution (1818)

Source: *The Works of John Adams* (Boston, 1856), vol. 10, pp. 282–89.

In this letter to Hezekiah Niles of Baltimore, the editor of the newspaper *Niles' Weekly Register*, John Adams outlined his view of the causes of the American Revolution. The real revolution, he insisted, had been a change in the mindset and allegiances of the people, which took place before the War of Independence. Adams believed it essential that young people born after the Revolution study its history, so as to develop a sense of national identity.

QUINCY, FEBRUARY 13, 1818

Mr. Niles,

The American Revolution was not a trifling nor a common event. Its effects and consequences have already been awful [inspiring awe] over a great part of the globe. And when and where are they to cease?

But what do we mean by the American Revolution? Do we mean the American War? The Revolution was effected before the War commenced. The Revolution was in the minds and hearts of the People. A change in their religious sentiments, of their duties and obligations. While the King, and all in authority under him, were believed to govern, in justice and mercy according to the laws and constitutions derived to them from the God of Nature, and transmitted to them by their ancestors—they thought themselves bound to pray for the King and Queen and all the royal family, and all the authority under them, as ministers ordained of God for their good. But when they saw those powers renouncing all the principles of authority, and bent upon the destruction of all the securities of their lives, liberties and properties, they thought it their duty to pray for the Continental Congress and all the thirteen State Congresses, etc.

There might be, and there were others, who thought less about religion and conscience, but had certain habitual sentiments of allegiance and loyalty derived from their education; but believing allegiance and protection to be reciprocal, when protection was withdrawn, they thought allegiance was dissolved.

Another alteration was common to all. The people of America had been educated in an habitual affection for England as their mother-country; and while they thought her a kind and tender parent, (erroneously enough, however, for she never was such a mother,) no affection could be more sincere. But when they found her a cruel bedlam willing, like Lady Macbeth, to "dash their Brains out," it is no wonder if their fillial affections ceased and were changed into indignation and horror.

This radical change in the principles, opinions sentiments and affection of the people, was the real American Revolution.

By what means, this great and important alteration in the religious, moral, political and social character of the people of thirteen Colonies, all distinct, unconnected and independent of each other, was begun, pursued and accomplished, it is surely interesting to Humanity to investigate, and perpetuate to posterity....

The Colonies had grown up under constitutions of government, so different, there was so great a variety of religions, they were composed of so many different nations, their customs, manners and habits had so little resemblance, and their intercourse had been so rare and their knowledge of each other so imperfect, that to unite them in the same principles in theory and the same system of action was certainly a very difficult enterprise. The complete accomplishment of it, in so short a time and by such simple means, was perhaps a singular example in the history of mankind. Thirteen clocks were made to strike together; a perfection of mechanism which no artist had ever before effected.

John Adams

Questions

1. Why does Adams believe that the War of Independence was not the essence of the American Revolution?

2. What does he see as the obstacles to forging a single sense of American identity?

37. Noah Webster on Equality (1787)

Source: Noah Webster, **An Examination into the Leading Principles of the Federal Constitution** *(Philadelphia, 1787), pp. 46–47.*

Americans of the revolutionary generation were preoccupied with the social conditions of freedom. Could a republic survive with a sizable dependent class of citizens? In the excerpt that follows, from a pamphlet published in 1787, the educator and political writer Noah Webster identified equality as essential for the stability of republican government. Citing and amending the teachings of the French political theorist Montesquieu, Webster proclaimed, "A general and tolerably equal distribution of landed property is the whole basis of national freedom." "Equality," he added, was "the very soul of a republic."

To most free Americans, "equality" meant equal opportunity, rather than equality of condition. Many leaders of the Revolution nevertheless assumed that in the exceptional circumstances of the New World, with its vast areas of available land and large population of independent farmers and artisans, the natural workings of society would enable all free Americans to acquire land and achieve, if not complete equality, at least the economic independence necessary for political "virtue."

IN AMERICA, WE begin our empire with more popular privileges than the Romans ever enjoyed. We have not to struggle against a monarch or an aristocracy—power is lodged in the mass of the people.

On reviewing the English history, we observe a progress similar to that in Rome—an incessant struggle for liberty from the date of Magna Charta, in John's reign, to the revolution. The struggle has been successful, by abridging the enormous power of the nobility. But we observe that the power of the people has increased in an exact proportion to their acquisitions of property. Wherever the right of primogeniture is established, property must accumulate and remain in families. Thus the landed property in England will never be sufficiently distributed, to give the powers of government wholly into the hands of the people. But to assist the struggle for liberty, commerce has interposed, and in conjunction with manufacturers, thrown a vast weight of property into the democratic scale. Wherever we cast our eyes, we see this truth, that *property* is the basis of *power;* and this, being established as a cardinal point, directs us to the means of preserving our freedom. Make laws, irrevocable laws in every state, destroying and barring entailments; leave real estates to revolve from hand to hand, as time and accident may direct; and no family influence can be acquired and established for a series of generations—no man can obtain dominion over a large territory— the laborious and saving, who are generally the best citizens, will possess each his share of property and power, and thus the balance of wealth and power will continue where it is, in the *body of the people.*

A general and tolerably equal distribution of landed property is the whole basis of national freedom: The system of the great Montesquieu will ever be erroneous, till the words *property or lands in fee simple* are substituted for *virtue*, throughout his *Spirit of Laws*.

Virtue, patriotism, or love of country, never was and never will be, till mens' natures are changed, a fixed, permanent principle and support of government. But in an agricultural country, a general possession of land in fee simple, may be rendered perpetual, and the inequalities introduced by commerce, are too fluctuating to endanger government. An equality of property, with a necessity of alienation, constantly operating to destroy combinations of powerful families, is the very *soul of a republic*—While this continues, the people will inevitably possess both *power* and *freedom;* when this is lost, power departs, liberty expires, and a commonwealth will inevitably assume some other form.

The liberty of the press, trial by jury, the Habeas Corpus writ, even Magna Charta itself, although justly deemed the palladia of freedom, are all inferior considerations, when compared with a general distribution of real property among every class of people. The power of entailing estates is more dangerous to liberty and republican government, than all the constitutions that can be written on paper, or even than a standing army. Let the people have property, and they *will* have power—a power that will for ever be exerted to prevent a restriction of the press, and abolition of trial by jury, or the abridgement of any other privilege. The liberties of America, therefore, and her forms of government, stand on the broadest basis. Removed from the fears of a foreign invasion and conquest, they are not exposed to the convulsions that shake other governments; and the principles of freedom are so general and energetic, as to exclude the possibility of a change in our republican constitutions.

Questions

1. Why does Webster consider an equal distribution of landed property more important to freedom than liberty of the press, trial by jury, and other rights?

2. Why does Webster believe the republican institutions of the United States will survive indefinitely?

---

38. Liberating Indentured Servants (1784)

Source: **New York Independent Journal,** *January 24, 1784.*

The upsurge of demands for equality during the Revolution brought into question many forms of inequality. In 1784, a group of "respectable" New Yorkers proposed to "liberate" a newly arrived shipload of indentured servants on the grounds that their status was "contrary to ... the idea of liberty this country has so happily established." The incident was one small contribution to the rapid decline of indentured servitude, which by 1800 had all but disappeared from the United States. This development sharpened the distinction between freedom and slavery, and between a northern economy relying on what would come to be called "free labor" (that is, working for wages or owning a farm or shop) and a South ever more heavily dependent on the labor of slaves.

WHEREAS THE TRAFFIC of *White people*, heretofore countenanced by this State while under the arbitrary control of the British Government, is contrary to the feelings of a number of respectable Citizens, and to the idea of *liberty* this country has so happily established.

And whereas it is necessary to encourage emigration to this country, upon the most liberal plan, and for that purpose, a number of Citizens of this State, have proposed to *liberate* a cargo of Servants just arrived, by paying their passage, and repaying themselves by a small rateable deduction out of the wages of such Servants, Such of the Citizens of this State as wish to encourage so laudable an undertaking, and if necessary, to petition the Legislature for a completion of their humane intentions, are requested to meet at the Hyderally Tavern, the lower end of King Street, *this Evening*, at Six of the Clock.

Questions

1. What practical reason does the notice give for eliminating indentured servitude?

2. Why do you think the notice singles out the sale of "White people" as contrary to liberty?

---

39. Letter of Phillis Wheatley (1774)

Source: **Connecticut Gazette; and the Universal Intelligencer,** *March 11, 1774.*

The revolutionary generation's emphasis on liberty inevitably raised questions about the future of slavery in the new republic. Many slaves saw the struggle for independence as an opportunity to assert their own claims to freedom. This letter to the Rev. Samson Occom, a Native American poet and Presbyterian minister, from the celebrated black poet Phillis Wheatley of Massachusetts, who would not gain her own freedom until 1778, is an early antislavery statement pointing to the contradiction between the revolutionary language of liberty and the continued reality of slavery. But the stark fact is that slavery survived the Revolution and continued to grow. The first national census, in 1790, revealed that despite the many who had become free through state laws, voluntary manumission, and escape, there were 700,000 slaves in the United states—200,000 more than in 1776.

REV'D AND HONOR'D SIR,

I have this Day received your obliging kind epistle, and am greatly satisfied with your reasons respecting the Negroes, and think highly reasonable what you offer in vindication of their natural rights: Those that invade them cannot be insensible that the divine light is chasing away the thick darkness which broods over the land of Africa; and the chaos which has reign'd so long, is converting into beautiful order, and reveals more and more clearly, the glorious dispensation of civil and religious Liberty, which are so inseparably limited, that there is little or no enjoyment of one without the other.

Otherwise, perhaps, the Israelites had been less solicitous for their freedom from Egyptian slavery; I do not say they would have been contented without it, by no means, for in every human breast, God has implanted a principle, which we call love of freedom; it is impatient of oppression, and pants for deliverance; and by the leave of our modern Egyptians I will assert, that the same principle lives in us. God grant deliverance in his own way and time, and get him honour upon all those whose avarice impels them to countenance and help forward the calamities of their fellow creatures.

This I desire not for their hurt, but to convince them of the strange absurdity of their conduct whose words and actions are so diametrically, opposite. How well the cry for liberty, and the reverse disposition for the exercise of oppressive power over others agree,—I humbly think it does not require the penetration of a philosopher to determine.

Questions

1. What does Wheatley mean by the "absurdity" of Americans' conduct?

2. How does she use the language of the white revolutionaries to argue for an end to slavery?

40. Benjamin Rush, Thoughts upon Female Education (1787)

Source: The Universal Asylum *and* The Columbian Magazine, *April 1790, pp. 209–13, May 1790, 288–92.*

A leader of the struggle for independence in Pennsylvania and a signer of the Declaration of Independence, Benjamin Rush was also a physician and a leading reformer, an advocate of the abolition of slavery and capital punishment, and a proponent of public education. In 1787, in a speech to the Board of Visitors of the Young Ladies Academy of Philadelphia, Rush explained why conditions of life in the United States and the republican form of government established by the Revolution made it imperative to extend educational opportunities to American women. Rush was hardly a believer in full equality for women. Their political role, he believed, was to train their sons in "the principles of liberty" so that they could act as virtuous citizens. But he also noted that many economic opportunities were open to American women that did not exist in Europe and that to take advantage of them, women needed greater access to education than they had enjoyed in the past. Rush's lecture illustrates how the struggle for independence threw into question many long-standing assumptions about how society should be organized.

THE EDUCATION OF young ladies, in this country, should be conducted upon principles very different from what it is in Great Britain, and in some respects different from what it was when we were part of a monarchical empire.

There are several circumstances in the situation, employments, and duties of women, in America, which require a peculiar mode of education.

I. The early marriages of our women, by contracting the time allowed for education, render it necessary to contract its plan, and to confine it chiefly to the more useful branches of literature.

II. The state of property, in America, renders it necessary for the greatest part of our citizens to employ themselves, in different occupations, for the advancement of their fortunes. This cannot be done without the assistance of the female members of the community. They must be the stewards, and guardians of their husbands' property. That education, therefore, will be most proper for our women, which teaches them to discharge the duties of those offices with the most success and reputation.

III. ... A principal share of the instruction of children naturally devolves upon the women. It becomes us therefore to prepare them by a suitable education, for the discharge of this most important duty of mothers.

IV. The equal share that every citizen has in the liberty, and the possible share he may have in the government, of our country, make it necessary that our ladies should be qualified to a certain degree by a peculiar and suitable education, to concur in instructing their sons in the principles of liberty and government....

The branches of literature most essential for a young lady, in this country, appear to be,

I. A knowledge of the English language. She should not only read, but speak and spell it correctly. The usual mode of teaching English syntax by means of rules committed to memory, appears to be as absurd as to teach a child to walk, by instructing it in the names and powers of the muscles which move the lower extremities.... Familiar conversations are alone proper for this purpose....

II. Pleasure and interest conspire to make the writing of a fair and legible hand, a necessary branch of female education....

III. Some knowledge of figures and book-keeping is absolutely necessary to qualify a young lady for the duties which await her in this country....

IV. An acquaintance with geography and some instruction in chronology will enable a young lady to read history, biography, and travels, with advantage; and thereby qualify her not only for a general intercourse with the world, but, to be an agreeable companion for a sensible man. To these branches of knowledge may be added, in some instances, a general acquaintance with the ... principles of chemistry, and natural philosophy, particularly with such parts of them as are applicable to domestic and culinary purposes.

V. Vocal music should never be neglected, in the education of a young lady, in this country. Besides preparing her to join in that part of public worship which consists in psalmody, it will enable her to soothe the cares of domestic life.

VI. Dancing is by no means an improper branch of education for an American lady. It promotes health and renders the figure and motions of the body easy and agreeable. I anticipate the time when the resources of conversation shall be so far multiplied, that the amusement of dancing shall be wholly confined to children. But in our present state of society and knowledge, I conceive it to be an agreeable substitute for the ignoble pleasures of drinking, and gaming, in our assemblies of grown people.

VII. The attention of our young ladies should be directed, as soon as they are prepared for it, to the reading of history-travels-poetry and moral essays ... they subdue that passion for reading novels, which so generally prevails among the fair sex.... They (novels) hold up life, it is true, but it is not as yet life, in America. Our passions have not as yet 'overstepped the modesty of nature.' ...

Let, therefore, all the branches of education which have been mentioned be connected with regular instruction in the Christian religion.... The female breast is the natural soil of Christianity.

Questions

1. What role does Rush foresee for women in the new American republic?

2. What benefits does he anticipate for society and the family from extending educational opportunities to women?

CHAPTER 7

Founding a Nation, 1783–1791

41. Petition of Inhabitants West of the Ohio River (1785)

Source: Petition, signed by sixty persons, April 11, 1785, in Archer B. Hulbert, ed., Ohio in the Time of the Confederation *(Marietta, 1918), pp. 103–6.*

After independence, American leaders believed that the republic's economic health required that farmers have access to land in the West. But they also saw land sales as a potential source of revenue and worried that unregulated settlement would produce endless conflicts with the Indians. Land companies, which lobbied Congress vigorously, hoped to profit by purchasing real estate and reselling it to settlers. The government, they insisted, should step aside and allow private groups to take control of the West's economic development.

The arrival of peace triggered a large population movement from settled parts of the original states into frontier areas like upstate New York and across the Appalachians into Kentucky, Tennessee, and Ohio. In 1785, a group of Ohioans who had suffered severely during the War of Independence petitioned Congress, assailing landlords and speculators who monopolized available acreage and asking that preference in access to "vacant lands" be given to "actual settlements." They proclaimed, "Grant us liberty."

To the honorable the President of the Honorable Congress of the United States of America.

The petition, of us the subscribers now residing on the western side of the Ohio, humbly show our grateful acknowledgments to those patriots of our country who under Divine Providence so wisely directed and steered the helm of government in that great and unparalleled conflict for liberty, bringing to a happy period the troubles of the states, laying the foundation . . . of the most glorious form of government any people on earth could ever yet boast of.

• • •

Notwithstanding when the joyful sound of peace had reached our ears, we had scarce enough left us to support the crying distresses of our families occasioned wholly by being exposed to the ravages of a cruel and savage enemy, on an open frontier where the most of us had the misfortune to reside through the whole continuance of the war, where the only recourse was to sit confined in forts for the preservation of our lives, by which we were reduced almost to the lowest ebb of poverty, the greatest part of us having no property in lands, our stocks reduced almost to nothing, our case seemed desperate.

But viewing as it appeared to us an advantage offering of vacant lands which the alarming necessities we were under joined with the future prospect of bettering our circumstances, invited us to enter on those lands fully determined to comply with every requisition of the legislature. . . . With hopes of future happiness we sat content in the enjoyment of our scanty morsel, thinking ourself safe under the protection of government, when on the fifth of this instant we were visited by a command of men sent by the commandant at Fort McIntosh, with orders from government . . . to dispossess us and to destroy our dwellings . . . by which order it now appears our conduct in settling here is considered by the legislature to be prejudicial to the common good, of which we had not the least conception until now. We are greatly distressed in our present circumstances, and humbly pray if you in your wisdom think proper to grant us liberty, to rest where we are and to grant us the preference to our actual settlements when the land is to be settled by order of the government.

• • •

Questions

1. Who do the authors of the petition consider to be the greatest enemies of their liberty?

2. Who do the authors claim ought to have preference when western land is distributed?

---

42. David Ramsey, American Innovations in Government (1789)

Source: David Ramsey, The History of the American Revolution *(2 vols.: Philadelphia, 1789), pp. 355–57.*

A member of the Continental Congress from South Carolina, David Ramsey published his history of the Revolution in the year the Constitution was ratified. In this excerpt, he lauds the principles of representative government, and the right of future amendment, embodied in the state constitutions and adopted in the national one, as unique American political principles and the best ways of securing liberty. Like many Americans of his era, Ramsey insisted that the political system of the United States was fundamentally different from that of Europe, and offered an opportunity to demonstrate to the rest of the world humankind's capacity for self-government.

THE FAMED SOCIAL compact between the people and their rulers, did not apply to the United States. The sovereignty was in the people. In their sovereign capacity by their representatives, they agreed on forms of government for their own security, and deputed certain individuals as their agents to serve them in public stations agreeably to constitutions, which prescribed their conduct.

The world has not hitherto exhibited so fair an opportunity for promoting social happiness. It is hoped for the honor of human nature, that the result will prove the fallacy of those theories that

mankind are incapable of self government. The ancients, not knowing the doctrine of representation, were apt in their public meetings
to run into confusion, but in America this mode of taking the sense
of the people, is so well understood, and so completely reduced to
system, that its most populous states are often peaceably convened
in an assembly of deputies, not too large for orderly deliberation,
and yet representing the whole in equal proportion. These popular
branches of legislature are miniature pictures of the community,
and from their mode of election are likely to be influenced by the
same interests and feelings with the people whom they represent. . . .
These circumstances give us as great a security that laws will be
made, and government administered for the good of the people, as
can be expected from the imperfection of human institutions.

In this view of the formation and establishment of the American
constitutions, we behold our species in a new situation. In no age
before, and in no other country, did man ever possess an election of
the kind of government, under which he would choose to live. The
constituent parts of the ancient free governments were thrown
together by accident. The freedom of modern European governments was, for the most part, obtained by concessions, or liberality
of monarchs, or military leaders. In America alone, reason and liberty concurred in the formation of constitutions. . . . In one thing
they were all perfect. They left the people in the power of altering
and amending them, whenever they pleased. In this happy pecu-
liarity they placed the science of politics on a footing with the other
sciences, by opening it to improvements from experience, and the
discoveries of future ages. By means of this power of amending
American constitutions, the friends of mankind have fondly hoped
that oppression will one day be no more.

Questions

1. In what ways, according to Ramsey, does the formation of governments
in the United States differ from precedents in other times and places?

2. Why does Ramsey feel that the power to amend the Constitution is so important a political innovation?

---

43. J. Hector St. John de Crèvecoeur, "What, Then, Is the American?" (1782)

Source: J. Hector St. John de Crèvecoeur, **Letters from an American Farmer** *(London, 1782), pp. 48–56.*

In the era of the Revolution, many foreigners celebrated the United States as not only an independent nation but a new society, in which individuals could enjoy opportunities unknown in the Old World and where a new nationality was being forged from the diverse populations of Europe. No one promoted this image of America more enthusiastically than J. Hector St. John de Crèvecoeur, who had settled in New York and married the daughter of a prominent landowner, after serving in the French army fighting the British during the Seven Years' War. He later returned to France and published a glowing account of life in the United States, entitled *Letters from an American Farmer.* As one who had lived in both Europe and the United States, he outlined the differences a newcomer was likely to note between the two societies. His description of the emergence of a "new man" from the diverse populations of Europe would later be popularized as the idea of the American melting pot.

I WISH I could be acquainted with the feelings and thoughts which must agitate the heart and present themselves to the mind of an enlightened Englishman, when he first lands on this continent. He must greatly rejoice that he lived at a time to see this fair country discovered and settled; he must necessarily feel a share of national pride, when he views the chain of settlements which embellishes these extended shores. When he says to himself, this is the work of my countrymen, who, when convulsed by factions, afflicted by a variety of miseries and wants, restless and impatient, took refuge here. They brought along with them their national genius, to which they principally owe what liberty they enjoy, and what substance they possess.

Here he sees the industry of his native country displayed in a new manner, and traces in their works the embryos of all the arts, sciences, and ingenuity which flourish in Europe. Here he beholds fair cities, substantial villages, extensive fields, an immense country filled with decent houses, good roads, orchards, meadows, and bridges, where a hundred years ago all was wild, woody and uncultivated! . . . He is arrived on a new continent; a modern society offers itself to his contemplation, different from what he had hitherto seen. It is not composed, as in Europe, of great lords who possess every thing and of a herd of people who have nothing. Here are no aristocratical families, no courts, no kings, no bishops, no ecclesiastical dominion, no invisible power giving to a few a very visible one; no great manufacturers employing thousands, no great refinements of luxury. The rich and the poor are not so far removed from each other as they are in Europe. Some few towns excepted, we are all tillers of the earth, from Nova Scotia to West Florida. We are a people of cultivators, scattered over an immense territory communicating with each other by means of good roads and navigable rivers, united by the silken bands of mild government, all respecting the laws, without dreading their power, because they are equitable. We are all animated with the spirit of an industry which is unfettered and unrestrained, because each person works for himself. If he travels through our rural districts he views not the hostile castle, and the haughty mansion, contrasted with the clay-built hut and miserable cabin, where cattle and men help to keep each other warm, and dwell in meanness, smoke, and indigence. A pleasing uniformity of decent competence appears throughout our habitations. The meanest of our log-houses is a dry and comfortable habitation. Lawyer or merchant are the fairest titles our towns afford; that of a farmer is the only appellation of the rural inhabitants of our country. . . . We have no princes, for whom we toil, starve, and bleed: we are the most perfect society now existing in the world. Here man is free; as he ought to be. . . .

The next wish of this traveler will be to know whence came all these people? they are mixture of English, Scotch, Irish, French, Dutch, Germans, and Swedes. From this promiscuous breed, that race now called Americans have arisen.... In this great American asylum, the poor of Europe have by some means met together.... Urged by a variety of motives, here they came. Every thing has tended to regenerate them; new laws, a new mode of living, a new social system; here they are become men: in Europe they were as so many useless plants, wanting vegitative mould, and refreshing showers; they withered, and were mowed down by want, hunger, and war....

What then is the American, this new man? He is either an European, or the descendant of an European, hence that strange mixture of blood, which you will find in no other country.... He is an American, who leaving behind him all his ancient prejudices and manners, receives new ones from the new mode of life he has embraced, the new government he obeys, and the new rank he holds.

Questions

1. What characteristics of American life does Crèvecoeur emphasize as being different from European society?

2. What aspects of society, and what parts of the American people, are left out of his description?

---

44. James Winthrop, The Anti-Federalist Argument (1787)

*Source: E. H. Scott, ed., **The Federalist and Other Constitutional Papers** (Chicago, 1894), vol. 2, pp. 515–16, 554–55.*

Opponents of the ratification of the Constitution, called Anti-Federalists, insisted that the document shifted the balance between liberty and power too far in the direction of the latter. Anti-Federalists repeatedly predicted that the new government would fall under the sway of merchants, creditors, and others hostile to the interests of ordinary Americans. Popular self-government, they claimed, flourished best in small communities, where rulers and ruled interacted daily. They warned that the absence of a Bill of Rights meant that the federal government could trample on such rights as trial by jury and freedom of speech and the press.

The excerpt below, from one of a series of newspaper articles published by James Winthrop, the librarian of Harvard College, under the pen name Agrippa, illustrates some of the Anti-Federalists' arguments. Winthrop repudiated Madison's equation of an "extensive republic" with security for liberty as "contrary to the whole experience of mankind." He insisted that large states inevitably sought to enforce a uniformity that ignored local difference. A Bill of Rights, moreover, was essential as a defense against tyranny. It was "as necessary," Winthrop wrote, "to defend an individual against the majority in a republic as against the king in a monarchy." The Anti-Federalists' insistence was the primary reason why Congress and the states added the Bill of Rights to the Constitution soon after ratification.

———

IT IS THE opinion of the ablest writers on the subject, that no extensive empire can be governed upon republican principles, and that such a government will degenerate to a despotism, unless it be made up of a confederacy of smaller states, each having the full powers of internal regulation. This is precisely the principle which has hitherto preserved our freedom. No instance can be found of any free government of considerable extent which has been supported upon any other plan. Large and consolidated empires may indeed dazzle the eyes of a distant spectator with their splendor, but if examined more nearly are always found to be full of misery. The reason is obvious. In large states the same principles of legislation will not apply to all the parts. The inhabitants of warmer climates are more dissolute in their manners, and less industrious, than in colder countries. A degree of severity is, therefore, necessary with one which would cramp the spirit of the other. We accordingly find that the very great empires have always been despotick. They have indeed tried to remedy the inconveniences to which the people were exposed by local regulations; but these contrivances have never answered the end. The laws not being made by the people, who felt the inconveniences, did not suit their circumstances. It is under such tyranny that the Spanish provinces languish, and such would be our misfortune and degradation, if we should submit to have the concerns of the whole empire managed by one legislature. To promote the happiness of the people it is necessary that there should be local laws; and it is necessary that those laws should be made by the representatives of those who are immediately subject to the want of them. By endeavoring to suit both extremes, both are injured.

It is impossible for one code of laws to suit Georgia and Massachusetts. They must, therefore, legislate for themselves. Yet there is, I believe, not one point of legislation that is not surrendered in the proposed plan. Questions of every kind respecting property are determinable in a continental court, and so are all kinds of criminal causes. The continental legislature has, therefore, a right to make rules in all cases by which their judicial courts shall proceed and decide causes. No rights are reserved to the citizens. The laws of Congress are in all cases to be the supreme law of the land, and paramount to the constitutions of the individual states. The Congress may institute what modes of trial they please, and no plea drawn from the constitution of any state can avail. This new system is, therefore, a consolidation of all the states into one large mass, however diverse the parts may be of which it is to be composed. The idea of an uncompounded republick, on an average one thousand miles in length, and eight hundred in breadth, and containing six millions of white inhabitants all reduced to the same standard of morals, of habits, and of laws, is in itself an absurdity, and contrary to the whole experience of mankind. The attempt made by Great Britain to introduce such a system, struck us with horror, and when it was proposed by some theorist that we should be represented in parliament, we uniformly declared that one legislature could not represent so many different interests for the purposes of legislation and taxation. This was the leading principle of the revolution, and makes an essential article in our creed. All that part, therefore, of the system, which relates to the internal government of the states, ought at once to be rejected.

• • •

It is now generally understood that it is for the security of the people that the powers of the government should be lodged in different branches. By this means public business will go on when they all agree, and stop when they disagree. The advantage of checks in government is thus manifested where the concurrence of different branches is necessary to the same act, but the advantage of a division of business is advantageous in other respects. As in every extensive empire, local laws are necessary to suit the different interests, no single legislature is adequate to the business. All human capacities are limited to a narrow space, and as no individual is capable of practicing a great variety of trades, no single legislature is capable of managing all the variety of national and state concerns. Even if a legislature was capable of it, the business of the judicial department must, from the same cause, be slovenly done. Hence arises the necessity of a division of the business into national and local. Each department ought to have all the powers necessary for executing its own business, under such limitations as tend to secure us from any inequality in the operations of government. I know it is often asked against whom in a government by representation is a bill of rights to secure us? I answer, that such a government is indeed a government by ourselves; but as a just government protects all alike, it is necessary that the sober and industrious part of the community should be defended from the rapacity and violence of the vicious and idle. A bill of rights, therefore, ought to set forth the purposes for which the compact is made, and serves to secure the minority against the usurpation and tyranny of the majority. It is a just observation of his excellency, Doctor [John] Adams, in his learned defence of the American constitutions that unbridled passions produce the same effect, whether in a king, nobility, or a mob. The experience of all mankind has proved the prevalence of a disposition to use power wantonly. It is therefore as necessary to defend an individual against the majority in a republic as against the king in a monarchy.

• • •

Questions

1. To what provisions of the Constitution does Winthrop refer in arguing that the new government will endanger liberty?

2. Why does Winthrop claim that the "leading principle of the revolution" is violated by the new Constitution?

45. Thomas Jefferson on Race and Slavery (1781)

Source: Thomas Jefferson, Notes on the State of Virginia *(Philadelphia, 1788), pp. 145–53, 172–73.*

No American of the revolutionary generation did more to shape prevailing views on race than Thomas Jefferson. His writings reflected a divided, even tortured mind. In *Notes on the State of Virginia*, written in 1781 and published a few years later, Jefferson ruminated on whether blacks should be considered inferior to whites. Although generally, Jefferson attributed different peoples' varying degrees of civilization to environmental factors, he concluded that what he considered blacks' inferiority was innate. Jefferson made clear that he understood that slavery violated the principles of the Declaration of Independence he had written. He looked forward to the day when slaves would be emancipated. But, he insisted, once freed, they must be removed from the United States. Blacks, in Jefferson's view, could never become equal members of the American nation.

MANY OF THE laws which were in force during the monarchy being relative merely to that form of government, or inculcating principles inconsistent with republicanism, the first assembly which met after the establishment of the commonwealth appointed a committee to revise the whole code.... The following are the most remarkable alterations proposed....

To emancipate all slaves born after passing the act. The bill reported by the revisors does not itself contain this proposition; but an amendment containing it was prepared, to be offered the legislature whenever the bill should be taken up, and further directing, that they should continue with their parents to a certain age, then be brought up, at the public expence, to tillage, arts or sciences, according to their geniusses, till the females should be eighteen, and the males twenty-one years of age, when they should be colonized to such place as the circumstances of the time should render most proper, sending them out with arms, implements of household and of the handicraft arts, seeds, pairs of the useful domestic animals, &c. to declare them a free and independant people, and extend to them our alliance and protection, till they have acquired strength; and to send vessels to the other parts of the world for an equal number of white inhabitants; to induce whom to migrate hither, proper encouragements were to be proposed. It will probably be asked, Why not retain and incorporate the blacks into the state, and thus save the expence of supplying, by importation of white settlers, the vacancies they will leave? Deep rooted prejudices entertained by the whites; ten thousand recollections, by the blacks, of the injuries they have sustained; new provocations; the real distinctions which nature has made; and many other circumstances, will divide us into parties, and produce convulsions which will probably never end but in the extermination of one or the other race.

• • •

—To these objections, which are political, may be added others, which are physical and moral. The first difference which strikes us is that of colour. Whether the black of the negro resides in the reticular membrane between the skin and scarf-skin, or in the scarf-skin itself; whether it proceeds from the colour of the blood, the colour of the bile, or from that of some other secretion, the difference is fixed in nature, and is as real as if its seat and cause were better known to us. And is this difference of no importance? Is it not the foundation of a greater or less share of beauty in the two races? Are not the fine mixtures of red and white, the expressions of every passion by greater or less suffusions of colour in the one, preferable to that eternal monotony, which reigns in the countenances, that immoveable veil of black which covers all the emotions of the other race? . . .

They seem to require less sleep. A black after hard labour through the day, will be induced by the slightest amusements to sit up till midnight, or later though knowing he must be out with the first dawn of the morning. They are at least as brave, and more adventuresome. But this may perhaps proceed from a want of forethought, which prevents their seeing a danger till it be present. When present, they do not go through it with more coolness or steadiness than the whites. They are more ardent after their female: but love seems with them to be more an eager desire, than a tender delicate mixture of sentiment and sensation. Their griefs are transient. Those numberless afflictions, which render it doubtful whether heaven has given life to us in mercy or in wrath, are less felt, and sooner forgotten with them. In general, their existence appears to participate more of sensation than reflection. . . .

—The opinion, that they are inferior in the faculties of reason and imagination, must be hazarded with great diffidence. To justify a general conclusion, requires many observations, even where the subject may be submitted to the anatomical knife, to optical glasses, to analysis by fire, or by solvents. How much more then where it is a faculty, not a substance, we are examining; where it eludes the research of all the senses; where the conditions of its existence are various and variously combined; where the effects of those which are present or absent bid defiance to calculation; let me add too, as a circumstance of great tenderness, where our conclusion would degrade a whole race of men from the rank in the scale of beings which their Creator may perhaps have given them.... I advance it therefore as a suspicion only, that the blacks, whether originally a distinct race, or made distinct by time and circumstances, are inferior to the whites in the endowments both of body and mind....

There must doubtless be an unhappy influence on the manners of our people produced by the existence of slavery among us. The whole commerce between master and slave is a perpetual exercise of the most boisterous passions, the most unremitting despotism on the one part, and degrading submissions on the other. Our children see this, and learn to imitate it; for man is an imitative animal. This quality is the germ of all education in him. From his cradle to his grave he is learning to do what he sees others do. If a parent could find no motive either in his philanthropy or his self-love, for restraining the intemperance of passion towards his slave, it would always be a sufficient one that his child is present. But generally it is not sufficient. The parent storms, the child looks on, catches the lineaments of wrath, puts on the same airs in the circle of smaller slaves, gives a loose to his worst of passions, and thus nursed, educated, and daily exercised in tyranny, cannot but be stamped by it with odious peculiarities. The man must be a prodigy who can retain his manners and morals undepraved by such circumstances. And with what execration should the statesman be loaded, who permitting one half the citizens thus to trample on the rights of the other, transforms those into despots, and these into enemies, destroys the morals of the one part, and the amor patriae of the other. For if a slave can have a country in this world, it must be any other in preference to that in which he is born to live and labour for another: in which he must lock up the faculties of his nature, contribute as far as depends on his individual endeavours to the evanishment of the human race, or entail his own miserable condition on the endless generations proceeding from him. With the morals of the people, their industry also is destroyed. For in a warm climate, no man will labour for himself who can make another labour for him. This is so true, that of the proprietors of slaves a very small proportion indeed are ever seen to labour. And can the liberties of a nation be thought secure when we have removed their only firm basis, a conviction in the minds of the people that these liberties are of the gift of God? That they are not to be violated but with his wrath? Indeed I tremble for my country when I reflect that God is just: that his justice cannot sleep for ever.

Questions

1. What reasons does Jefferson offer for colonizing blacks outside the United States in the event of emancipation?

2. How does Jefferson describe the effect of slavery on the morals and behavior of white Virginians?

CHAPTER 8

Securing the Republic, 1791–1815

46. Benjamin F. Bache, A Defense of the French Revolution (1792–1793)

Source: The General Advertiser *(Philadelphia), December 12, 1792, January 25, 1793.*

The French Revolution reverberated strongly in the United States. From its outbreak in 1789, Americans eagerly followed the course of events. Initially, nearly all Americans hailed the overthrow of the monarchy as a fulfillment of the ideals of their own revolution. But as France descended into bloodshed and war broke out between Great Britain and France, Federalists condemned the Revolution, and Republicans remained sympathetic while criticizing its excesses. In his editorials for the Philadelphia newspaper he edited, Benjamin Franklin Bache, a grandson of Benjamin Franklin and himself a leading Republican, defended the actions of the French revolutionaries, insisting that a long-established system of "despotism" could not be overthrown without turmoil. The opposition to change, he insisted, was more deeply entrenched in France than it had been in America, and hence the struggle for liberty had to be more extreme.

Later, in the 1790s, Bache was arrested under the Sedition Act, which made it a crime to criticize the policies of President John Adams. His experience illustrates how early American politics was profoundly influenced by events elsewhere in the Atlantic world.

IN ADVERTING TO the present disastrous situation of France, many, perhaps may be inclined to reprobate that revolution which has produced effects so horrible. But if we survey the effects with the eye of cool deliberation, we shall find that though they certainly emanated from the revolution, yet that our reprobation ought to be turned into another channel. The change which took place in the system of government, emancipated twenty-four millions of the human species.—Prima facie, therefore, the most cautious reasoning must allow it to be an event of infinite advantage to the world.

But though it was effected with the consent and support of nine parts out of ten, yet the tenth part viewed it in a different light. A long series of years had transmitted to them hereditary rights & privileges which placed them above the great body of the nation. The King exercised a despotic power without restraint. The nobles described around them a circle equally tyrannical, though of extent less ample. To those who know how dear the possession of power to the human mind, it will not appear strange that such persons should view the revolution with the eye of anger, in as much as it wrested from them those exclusive rights which had descended to them covered with the reverend rust of antiquity; neither will it be a matter of wonder that they should attempt to impede the progress of a system to them so distasteful.... Let us recollect, that though much blood may be shed ere Liberty be firmly established; yet that when it shall be established the effusion will cease. A system of Despotism, however, cannot be supported without blood, and we have no reason to believe that as long as it continues, the sanguinary torrent will ever cease. Until we know the real cause of those ferocious acts, which no honest man can approve nor no honest man contemplate without horror, it is treason against a good cause to attribute them to the friends of the Revolution....

There is that difference between the French and American Revolutions, that the latter was not opposed by cunning priests, nor cruel aristocrats determined to overthrow every principle of honesty and humanity.... A royal puppet on this spot, did not dance on the wire of a band of courtiers; the most despicable and abandoned wretches that ever disgraced mankind. The focus of both despotism and nobility was far from this land of liberty, and its glorious adherents could not be infected with the pernicious breath of mad royalty and impudent aristocracy. The popular cause was opposed openly, sword in hand, and victoriously fought by the friends to the rights of men; had the French republicans met with such opponents, they had not done those excesses, the king, the nobles and clergy have roused them to by the most perfidious contrivances. A king did not forswear himself in America, nor had the American people more than one [Benedict] Arnold; their tempers were soured neither by misery nor by a complicated system of treachery, framed coolly and pursued with the greatest obstinacy. The American people were not loaded with enormous taxes that had reduced millions of their fellow citizens to the utmost misery to maintain haughty plunderers in sloth and profligacy. All this odds must be reckoned by impartial men; to explain the difference insidiously delineated between the two revolutions, by some desperate royalty, or a narrow minded plan.

Questions

1. Why does Bache believe that Americans should support the French Revolution despite the bloodshed taking place in France?

2. What does he see as the similarities and differences between the American and French Revolutions?

––––––

47. Address of the Democratic-Republican Society of Pennsylvania (1794)

Source: Democratic-Republican Society of Pennsylvania, Excerpt from Minutes, December 18, 1794, Democratic Society of Pennsylvania Minutes [Am.315], Historical Society of Pennsylvania.

Another example of the spread of public involvement in politics during the 1790s was the emergence in 1793 and 1794 of the Democratic-Republic societies. The societies harshly criticized the policies of George Washington's administration, which they claimed were planting the seeds of aristocracy in the United States.

Federalists saw the societies as an example of how American freedom was getting out of hand. The government, not "self-created societies," declared the president, was the authentic voice of the American people. They also accused the societies of helping to foment the Whiskey Rebellion of 1794, in which farmers in western Pennsylvania resisted paying a new federal tax on distilled liquor. Forced to justify their existence, the societies developed a defense of the right of the people to debate political issues and organize to affect public policy. As a statement adopted by the Democratic-Republican Society of Pennsylvania insisted, "freedom of opinion" was the "bulwark of liberty," a natural right that no government could restrict.

THE DEMOCRATIC SOCIETY of Pennsylvania, established in Philadelphia, to their Fellow Citizens throughout the United States.

FELLOW CITIZENS,

The principles and proceedings of our Association have lately been calumniated. We should think ourselves unworthy to be ranked as Freemen, if awed by the name of any man, however he may command the public gratitude for past services, we could suffer in silence so sacred a right, so important a principle, as the freedom of opinion to be infringed, by attack on Societies which stand on that constitutional basis.

We shall not imitate our opponents, by resorting to declamation and abuse, instead of calm reasoning, and substituting assertion for proof. They have termed us anarchists; they have accused us of fomenting the unfortunate troubles in the western counties of this State:—yet not a single fact have they been able to adduce in support of the charge,—They have accused us of aiming at the overthrow of the Constitution; and this also rests upon their bare assertion. Neither shall we recriminate; though we might with at least as much plausibility assert, that endeavours to crush the freedom of opinion and of speech, denote liberticide intentions. But we shall content ourselves with a bare examination of the question, which has agitated the public mind; and refute the calumnies heaped on our Institution.

Freedom of thought, and a free communication of opinions by speech or through the medium of the press, are the safeguards of our Liberties. Apathy as to public concerns, too frequent even in Republics, is the reason for usurpation: by the communication or collision of sentiments, knowledge is increased, and truth prevails.

By the freedom of opinion, cannot be meant the right of thinking merely; for of this right the greatest Tyrant cannot deprive his meanest slave; but, it is freedom in the communication of sentiments, [by] speech or through the press. This liberty is an imprescriptable right, independent of any Constitution or social compact: it is as complete a right as that which any man has to the enjoyment of his life. These principles are eternal—they are recognized by our Constitution; and that nation is already enslaved that does not acknowledge their truth.

In the expression of sentiments, speech is the natural organ—the press an artificial one and though the latter, from the services it has rendered, has obtained the just appellation of Bulwark of Liberty; it would not be difficult to show that the former should be more prized because more secure from usurpation.

If freedom of opinion, in the sense we understand it, is the right of every Citizen, by what mode of reasoning can that right be denied to an assemblage of Citizens? A conviction that the exercise of this right collectively could not be questioned, led to the formation of our institution; and in the conduct the Society have held since their first establishment, they trust, no instance can be adduced in which they have overstepped the just bounds of the right, of which they claim the enjoyment. . . .

• • •

The Society are free to declare that they never were more strongly impressed with a sentiment of the importance of associations, on the principles which they hold, than at the present time. The germ of an odious Aristocracy is planted among us—it has taken root,—and has indeed already produced fruit worthy of the parent stock. If it be imprudent to eradicate this baneful exotic, let us at least unite in checking its growth. Let us remain firm in attachment to principles, and with a jealous eye guard our rights against the least infringement. The enlightened state of the public mind in this country, frees us, we trust, of all apprehension from bold and open usurpation; but the gradual approaches of artful ambition, are the source of great danger. Let us especially guard, with firmness, the outposts of our Liberties: and, if we wish to baffle the efforts of the enemies of freedom, whatever garb they may assume, let us be particularly watchful to preserve inviolate the freedom of opinion, assured that it is the most effectual weapon for the protection of our liberty.

Resolved, That the said Address be signed by the President and attested by the Acting Secretary: and that it be published.

Questions

1. How do the members of the Democratic-Republican Society defend their right to form a society that comments on public affairs?

2. What do they mean by writing that "the germ of an odious Aristocracy" has been planted in the United States?

---

48. Judith Sargent Murray, "On the Equality of the Sexes" (1790)

Source: Judith Sargent Murray, "On the Equality of the Sexes," Massachusetts Magazine, *vol. 2 (March 1790), pp. 132–35.*

The expansion of the public sphere during the era of the Revolution offered women an opportunity to take part in political discussions, read newspapers, and hear orations even though outside of New Jersey they could not vote. Judith Sargent Murray, one of the era's most accomplished American women, wrote plays, novels, and poetry. She also wrote essays on public issues for the *Massachusetts Magazine* and other journals under the pen name "The Gleaner."

Although Murray could not attend college because of her sex, she studied alongside her brother with a tutor preparing the young man for admission to Harvard. In her essay "On the Equality of the Sexes," written in 1779 and published in 1790, Murray insisted that women had as much right as men to exercise all their talents and should be allowed equal educational opportunities to enable them to do so. Murray forthrightly demanded "equality" for women and attacked the common idea that women's happiness rested on devoting themselves to their duties within the family.

• • •

IS IT UPON mature consideration we adopt the idea, that nature is thus partial in her distributions? Is it indeed a fact, that she hath yielded to one half of the human species so unquestionable a mental superiority? I know that to both sexes elevated understandings, and the reverse, are common. But, suffer me to ask, in what the minds of females are so notoriously deficient, or unequal. May not the intellectual powers be ranged under these four heads—imagination, reason, memory and judgment. The province of imagination hath long since been surrendered up to us, and we have been crowned undoubted sovereigns of the regions of fancy. Invention is perhaps the most arduous effort of the mind; this branch of imagination hath been particularly ceded to us, and we have been time out of mind invested with that creative faculty. Observe the variety of fashions (here I bar the contemptuous smile) which distinguish and adorn the female world; how continually are they changing, insomuch that they almost render the wise man's assertion problematical, and we are ready to say, *there is something new under the sun.* Now what a playfulness, what an exuberance of fancy, what strength of inventive imagination, doth this continual variation discover?

Again, it hath been observed, that if the turpitude of the conduct of our sex, hath been ever so enormous, so extremely ready are we, that the very first thought presents us with an apology, so plausible, as to produce our actions even in an amiable light. Another instance of our creative powers, is our talent for slander; how ingenious are we at inventive scandal? what a formidable story can we in a moment fabricate merely from the force of a prolifick imagination? how many reputations, in the fertile brain of a female, have been utterly despoiled? how industrious are we at improving a hint? suspicion how easily do we convert into conviction, and conviction, embellished by the power of eloquence, stalks abroad to the surprise and confusion of unsuspecting innocence. Perhaps it will be asked if I furnish these facts as instances of excellency in our sex. Certainly not; but as proofs of a creative faculty, of a lively imagination. Assuredly great activity of mind is thereby discovered, and was this activity properly directed, what beneficial effects would follow. Is the needle and kitchen sufficient to employ the operations of a soul thus organized? I should conceive not. Nay, it is a truth that those very departments leave the intelligent principle vacant, and at liberty for speculation.

Are we deficient in reason? we can only reason from what we know, and if an opportunity of acquiring knowledge hath been denied us, the inferiority of our sex cannot fairly be deduced from thence. Memory, I believe, will be allowed us in common, since every one's experience must testify, that a loquacious old woman is as frequently met with, as a communicative old man; their subjects are alike drawn from the fund of other times, and the transactions of their youth, or of maturer life, entertain, or perhaps fatigue you, in the evening of their lives. "But our judgment is not so strong—we do not distinguish so well."—Yet it may be questioned, from what doth this superiority, in this determining faculty of the soul, proceed. May we not trace its source in the difference of education, and continued advantages?

Will it be said that the judgment of a male of two years old, is more sage than that of a female's of the same age? I believe the reverse is generally observed to be true. But from that period what partiality! how is the one exalted, and the other depressed, by the contrary modes of education which are adopted! the one is taught to aspire, and the other is early confined and limited. As their years increase, the sister must be wholly domesticated, while the brother is led by the hand through all the flowery paths of science. Grant that their minds are by nature equal, yet who shall wonder at the *apparent* superiority, if indeed custom becomes *second nature*; nay if it taketh place of nature, and that it doth the experience of each day will evince. At length arrived at womanhood, the uncultivated fair one feels a void, which the employments allotted her are by no means capable of filling. What can she do? to books she may not apply; or if she doth, *to those only of the novel kind,* lest she merit the appellation of a *learned lady*; and what ideas have been affixed to this term, the observation of many can testify. Fashion, scandal, and sometimes what is still more reprehensible, are then called in to her relief; and who can say to what lengths the liberties she takes may proceed. Meantime she herself is most unhappy; she feels the want of a culti-vated mind. Is she single, she in vain seeks to fill up time from sexual employments or amusements. Is she united to a person whose soul nature made equal to her own, education hath set him so far above her, that in those entertainments which are productive of such ratio-nal felicity, she is not qualified to accompany him. She experiences a mortifying consciousness of inferiority, which embitters every enjoy-ment. Doth the person to whom her adverse fate hath consigned her, possess a mind incapable of improvement, she is equally wretched, in being so closely connected with an individual whom she cannot but despise. Now, was she permitted the same instructors as her brother, (with an eye however to their particular departments) for the employ-ment of a rational mind an ample field would be opened....

Will it be urged that those acquirements would supersede our domestic duties. I answer that every requisite in female economy is easily attained; and, with truth I can add, that when once attained, they require no further *mental attention*. Nay, while we are pursuing the needle, or the superintendency of the family, I repeat, that our minds are at full liberty for reflection; that imagination may exert itself in full vigor; and that if a just foundation is early laid, our ideas will then be worthy of rational beings. If we were industrious we might easily find time to arrange them upon paper, or should avocations press too hard for such an indulgence, the hours allotted for conversation would at least become more refined and rational. Should it still be vociferated, "Your domestic employments are sufficient"—I would calmly ask, is it reasonable, that a candidate for immortality, for the joys of heaven, an intelligent being, who is to spend an eternity in contemplating the works of Deity, should at present be so degraded, as to be allowed no other ideas, than those which are suggested by the mechanism of a pudding, or the sewing the seams of a garment? Pity that all such censurers of female improvement do not go one step further, and deny their future existence; to be consistent they surely ought.

Yes, ye lordly, ye haughty sex, our souls are by nature *equal* to yours; the same breath of God animates, enlivens, and invigorates us; and that we are not fallen lower than yourselves, let those witness who have greatly towered above the various discouragements by which they have been so heavily oppressed.... Were we to grant that animal strength proved any thing, taking into consideration the accustomed impartiality of nature, we should be induced to imagine, that she had invested the female mind with superior strength as an equivalent for the bodily powers of man. But waving this however palpable advantage, for *equality only*, we wish to contend.

• • •

Questions

1. Why does Murray refer to the "variety of fashions" among women as an argument for their intellectual capacity?

2. How does she answer the charge that offering educational opportunities to women will lead to neglect of their "domestic duties"?

---

49. Protest against the Alien and Sedition Acts (1798)

Source: Jonathan Elliott, ed., The Debates in the Several State Conventions on the Adoption of the Federal Constitution, *2nd ed. (Philadelphia: J. B. Lippincott & Co., 1836–59), vol. 5, pp. 528–29.*

From the adoption of the Constitution, the relative powers of the state and federal governments have remained a point of dispute. In 1798, faced with mounting opposition from opponents (among them foreign-born Jeffersonian newspaper editors), President John Adams and the Federalist Party moved to silence criticism of the administration. Congress passed the Alien Act, which allowed the deportation of "dangerous" foreigners, and the Sedition Act, set to expire after the presidential election of 1800, which made it a crime to criticize the government in print or a public assembly. In response, James Madison and Thomas Jefferson wrote resolutions of protest. Virginia's legislature approved Madison's and Kentucky adopted Jefferson's. Both claimed that states could "interpose" their power to prevent the federal government from acting in a despotic manner. Southern advocates of nullification and secession later cited the resolutions to justify their position.

RESOLVED, THAT THE General Assembly of Virginia doth unequivocally express a firm resolution to maintain and defend the Constitution of the United States, and the Constitution of this state, against every aggression, either foreign or domestic; and that they will support the government of the United States in all measures warranted by the former.

That this Assembly most solemnly declares a warm attachment to the union of the states, to maintain which it pledges its powers;

and that, for this end, it is their duty to watch over and oppose every infraction of those principles which constitute the only basis of that union, because a faithful observance of them can alone secure its existence and the public happiness.

That this Assembly doth explicitly and peremptorily declare, that it views the powers of the federal government as resulting from the compact to which the states are parties, as limited by the plain sense and intention of the instrument constituting that compact, as no further valid than they are authorized by the grants enumerated in that compact; and that, in case of a deliberate, palpable, and dangerous exercise of other powers, not granted by the said compact, the states, who are parties thereto, have the right, and are in duty bound, to interpose, for arresting the progress of the evil, and for maintaining, within their respective limits, the authorities, rights, and liberties, appertaining to them.

That the General Assembly doth also express its deep regret, that a spirit has, in sundry instances, been manifested by the federal government to enlarge its powers by forced constructions of the constitutional charter which defines them; and that indications have appeared of a design to expound certain general phrases (which, having been copied from the very limited grant of powers in the former Articles of Confederation, were the less liable to be misconstrued) so as to destroy the meaning and effect of the particular enumeration which necessarily explains and limits the general phrases, and so as to consolidate the states, by degrees, into one sovereignty, the obvious tendency and inevitable result of which would be, to transform the present republican system of the United States into an absolute, or, at best, a mixed monarchy.

That the General Assembly doth particularly PROTEST against the palpable and alarming infractions of the Constitution, in the two late cases of the "Alien and Sedition Acts," passed at the last session of Congress; the first of which exercises a power nowhere delegated to the federal government, and which, by uniting legislative and judicial powers to those of executive, subverts the general principles of free government, as well as the particular organization and positive provisions of the Federal Constitution; and the other of which acts exercises, in like manner, a power not delegated by the Constitution, but, on the contrary, expressly and positively forbidden by one of the amendments thereto,—a power which, more than any other, ought to produce universal alarm, because it is levelled against the right of freely examining public characters and measures, and of free communication among the people thereon, which has ever been justly deemed the only effectual guardian of every other right.

That this state having, by its Convention, which ratified the Federal Constitution, expressly declared that, among other essential rights, "the liberty of conscience and the press cannot be cancelled, abridged, restrained, or modified, by any authority of the United States," and from its extreme anxiety to guard these rights from every possible attack of sophistry and ambition, having, with other states, recommended an amendment for that purpose, which amendment was, in due time, annexed to the Constitution,—it would mark a reproachful inconsistency, and criminal degeneracy, if an indifference were now shown to the most palpable violation of one of the rights thus declared and secured, and to the establishment of a precedent which may be fatal to the other.

That the good people of this commonwealth, having ever felt, and continuing to feel, the most sincere affection for their brethren of the other states; the truest anxiety for establishing and perpetuating the union of all; and the most scrupulous fidelity to that Constitution, which is the pledge of mutual friendship, and the instrument of mutual happiness,—the General Assembly doth solemnly appeal to the like dispositions in the other states, in confidence that they will concur with this commonwealth in declaring, as it does hereby declare, that the acts aforesaid are unconstitutional; and that the necessary and proper measures will be taken by each for cooperating with this state, in maintaining unimpaired the authorities, rights, and liberties, reserved to the states respectively, or to the people.

Questions

1. In what ways does the resolution claim that the Alien and Sedition Acts violate the principles of "free government"?

2. How does the resolution define the relationship between the federal government and the states under the Constitution?

50. George Tucker on Gabriel's Rebellion (1801)

Source: **Letter to a Member of the General Assembly of Virginia on the Subject of the Late Conspiracy of the Slaves; With a Proposal for Their Colonization** *(Baltimore, 1801), pp. 5–18.*

In 1800, a plot by slaves in Virginia to gain their freedom was organized by a Richmond blacksmith, Gabriel. The plot was soon discovered and the leaders arrested. Twenty-six slaves, including Gabriel, were hanged and dozens more transported out of the state. The conspiracy, commented George Tucker, a member of one of the state's most prominent families, demonstrated that slaves possessed "the love of freedom" as fully as other men. Gabriel's language, he added, reflected "the advance of knowledge" among Virginia's slaves, which would inevitably continue.

Like Thomas Jefferson, James Madison, and many others of his generation, Tucker opposed slavery but could not envision the United States as a biracial society of free citizens. He proposed that the Virginia legislature adopt a plan to emancipate the slaves and settle them outside of the state, somewhere "on the western side" of the Mississippi River (an area then under the control of Spain). The legislature, however, moved in the opposite direction. It tightened controls over the black population and severely restricted the ability of masters to free their slaves voluntarily.

———

THERE IS OFTEN a progress in human affairs which may indeed be retarded, but which nothing can arrest. Moving on with slow and silent steps, it is marked only by comparing distant periods. The causes which produce it are either so minute as to be invisible, or, if perceived, are too numerous and complicated to be subject to human controul. Of such sort is the advancement of knowledge among the negroes of this country. It is so striking, as to be obvious to a man of the most ordinary observation. Every year adds to the number of those who can read and write; and he who has made any proficiency in letters, becomes a little centre of instruction to others. This increase of knowledge is the principal agent in evolving the spirit we have to fear. The love of freedom, sir, is an inborn sentiment, which the God of nature has planted deep in the heart: long may it be kept under by the arbitrary institutions of society; but, at the first favourable moment, it springs forth, and flourishes with a vigour that defies all check. This celestial spark, which fires the breast of the savage, which glows in that of the philosopher, is not extinguished in the bosom of the slave. It may be buried in the embers; but it still lives; and the breath of knowledge kindles it into flame. Thus we find, sir, there never have been slaves in any country, who have not seized the first favorable opportunity to revolt.

• • •

In our infant country, where population and wealth increase with unexampled rapidity, the progress of liberal knowledge is proportionally great. In this vast march of the mind, the blacks, who are far behind us, may be supposed to advance at a pace equal to our own; but, sir, the fact is, they are likely to advance much faster. The growth and multiplication of our towns tend a thousand ways to enlighten and inform them. The very nature of our government, which leads us to recur perpetually to the discussion of natural rights, favors speculation and enquiry.

• • •

There is one argument to which I have not even hinted; but which some may think of more weight than any other;—I mean the ease with which they may become the tools of a foreign enemy. Granting that the danger from themselves is slight or remote, this, it must be confessed, depends upon an event that is altogether uncertain. War is sometimes inevitable; no human prudence can guard against an event that may be brought about by the insolence, the injustice, or the caprice of *any* nation. Whenever we are involved in this calamity, if our enemies hold out the lure of freedom, they will have, in every negro, a decided friend. The passage is easy from friends to auxiliaries: little address would be necessary to excite insurrection; to put arms into their hands, and to convert a willing multitude into a compact and disciplined army.

• • •

The following hints I submit to your serious and candid consideration.

That application be made to the United States, to procure from the Spanish government, or to furnish from its own territory, such a tract of country as shall be deemed sufficient for the colony proposed. The consideration of future peace would recommend the western side of the Mississippi. Present convenience and economy would advise a purchase of some part of the Indian country, comprehended within the limits of the state of Georgia.

That this colony be under the protection and immediate government of this state, or the United States, until it contained a number of inhabitants sufficient to manage their own concerns: and that it be exclusively appropriated to the colonization and residence of people of colour.

Questions

1. Why does Tucker think that "progress in human affairs" will inevitably lead slaves to become more discontented?

2. In what ways does Tucker believe that living in Virginia has affected the ideas of the slaves?

51. Tecumseh, Speech to the Osage (1810)

Source: John D. Hunter, **Memoirs of a Captivity among the Indians of North America, from Childhood to the Age of Nineteen,** *2nd ed. (London: Longman, Hurst, Rees, Orme, Brown, and Green, 1823), pp. 45–48.*

By 1800, nearly 400,000 American settlers lived west of the Appalachian Mountains. They far outnumbered remaining Indians. While some Native Americans claimed rights as Americans, others asserted a pan-Indian iden-tity, insisting that all Indian nations shared a common set of values and a common future of freedom and autonomy rather than assimilation or removal. The Shawnee leader Tecumseh sought to rally Indians to unite as one people. He hoped to root out European influences and resist further white encroachment on Indian lands. This speech, to Osage Indians, was recorded by John P. Hunter, who had been held captive by the Osage since childhood.

———

BROTHERS—WE ALL belong to one family; we are all children of the Great Spirit; we walk in the same path; slake our thirst at the same spring; and now affairs of the greatest concern lead us to smoke the pipe around the same council fire!

Brothers—we are friends; we must assist each other to bear our burdens. The blood of many of our fathers and brothers has run like water on the ground, to satisfy the avarice of the white men. We, ourselves, are threatened with a great evil; nothing will pacify them but the destruction of all the red men.

Brothers—When the white men first set foot on our grounds, they were hungry; they had no place on which to spread their blankets, or to kindle their fires. They were feeble; they could do nothing for them-selves. Our fathers commiserated their distress, and shared freely with them whatever the Great Spirit had given his red children. They gave them food when hungry, medicine when sick, spread skins for them to sleep on, and gave them grounds, that they might hunt and raise corn.

Brothers—The white people are like poisonous serpents: when chilled they are feeble, and harmless; but invigorate them, with warmth, and they sting their benefactors to death. The white people came among us feeble; and now we have made them strong, they wish to kill us, or drive us back, as they would wolves and panthers.

Brothers—The white men are not friends to the Indians: at first, they only asked for land sufficient for a wigwam; now, nothing will satisfy them but the whole of our hunting grounds, from the rising to the setting sun....

Brothers—My people wish for peace; the red men all wish for peace: but where the white people are, there is no peace for them, except it be on the bosom of our mother.

Brothers—The white men despise and cheat the Indians; they abuse and insult them; they do not think the red men sufficiently good to live. The red men have borne many and great injuries; they ought to suffer them no longer. My people will not; they are determined on vengeance; they have taken up the tomahawk; they will make it fat with blood; they will drink the blood of the white people.

Brothers—My people are brave and numerous; but the white people are too strong for them alone. I wish you to take up the tomahawk with them. If we all unite, we will cause the rivers to stain the great waters with their blood.

Brothers—if you do not unite with us, they will first destroy us, and then you will fall an easy prey to them. They have destroyed many nations of red men because they were not united...they wish to make us enemies, that they may sweep over and desolate our hunting grounds, like devastating winds, or rushing waters.

Brothers—Our Great Father over the great waters [the king of England] is angry with the white people, our enemies. He will send his brave warriors against them; he will send us rifles, and whatever else we want—he is our friend, and we are his children....

Brothers—We must be united; we must smoke the same pipe; we must fight each other's battles; and more than all, we must love the

Great Spirit; he is for us; he will destroy our enemies, and make his
red children happy.

Questions:

1. How does Tecumseh's understanding of national identity compare with
that of most white Americans of his era?

2. Why does he claim that the king of England is the Indians' ally and
what does this suggest about his attitudes toward white people?

---

52. Felix Grundy, Battle Cry of the War Hawks (1811)

Source: Annals of Congress, *12th Congress, 1st Session, pp. 425–27
(December 10, 1811).*

In the months leading up to the War of 1812, a group of younger
congressmen, mostly from the West, called for war with Britain. Known
as the War Hawks, this new generation of political leaders had come of
age after the winning of independence and were ardent nationalists.
Their leaders included Henry Clay of Kentucky, elected Speaker of the
House of Representatives in 1810, and John C. Calhoun of South Carolina. The War Hawks spoke passionately of defending the national
honor against British insults, but also had more practical goals in mind,
notably the annexation of Canada. Their views were expressed in a
speech in the House of Representatives by Felix Grundy of Tennessee.
To British interference with American shipping, the main concern of
the Madison administration, Grundy added the aim of acquiring Canada
(British territory) and Florida (owned by Spain) to the United States,
thereby expanding the Union and undermining the remaining power
of Indian tribes.

WHAT, MR. SPEAKER, are we now called on to decide? It is, whether we will resist by force the attempt, made by [the British] Government, to subject our maritime rights to the arbitrary and capricious rule of her will; for my part I am not prepared to say that this country shall submit to have her commerce interdicted or regulated, by any foreign nation. Sir, I prefer war to submission.

Over and above these unjust pretensions of the British Government, for many years past they have been in the practice of impressing our seamen, from merchant vessels; this unjust and lawless invasion of personal liberty, calls loudly for the interposition of this Government. To those better acquainted with the facts in relation to it, I leave it to fill up the picture. My mind is irresistibly drawn to the West....

It cannot be believed by any man who will reflect, that the savage tribes, uninfluenced by other Powers, would think of making war on the United States. They understand too well their own weakness, and our strength. They have already felt the weight of our arms; they know they hold the very soil on which they live as tenants at sufferance. How, then, sir, are we to account for their late conduct? In one way only; some powerful nation must have intrigued with them, and turned their peaceful disposition towards us into hostilities. Great Britain alone has intercourse with those Northern tribes; I therefore infer, that if British gold has not been employed, their baubles and trinkets, and the promise of support and a place of refuge if necessary, have had their effect....

This war, if carried on successfully, will have its advantages. We shall drive the British from our Continent—they will no longer have an opportunity of intriguing with our Indian neighbors, and setting on the ruthless savage to tomahawk our women and children. That nation will lose her Canadian trade, and, by having no resting place in this country, her means of annoying us will be diminished.... I am willing to receive the Canadians as adopted brethren; it will have beneficial political effects; it will preserve the equilibrium of the Government. When Louisiana shall be fully peopled, the Northern

States will lose their power; they will be at the discretion of others; they can be depressed at pleasure, and then this Union might be endangered—I therefore feel anxious not only to add the Floridas to the South, but the Canadas to the North of this empire....

Questions

1. Why does Grundy think that acquiring Canada will strengthen the American Union?

2. Whom does Grundy hold responsible for Tecumseh's uprising (the "late conduct" of the Indian tribes he mentions)?

53. Mercy Otis Warren on Religion and Virtue (1805)

Source: *Mercy Otis Warren*, History of the Rise, Progress and Termination of the American Revolution *(3 vols.: Boston, 1805), vol. 3, pp. 412–18.*

A sister of the Massachusetts patriot leader James Otis and wife of James Warren, who was paymaster for George Washington's army, Mercy Otis Warren emerged as one of the leading women writers of her generation and an insightful commentator on political events. She promoted the revolutionary cause in poetry and dramas, and advocated the addition of a Bill of Rights to the Constitution. In 1805 she published a three-volume history of the American Revolution. In one section, she worried about what she considered the spread of religious infidelity and declining virtue in Europe, and wondered if the United States would eventually go down this road. But she remained confident that Americans would not soon emulate Europe in the loss of liberty.

IT IS NEITHER a preference to republican systems, nor an attachment to monarchic or aristocratic forms of government that disseminates the wild opinions of infidelity. It is the licentious manners of courts of every description, the unbridled luxury of wealth, and the worst passions of men let loose on the multitude by the example of their superiors. Bent on gratification, at the expense of every moral tie, they have broken down the barriers of religion, and the spirit of infidelity is nourished at the fount; thence the poisonous streams run through every grade that constitutes the mass of nations.

It may be further observed, that there is a variety of additional causes which have led to a disposition among some part of mankind, to reject the obligations of religion, and even to deny their God. This propensity in some may easily be elucidated, without casting any part of the odium on the spirit of free inquiry relative to civil and political liberty, which had been widely disseminated, and had produced two such remarkable revolutions as those of America and France. It may be imputed to the love of novelty, the pride of opinion, and an extravagant propensity to speculate and theorize on subjects beyond the comprehension of mortals, united with a desire of being released from the restraints on their appetites and passions: restraints dictated both by reason and revelation; and which, under the influence of sober reflection, forbid the indulgence of all gratifications that are injurious to man. Further elucidations, or more abstruse causes, which contribute to lead the vain inquirer, who steps over the line prescribed by the Author of nature, to deviations from, and forgetfulness of its Creator, and to involve him in a labyrinth of darkness, from which his weak reasonings can never disentangle him, may be left to those who delight in metaphysical disquisitions.

The world might reasonably have expected, from the circumstances connected with the first settlement of the American colonies, which was in consequence of their attachment to the religion of their fathers, united with a spirit of independence relative to civil government, that there would have been no observable dereliction of those honorable principles, for many ages to come. From the sobriety of their manners, their simple habits, their attention to the education and moral conduct of their children, they had the highest reason to hope, that it might have been long, very long, before the faith of their religion was shaken, or their principles corrupted, either by the manners, opinions, or habits of foreigners, bred in the courts of despotism, or the schools of licentiousness.

This hope shall not yet be relinquished. There has indeed been some relaxation of manners, and the appearance of a change in public opinion not contemplated when revolutionary scenes first shook the western world. But it must be acknowledged, that the religious and moral character of Americans yet stands on a higher grade of excellence and purity, than that of most other nations. It has been observed, that "a violation of manners has destroyed more states than the infraction of laws." It is necessary for every *American*, with becoming energy to endeavour to stop the dissemination of principles evidently destructive of the cause for which they have bled. It must be the combined virtue of the rulers and of the people to do this, and to rescue and save their civil and religious rights from the outstretched arm of tyranny, which may appear under any mode or form of government.

Let not the frivolity of the domestic taste of the children of Columbia, nor the examples of strangers of high or low degree, that may intermix among them, or the imposing attitude of distant nations, or the machinations of the bloody tyrants of Europe, who have united themselves, and to the utmost are exerting their strength to extirpate the very name of *republicanism*, rob them of their character, their morals, their religion, or their liberty....

It is to be regretted that Americans are so much divided on this point as well as on many other questions: we hope the spirit of division will never be wrought up to such a height as to terminate in a disseveration of the states, or any internal hostilities. Any civil convulsions would shake the fabric of government, and perhaps entirely subvert the present excellent constitution; a strict adherence to which, it may be affirmed, is the best security of the rights and liberties of a country that has bled at every vein, to purchase and transmit them to posterity. The sword now resheathed, the army dismissed, a wise, energetic government established and organized, it is to be hoped many generations will pass away in the lapse of time, before America again becomes a theatre of war.

Indeed the United States of America embrace too large a portion of the globe, to expect their isolated situation will forever secure them from the encroachments of foreign nations, and the attempts of potent Europeans to interrupt their peace. But if the education of youth, both public and private, is attended to, their industrious and economical habits maintained, their moral character and that assemblage of virtues supported, which is necessary for the happiness of individuals and of nations, there is not much danger that they will for a long time be subjugated by the arms of foreigners, or that their republican system will be subverted by the arts of domestic enemies. Yet, probably some distant day will exhibit the extensive continent of America, a portrait analogous to the other quarters of the globe, which have been laid waste by ambition, until misery has spread her sable veil over the inhabitants. But this will not be done, until ignorance, servility and vice, have led them to renounce their ideas of freedom, and reduced them to that grade of baseness which renders them unfit for the enjoyment of that rational liberty which is the natural inheritance of man. The expense of blood and treasure, lavished for the purchase of freedom, should teach Americans to estimate its real worth, nor ever suffer it to be depreciated by the vices of the human mind, which are seldom single. The sons of America ought ever to bear in grateful remembrance the worthy band of patriots, who first supported an opposition to the tyrannic measures of Great Britain. Though some of them have long since been consigned to the tomb, a tribute of gratitude is ever due to their memory, while the advantages of freedom and independence are felt by their latest posterity.

Questions

1. What does Warren consider the greatest threats to freedom?

2. What does she consider the most significant legacy of the American Revolution?

CHAPTER 9

The Market Revolution, 1800–1840

54. Sarah Bagley, Freedom and Necessity at Lowell (1845)

Source: **Voice of Industry,** *September 18, 1845.*

The early industrial revolution centered on factories producing cotton textiles with water-powered spinning and weaving machinery. In the 1820s, a group of merchants created an entirely new factory town near Boston, incorporated as the city of Lowell in 1836. Here they built a group of modern textile factories that brought together all phases of production from the spinning of thread to the weaving and finishing of cloth. By 1850, Lowell's fifty-two mills employed more than 10,000 workers.

Closely supervised work tending a machine seemed to violate the independence Americans considered an essential element of freedom. As a result, few native-born men could be attracted to work in the early factories. At Lowell, young unmarried women from Yankee farm families dominated the workforce that tended spinning machines. The women typically remained in the factories for only a few years, after which they returned home, married, or moved west.

Born to a New Hampshire farm family in 1806, Sarah Bagley came to Lowell in 1837 after her father suffered financial reverses. She soon became one of the most outspoken leaders of the labor movement among the city's "mill girls." In 1845 she became the editor of the *Voice of Industry,* which spoke for the male and female labor movement of New England. Her critique of the northern labor system was similar to arguments advanced by proslavery thinkers such as George Fitzhugh (see his document in Chapter 11).

───────

WHENEVER I RAISE the point that it is immoral to shut us up in a close room twelve hours a day in the most monotonous and tedious of employment, I am told that we have come to the mills voluntarily and we can leave when we will. Voluntary! Let us look a little at this remarkable form of human freedom. Do we from mere choice leave our fathers' dwellings, the firesides where all of our friends, where too our earliest and fondest recollections cluster, for the factory and the corporation's boarding house?... A slave too goes voluntarily to his task, but his will is in some manner quickened by the whip of the overseer.

The whip which brings us to Lowell is NECESSITY. We must have money; a father's debts are to be paid, an aged mother to be supported, a brother's ambition to be aided, and so the factories are supplied. Is this to act from free will?... Is any one such a fool as to suppose that out of six thousand factory girls of Lowell, sixty would be there if they could help it? Everybody knows that it is necessity alone, in some form or other, that takes us to Lowell and keeps us there. Is this freedom? To my mind it is slavery quite as really as any in Turkey or Carolina. It matters little as to the fact of slavery, whether the slave be compelled to his task by the whip of the overseer or the wages of the Lowell Corporation. In either case it is not free will, leading the laborer to work, but an outward necessity that puts free will out of the question....

We are engaged in a movement, the aim of which is the elevation of the whole human race into a social condition of complete and universal justice. While thus seeking the good of all men, of all orders and conditions, we cannot be blind to the fact that the laboring classes are everywhere greater sufferers than any others. In barbarian society, the slaves of arbitrary power and of brute force. In Civilized society, the slaves of money and their physical necessities, they are universally oppressed, degraded, and regarded as an inferior order of beings. But they are beginning to understand that they have all the attributes of men, and will soon demand their rights.

Questions

1. Why does Bagley compare the situation of female factory workers with slavery?

2. Why does she question the idea that the "mill girls" have freely chosen factory work?

55. Joseph Smith, The Wentworth Letter (1842)

Source: Times and Seasons *(March–May 1842).*

Among the most successful of the religions that sprang up in pre–Civil War America was the Church of Jesus Christ of Latter-day Saints, or Mormons. The Mormons were founded in the 1820s by Joseph Smith, a farmer in upstate New York who as a youth began to experience religious visions. He claimed to have been led by an angel to a set of golden plates covered with strange writing. Smith translated and published them as *The Book of Mormon*, after a fourth-century prophet. In 1842, at the request of John Wentworth, a Chicago editor, Smith wrote an account of his life to that point and his religious beliefs, which Wentworth republished in a magazine Smith edited. Not long afterward, Smith was arrested in Nauvoo, Illinois, where the Mormons had settled after being driven out of New York, Ohio, and Missouri because of popular outrage at Smith's insistence that *The Book of Mormon* was as much the word of God as the Bible, and his doctrine of polygamy (that one man may have several wives). While in jail, Smith was murdered by a group of intruders. In 1847, his successor as Mormon leader, Brigham Young, led more than 2,000 followers across the Great Plains and Rocky Mountains to the shores of the Great Salt Lake in present-day Utah.

―――――――

MY FATHER WAS a farmer and taught me the art of husbandry. When about fourteen years of age I began to reflect upon the importance of being prepared for a future state, and upon enquiring [of] the plan of salvation I found that there was a great clash in religious sentiment; if I went to one society they referred me to one plan, and another to another, each one pointing to his own particular creed as the summum bonum of perfection: considering that all could not be right, and that God could not be the author of so much confusion I determined to investigate the subject more fully, believing that if God had a church it would not be split up into factions, and that if he taught one society to worship one way, and administer in one set of ordinances, He would not teach another, principles which were diametrically opposed. Believing the word of God I had confidence in the declaration of James; "If any man lack wisdom let him ask of God who giveth to all men liberally and upbraideth not and it shall be given him." I retired to a secret place in a grove and began to call upon the Lord, while fervently engaged in supplication my mind was taken away from the objects with which I was surrounded, and I was enwrapped in a heavenly vision and saw two glorious personages who exactly resembled each other in features and likeness, surrounded with a brilliant light which eclipsed the sun at noon-day. They told me that all religious denominations were believing in incorrect doctrines and that none of them was acknowledged of God as His Church and kingdom. And I was expressly commanded to "go not after them," at the same time receiving a promise that the fullness of the gospel should at some future time be made known unto me....

I was informed that I was chosen to be an instrument in the hands of God to bring about some of His purposes in this glorious dispensation.

I was also informed concerning the aboriginal inhabitants of this country [America], and shown who they were, and from whence they came; a brief sketch of their origin, progress, civilization, laws, governments, of their righteousness and iniquity, and the blessings of God being finally withdrawn from them as a people was made known unto me: I was also told where there was deposited some plates on which were engraven an abridgment of the records of the ancient prophets that had existed on this continent. The angel appeared to me three times the same night and unfolded the same things. After having received many visits from the angels of God unfolding the majesty and glory of the events that should transpire in the last days, on the morning of the 22d of September, A.D. 1827, the angel of the Lord delivered the records into my hands.

These records were engraven on plates which had the appearance of gold, each plate was six inches wide and eight inches long and not quite so thick as common tin. They were filled with engravings, in Egyptian characters and bound together in a volume, as the leaves of a book with three rings running through the whole. The volume was something near six inches in thickness, a part of which was sealed. The characters on the unsealed part were small, and beautifully engraved. The whole book exhibited many marks of antiquity in its construction and much skill in the art of engraving. With the records was found a curious instrument which the ancients called "Urim and Thummim," which consisted of two transparent stones set in the rim of a bow fastened to a breastplate. . . .

As soon as the news of this discovery was made known, false reports, misrepresentation, and slander flew as on the wings of the wind in every direction, the house was frequently beset by mobs, and evil designing people, several times I was shot at, and very narrowly escaped, and every device was made use of to get the plates away from me, but the power and blessing of God attended me, and several began to believe my testimony. . . .

In the situation before alluded to we arrived in the state of Illinois in 1839, where we found a hospitable people and a friendly home; a people who were willing to be governed by the principles of law and humanity. We have commenced to build a city called "Nauvoo" in Hancock co., we number from six to eight thousand here besides vast numbers in the county around and in almost every county of the state. We have a city charter granted us and a charter for a legion the troops of which now number 1500. We have also a charter for a university, for an agricultural and manufacturing society, have our own laws and administrators, and possess all the privileges that other free and enlightened citizens enjoy.

Persecution has not stopped the progress of truth, but has only added fuel to the flame, it has spread with increasing rapidity, proud of the cause which they have espoused and conscious of our innocence and of the truth of their system amidst calumny and reproach have the elders of this Church gone forth, and planted the gospel in almost every state in the Union; it has penetrated our cities, it has spread over our villages and has caused thousands of our intelligent, noble, and patriotic citizens to obey its divine mandates, and be governed by its sacred truths. It has also spread into England, Ireland, Scotland, and Wales: in the year 1839 where a few of our missionaries were sent over five thousand joined the standard of truth, there are numbers now joining in every land.

Questions

1. What does the Mormon experience suggest about the extent and limits of religious freedom in the pre–Civil War United States?

2. What in Smith's letter might offend non-Mormon Americans?

56. Margaret McCarthy to Her Family in Ireland (1850)

Source: Margaret McCarthy, from "State-Aided Emigration Schemes from Crown Estates in Ireland c. 1850" by Eilish Ellis. Analecta Hibernica *22 (1960), pp. 390–93. Reprinted by permission of the estate of Eilish Ellis.*

America's economic expansion fueled a demand for labor that was met, in part, by increased immigration from abroad. Between 1840 and 1860, over 4 million people (more than the entire population of 1790) entered the United States, the majority from Ireland and Germany. The Irish were fleeing a devastating famine that killed hundreds of thousands of persons and led millions of others to emigrate. About 90 percent of immigrants headed for the northern states, where job opportunities were most abundant and the new arrivals would not have to compete with slave labor. Many sent money home to help family members join them, a process today sometimes called chain migration. In this letter, Margaret McCarthy, a young immigrant writing from New York City, offers advice to her family in Ireland about coming to the United States.

<hr>

NEW YORK, SEPTEMBER 22, 1850

My dear father and mother brothers and sisters.

I write these few lines to you hoping that [they] may find you all in as good state of health as I am at present thank God.... My dear father I must only say that this is a good place and a good country for if one place does not suit a man he can go to another and can very easy please himself.... [But] I would advise no one to come to America that would not have some money after landing here that [will] enable them to go west in case they would get no work to do here. But any man or woman without a family are fools that would not venture and come to this plentiful country where no man or woman ever hungered or ever will....

Come you all together courageously and bid adieu to that lovely place the land of our birth.... But alas I am now told it's the gulf of misery, oppression, degradation and ruin of every description which I am sorry to hear of so doleful a history to be told of our dear country. This, my dear father induces me to remit to you in this letter 20 dollars.... Believe me I cannot express how great would be my joy at seeing you all here together where you would never want or be at a loss for a good breakfast or dinner. So prepare as soon as possible for this will be my last remittance until I see you all here.

Dan Keliher tells me that you knew more of the house carpentry than he did himself and he can earn from twelve to fourteen shilling a day and he also tells me that Florence will do very well and that Michael can get a place right off.... It's not for slavery I want you to come here. No its for affording my brothers and sisters and I an opportunity of showing our kindness and gratitude and coming on your seniour days... [so] that you my dear father and mother could walk about leisurely and independently....

Oh how happy I feel [that] the Lord had not it destined for me to get married... at home [and] after a few months he and I may be an encumbrance on you or perhaps in the poor house....

And dear father when you are coming here if you possibly can bring my uncle Con I would be glad that you would and I am sure he would be of the greatest acquisition to you on board and also tell Mary Keeffe that if her child died that I will pay her passage very shortly and when you are coming do not be frightened. Take courage and be determined and bold in your undertaking as the first two or three days will be the worst to you and mind whatever happens on board keep your temper and do not speak angry to any.

Questions

1. What aspirations seem to be uppermost in Margaret McCarthy's mind?

2. Why do you think McCarthy's account of economic opportunities in the United States differs so strongly from Sarah Bagley's above?

57. Ralph Waldo Emerson, "The American Scholar" (1837)

Source: "The American Scholar [1837]," in Ralph Waldo Emerson, Nature, Addresses, and Lectures *(Boston, 1892), pp. 79–80, 99–103.*

Ralph Waldo Emerson was perhaps the most prominent member of a group of New England intellectuals known as the Transcendentalists, who insisted on the primacy of individual judgment over existing social traditions and institutions. Emerson was a proponent of "individualism," a word that entered the language in the 1820s. The keynote of the times, he declared, was "the new importance given to the single person." In a widely reprinted 1837 address, "The American Scholar," delivered at Harvard College, he called on Americans engaged in writing and thinking to trust their own judgment and "never defer to the popular cry." In Emerson's own definition, rather than a preexisting set of rights or privileges, freedom was an open-ended process of self-realization by which individuals could remake themselves and their own lives. He particularly urged young scholars to free themselves from European literary and artistic ideas and create their own intellectual traditions based on American life.

Mr. President, and Gentlemen,

I greet you on the re-commencement of our literary year. Our anniversary is one of hope, and, perhaps, not enough of labor. We do not meet for games of strength or skill, for the recitation of histories, tragedies and odes, like the ancient Greeks; for parliaments of love and poesy, like the Troubadours; nor for the advancement of science, like our contemporaries in the British and European capitals. Thus far, our holiday has been simply a friendly sign of the survival of the love of letters amongst a people too busy to give to letters any more. As such, it is precious as the sign of an indestructible instinct. Perhaps the time is already come, when it ought to be, and will be something else; when the sluggard intellect of this continent will look from under its iron lids and fill the postponed expectation of the world with something better than the exertions of mechanical skill. Our day of dependence, our long apprenticeship to the learning of other lands, draws to a close. The millions that around us are rushing into life, cannot always be fed on the sere remains of foreign harvests. Events, actions arise, that must be sung, that will sing themselves. Who can doubt that poetry will revive and lead in a new age, as the star in the constellation Harp which now flames in our zenith, astronomers announce, shall one day be the pole-star for a thousand years.

• • •

In self-trust, all the virtues are comprehended. Free should the scholar be,—free and brave. Free even to the definition of freedom, "without any hindrance that does not arise out of his own constitution." Brave; for fear is a thing which a scholar by his very function puts behind him. Fear always springs from ignorance. It is a shame to him if his tranquility, amid dangerous times, arise from the presumption that like children and women, his is a protected class; or if he seek a temporary peace by the diversion of his thoughts from politics or vexed questions, hiding his head like an ostrich in the flowering bushes, peeping into microscopes, and turning rhymes, as a boy whistles to keep his courage up. So is the danger a danger still: so is the fear worse. Manlike let him turn and face it. Let him look into its eye and search its nature, inspect its origin—see the whelping of this lion,—which lies no great way back; he will then find in himself a perfect comprehension of its nature and extent; he will have made his hands meet on the other side, and can henceforth defy it, and pass on superior. The world is his who can see through its pretension. What deafness, what stoneblind custom, what overgrown error you behold, is there only by sufferance,—by your sufferance. See it to be a lie, and you have already dealt it its mortal blow.

Yes, we are the cowed,—we the trustless. It is a mischievous notion that we are come late into nature; that the world was finished a long time ago. As the world was plastic and fluid in the hands of God, so it is ever to so much of his attributes as we bring to it. To ignorance and sin, it is flint. They adapt themselves to it as they may; but in proportion as a man has anything in him divine, the firmament flows before him, and takes his signet [seal] and form. Not he is great who can alter matter, but he who can alter my state of mind. They are the kings of the world who give the color of their present thought to all nature and all art, and persuade men by the cheerful serenity of their carrying the matter, that this thing which they do, is the apple which the ages have desired to pluck, now at last ripe, and inviting nations to the harvest. The great man makes the great thing.... The day is always his, who works in it with serenity and great aims. The unstable estimates of men crowd to him whose mind is filled with a truth, as the heaped waves of the Atlantic follow the moon.

• • •

Another sign of our times, also marked by an analogous political movement is, the new importance given to the single person. Every thing that tends to insulate the individual,—to surround him with barriers of natural respect, so that each man shall feel the world is his, and man shall treat with man as a sovereign state with a sovereign state:—tends to true union as well as greatness. "I learned," said the melancholy Pestalozzi, [a Swiss educator] "that no man in God's wide earth is either willing or able to help any other man." Help must come from the bosom alone. The scholar is that man who must take up into himself all the ability of the time, all the contributions of the past, all the hopes of the future. He must be an university of knowledges. If there be one lesson more than another which should pierce his ear, it is, The world is nothing, the man is all; in yourself is the law of all nature, and you know not yet how a globule of sap ascends; in yourself slumbers the whole of Reason; it is for you to know all, it is for you to dare all. Mr. President and Gentlemen, this confidence in the unsearched might of man, belongs by all motives, by all prophecy, by all preparation, to the American Scholar. We have listened too long to the courtly muses of Europe. The spirit of the American freeman is already suspected to be timid, imitative, tame. Public and private avarice make the air we breathe thick and fat. The scholar is decent, indolent, complaisant. See already the tragic consequence. The mind of this country taught to aim at low objects, eats upon itself.

There is no work for any but the decorous and the complaisant. Young men of the fairest promise, who begin life upon our shores, inflated by the mountain winds, shined upon by all the stars of God, find the earth below not in unison with these,—but are hindered from action by the disgust which the principles on which business is managed inspire, and turn drudges, or die of disgust,—some of them suicides. What is the remedy? They did not yet see, and thousands of young men as hopeful now crowding to the barriers for the career, do not yet see, that if the single man plant himself indomitably on his instincts, and there abide, the huge world will come round to him. Patience—patience;—with the shades of all the good and great for company; and for solace, the perspective of your own infinite life; and for work, the study and the communication of principles, the making those instincts prevalent, the conversion of the world. It is not the chief disgrace in the world, not to be an unit;—not to be reckoned one character;—not to yield that peculiar fruit which each man was created to bear, but to be reckoned in the gross, in the hundred, or the thousand, of the party, the section, to which we belong; and our opinion predicted geographically, as the north, or the south. Not so, brothers and friends,—please God, ours shall not be so. We will walk on our own feet; we will work with our own hands; we will speak our own minds. Then shall man be no longer a name for pity, for doubt, and for sensual indulgence. The dread of man and the love of man shall be a wall of defence and a wreath of love around all. A nation of men will for the first time exist, because each believes himself inspired by the Divine Soul which also inspires all men.

Questions

1. Why does Emerson feel that American writers and artists are "cowed" and need to develop more boldness and originality?

2. Why does Emerson describe self-reliance as a "manlike" quality?

58. Henry David Thoreau, *Walden* (1854)

Source: Henry David Thoreau, Walden *(Boston, 1854), pp. 10–17.*

Henry David Thoreau, Emerson's neighbor in Concord, Massachusetts, became persuaded that modern society stifled individual judgment by making men "tools of their tools," trapped in stultifying jobs by their obsession with acquiring wealth. Americans, he believed, were so preoccupied with material things that they had no time to contemplate the beauties of nature.

To escape this fate, Thoreau retreated from 1845 to 1847 to a cabin on Walden Pond in Concord, where he could enjoy the freedom of isolation from the misplaced values he believed ruled American society. He subsequently wrote *Walden* (1854), an account of his experiences. Unlike writers who celebrated the market revolution, Thoreau insisted that it was degrading both Americans' values and the natural environment. Americans, he believed, should adopt a pace of life more attuned to the rhythms of nature. Genuine freedom, he insisted, lay not in the accumulation of material goods, but within. One of the most influential works of American literature ever written, *Walden* would be rediscovered by later generations who criticized social conformity, materialism, and the degradation of the natural environment.

• • •

THE MASS OF men lead lives of quiet desperation. What is called resignation is confirmed desperation. From the desperate city you go into the desperate country, and have to console yourself with the bravery of minks and muskrats. A stereotyped but unconscious despair is concealed even under what are called the games and amusements of mankind. There is no play in them, for this comes after work. But it is a characteristic of wisdom not to do desperate things.

The greater part of what my neighbours call good I believe in my soul to be bad, and if I repent of anything, it is very likely to be my good behaviour. What demon possessed me that I behaved so well? You may say the wisest thing you can, old man—you who have lived seventy years, not without honour of a kind—I hear an irresistible voice which invites me away from all that. One generation abandons the enterprises of another like stranded vessels.

I think that we may safely trust a good deal more than we do. We may waive just so much care of ourselves as we honestly bestow elsewhere. Nature is as well adapted to our weakness as to our strength.... Let us consider for a moment what most of the trouble and anxiety which I have referred to is about, and how much it is necessary that we be troubled, or at least, careful. It would be some advantage to live a primitive and frontier life, though in the midst of an outwards civilisation, if only to learn what are the gross necessaries of life and what methods have been taken to obtain them; or even to look over the old day-books of the merchants, to see what it was that the men most commonly bought at the stores, what they stored, that is, what are the grossest groceries. For the improvements of ages have had but little influence on the essential laws of man's existence: as our skeletons, probably, are not to be distinguished from those of our ancestors.

By the words, *necessary of life*, I mean whatever, of all that man obtains by his own exertions, has been from the first, or from long use has become, so important to human life that few, if any, whether from savageness, or poverty, or philosophy, ever attempt to do without it.... Most of the luxuries, and many of the so-called comforts of life, are not only not indispensable, but positive hindrances to the elevation of mankind. With respect to luxuries and comforts, the wisest have ever lived a more simple and meagre life than the poor. The ancient philosophers, Chinese, Hindoo, Persian, and Greek, were a class than which none has been poorer in outward riches, none so rich in inward....

• • •

I went to the woods because I wished to live deliberately, to [confront] only the essential facts of life, and see if I could not learn what it had to teach, and not, when I came to die, discover that I had not lived. I did not wish to live what was not life, living is so dear, nor did I wish to practice resignation, unless it was quite necessary. I wanted to live deep and suck out all the marrow of life, to live so sturdily and Spartan-like as to put rout all that was not life, to cut a broad swath and shave close, to drive life into a corner, and reduce it to its lowest terms, and, if it proved to be mean, why then to get the whole and genuine meanness of it, and publish its meanness to the world; or if it were sublime, to know it by experience, and be able to give a true account of it in my next excursion. For most men, it appears to me, are in a strange uncertainty about it, whether it is of the devil or of God, and have somewhat hastily concluded that it is the chief end of man here to "glorify God and enjoy him forever."

Still we live meanly, like ants; though the fable tells us that we were long ago changed into men; like pygmies we fight with cranes; it is error upon error, and clout upon clout, and our best virtue has for its occasion a superfluous and inevitable wretchedness. Our life is frittered away by detail. An honest man has hardly need to count more than his ten fingers, or in extreme cases he may add his ten toes, and lump the rest. Simplicity, simplicity, simplicity! I say, let your affairs be as two or three, and not a hundred or a thousand; instead of a million, count half a dozen, and keep your accounts on your thumb nail.... Simplify, simplify. Instead of three meals a day, if it be necessary eat but one; instead of a hundred dishes, five; and reduce other things in proportion....

The nation itself, with all its so called internal improvements, which, by the way, are all external and superficial, is just such an unwieldy and overgrown establishment, cluttered with furniture and tripped up by its own traps, ruined by luxury and heedless expense, by want of calculation and a worthy aim, as the million households in the land; and the only cure for them is in a rigid economy, a stern and more than Spartan simplicity of life and elevation of purpose. It lives too fast. Men think that it is essential that the Nation have commerce, and export ice, and talk through a telegraph, and ride thirty miles an hour, without a doubt, whether they do or not; but whether we should live like baboons or like men, is a little uncertain.

If we do not get our sleepers, and forge rails, and devote days and nights to the work, but go tinkering upon our lives to improve them, who will build railroads? And if railroads are not built, how shall we get to heaven in season? But if we stay at home and mind our business, who will want railroads? We do not ride on the railroad; it rides upon us. Did you ever think what those sleepers are that underlie the railroad? Each one is a man, an Irishman, or a Yankee man. The rails are laid on them, and they are covered with sand, and the cars run smoothly over them. They are sound sleepers, I assure you. And every few years a new lot is laid down and run over; so that if some have the pleasure of riding on a rail, others have the misfortune to be ridden upon.

Why should we live with such a hurry and waste of life? We are determined to be starved before we are hungry. Men say that a stitch in time saves nine, and so they take a thousand stitches today to save nine tomorrow.

• • •

Questions

1. Thoreau's statement, "The mass of men lead lives of quiet desperation," is one of the most famous lines in American literature. What does he mean, and what does he think is the cause?

2. What does Thoreau mean when he writes, "We do not ride on the railroad; it rides upon us"?

59. Charles G. Finney, "Sinners Bound to Change Their Own Hearts" (1836)

Source: "Sinners Bound to Change Their Own Hearts," in Charles G. Finney, Sermons on Important Subjects, *3rd ed. (New York, 1836), pp. 3–42.*

Beginning in the early nineteenth century, a series of religious revivals, known as the Second Great Awakening, swept over the United States. They reached a crescendo in the 1820s and early 1830s, when the Rev. Charles Grandison Finney held months-long revival meetings in upstate New York and New York City. His sermons warned of hell in vivid language while offering the promise of salvation to converts who abandoned their sinful ways. He rejected the idea that man is a sinful creature with a preordained fate, promoting instead the doctrine of free will and the possibility of salvation. Every person, Finney insisted, was a moral free agent, that is, a person free to choose between a Christian life and a life of sin.

The Second Great Awakening democratized American Christianity, making it a truly mass enterprise. At the time of independence, fewer than 2,000 Christian ministers preached in the United States. In 1845, they numbered 40,000. Americans, wrote Alexis de Tocqueville when he visited the United States in the 1830s, "combine the notions of Christianity and of liberty so intimately in their minds that it is impossible to make them conceive the one without the other."

Ezek. xviii, 31: Make you a new heart and a new spirit, for why will ye die?

• • •

A CHANGE OF HEART ... consists in changing the controlling preference of the mind in regard to the *end* of pursuit. The selfish heart is a preference of self-interest to the glory of God and the interests of his kingdom. A new heart consists in a preference of the glory of God and the interests of his kingdom to one's own happiness. In other words, it is a change from selfishness to benevolence, from having a supreme regard to one's own interest to an absorbing and controlling choice of the happiness and glory of God and his kingdom.

It is a change in the choice of a *Supreme Ruler.* The conduct of impenitent sinners demonstrates that they prefer Satan as the ruler of the world, they obey his laws, electioneer for him, and are zealous for his interests, even to martyrdom. They carry their attachment to him and his government so far as to sacrifice both body and soul to promote his interest and establish his dominion. A new heart is the choice of JEHOVAH as the supreme ruler; a deep-seated and abiding preference of his laws, and government, and character, and person, as the supreme Legislator and Governor of the universe.

Thus the world is divided into two great political parties; the difference between them is, that one party choose Satan as the god of this world, yield obedience to his laws, and are devoted to his interest. Selfishness is the law of Satan's empire, and all impenitent sinners yield it a willing obedience. The other party choose Jehovah for their governor, and consecrate themselves, with all their interests, to his service and glory. Nor does this change imply a constitutional alteration of the powers of body or mind, any more than a change of mind in regard to the form or administration of a human government. . . .

God has established a government, and proposed by the exhibition of his own character, to produce the greatest practicable amount of happiness in the universe. He has enacted laws wisely calculated to promote this object, to which he conforms all his own conduct, and to which he requires all his subjects perfectly and undeviatingly to conform theirs. After a season of obedience, Adam changed his heart, and set up for himself. So with every sinner, although he *does not first obey, as Adam did;* yet his wicked heart consists in setting up his own interest in opposition to the interest and government of God. In aiming to promote his own private happiness, in a way that is opposed to the general good. Self-gratification becomes the law to which he conforms his conduct. It is that minding of the flesh, which is enmity against God. A change of heart, therefore, is to prefer a different *end.* To prefer supremely the glory of God and the public good, to the promotion of his own interest; and whenever this preference is changed, we see of course a corresponding change of conduct. If a man change sides in politics, you will see him meeting with those that entertain the same views and feelings with himself; devising plans and using his influence to elect the candidate which he has now chosen. He has new political friends on the one side, and new political enemies on the other. So with a sinner; if his heart is changed, you will see that Christians become his friends—Christ his candidate. He aims at honoring him and promoting his interest in all his ways. Before, the language of his conduct was, "Let Satan govern the world." Now, the language of his heart and of his life is, "Let Christ rule King of nations, as he is King of saints." Before, his conduct said, "O Satan, let thy kingdom come, and let thy will be done." Now, his heart, his life, his lips cry out, "O Jesus, let thy kingdom come, let thy will be done on earth as it is in heaven." . . .

• • •

As God requires men to make to themselves a new heart, on pain of eternal death, it is the strongest possible evidence that they are able to do it. To say that he has commanded them to do it, without telling them they are able, is consummate trifling. Their ability is implied as strongly as it can be, in the command itself. . . .

The strivings of the Spirit of God with men, is not a physical scuffling, but a debate; a strife not of body with body, but of mind with mind; and that in the action and reaction of vehement argumentation. From these remarks, it is easy to answer the question sometimes put by individuals who seem to be entirely in the dark upon this subject, whether in converting the soul the Spirit acts directly on the mind, or on the truth. This is the same nonsense as if you should ask, whether an earthly advocate who had gained his cause, did it by acting directly and physically on the jury, or on his argument. . . .

You see from this subject that a sinner, under the influence of the Spirit of God, is just as free as a jury under the arguments of an advocate. . . .

• • •

So if a minister goes into a desk to preach to sinners, believing that they have no power to obey the truth, and under the impression that a direct physical influence must be exerted upon them before they *can* believe, and if his audience be of the same opinion, in vain does he preach, and in vain do they hear, "for they are yet in their sins"; they sit and quietly wait for some invisible hand to be stretched down from heaven, and perform some surgical operation, infuse some new principle, or implant some constitutional taste; *after* which they suppose they shall be *able* to obey God. Ministers should labor with sinners, as a lawyer does with a jury, and upon the same principles of mental philosophy; and the sinner should weigh his arguments, and make up his mind as upon oath and for his life, and give a verdict upon the spot, according to law and evidence....

Sinner! instead of waiting and praying for God to change your heart, you should at once summon up your powers, put forth the effort, and change the governing preference of your mind....

Sinner! your obligation to love God is equal to the excellence of his character, and your guilt in not obeying him is of course equal to your obligation. You cannot therefore for an hour or a moment defer obedience to the commandment in the text, without deserving eternal damnation....

And now, sinner; while the subject is before you, will you yield? To keep yourself away from under the motives of the gospel, by neglecting church, and neglecting your Bible, will prove fatal to your soul. And to be careless when you do attend, or to hear with attention and refuse to make up your mind and yield, will be equally fatal. And now, "I beseech you, by the mercies of God, that you at *this time* render your body and soul, a living sacrifice to God, which is your reasonable service." Let the truth take hold upon your conscience— throw down your rebellious weapons—give up your refuges of lies— fix your mind steadfastly upon the world of considerations that should instantly decide you to close in with the offer of reconciliation while it now lies before you. Another moment's delay, and it may be too late forever. The Spirit of God may depart from you—the offer of life may be made no more, and this one more slighted offer of mercy may close up your account, and seal you over to all the horrors of eternal death. Hear, then, O sinner, I beseech you, and obey the word of the Lord—"Make you a new heart and a new spirit, for why will ye die?"

Questions

1. What precisely does Finney mean by a "change of heart"?

2. How does the fact that he is preaching in an era of mass political democracy affect Finney's language?

CHAPTER 10

Democracy in America, 1815–1840

60. The Monroe Doctrine (1823)

Source: James D. Richardson, ed., A Compilation of the Messages and Papers of the Presidents *(10 vols.: Washington, D.C., 1896–99), vol. 2, pp. 778, 786–88.*

Between 1810 and 1822, Spain's Latin American colonies rose in rebellion and established a series of independent nations, including Mexico, Venezuela, Ecuador, and Peru. By 1825, Spain's once vast American empire had been reduced to the islands of Cuba and Puerto Rico. The uprisings inspired a wave of sympathy in the United States. In 1822, the Monroe administration became the first government to extend diplomatic recognition to the new Latin American republics. The following year, President James Monroe included in his annual message a passage, written by Secretary of State John Quincy Adams, that became known as the Monroe Doctrine. It outlined principles that would help to govern the country's relations with the rest of the world for nearly a century—that the Western Hemisphere was no longer open to European colonization and that the United States would remain uninvolved in the wars of Europe. In effect, Monroe declared the Americas a sphere of influence of the United States.

AT THE PROPOSAL of the Russian Imperial government, made through the minister of the Emperor residing here, a full power and instructions have been transmitted to the minister of the United States at St. Petersburg to arrange by amicable negotiation the respective rights and interests of the two nations on the northwest coast of this continent. A similar proposal has been made by His Imperial Majesty to the government of Great Britain, which has likewise been acceded to. The government of the United States has been desirous by this friendly proceeding of manifesting the great value which they have invariably attached to the friendship of the Emperor and their solicitude to cultivate the best understanding with his government.

In the discussions to which this interest has given rise and in the arrangements by which they may terminate the occasion has been judged proper for asserting, as a principle in which the rights and interests of the United States are involved, that the American continents, by the free and independent condition which they have assumed and maintain, are henceforth not to be considered as subjects for future colonization by any European powers....

It was stated at the commencement of the last session that a great effort was then making in Spain and Portugal to improve the condition of the people of those countries, and that it appeared to be conducted with extraordinary moderation. It need scarcely be remarked that the results have been so far very different from what was then anticipated. Of events in that quarter of the globe, with which we have so much intercourse and from which we derive our origin, we have always been anxious and interested spectators. The citizens of the United States cherish sentiments the most friendly in favor of the liberty and happiness of their fellow-men on that side of the Atlantic. In the wars of the European powers in matters relating to themselves we have never taken any part, nor does it comport with our policy to do so. It is only when our rights are invaded or seriously menaced that we resent injuries or make preparation for our defense. With the movements in this hemisphere we are of necessity more immediately connected, and by causes which must be obvious to all enlightened and impartial observers. The political system of the allied powers [of Europe] is essentially different in this respect from that of America. ...

We owe it, therefore, to candor and to the amicable relations existing between the United States and those powers to declare that we should consider any attempt on their part to extend their system to any portion of this hemisphere as dangerous to our peace and safety. With the existing colonies or dependencies of any European power we have not interfered and shall not interfere. But with the Governments who have declared their independence and maintain it, and whose independence we have, on great consideration and on just principles, acknowledged, we could not view any interposition for the purpose of oppressing them, or controlling in any other manner their destiny, by any European power in any other light than as the manifestation of an unfriendly disposition toward the United States. ...

It is impossible that the allied powers should extend their political system to any portion of [North or South America] without endangering our peace and happiness; nor can anyone believe that our southern brethren, if left to themselves, would adopt it of their own accord. It is equally impossible, therefore, that we should behold such interposition in any form with indifference. If we look to the comparative strength and resources of Spain and those new governments, and their distance from each other, it must be obvious that she can never subdue them. It is still the true policy of the United States to leave the parties to themselves, in hope that other powers will pursue the same course.

Questions

1. Why does Monroe think that the "systems" of Europe and the Western Hemisphere are fundamentally different?

2. Why does Monroe mention Russia at the beginning of his address?

61. John Quincy Adams on the Role of the National Government (1825)

Source: James D. Richardson, ed., A Compilation of the Messages and Papers of the Presidents *(10 vols.: Washington, D.C., 1896–99), vol. 2., pp. 878–82.*

Many Americans in the first half of the nineteenth century saw a powerful federal government as a threat to individual liberty. Others, however, believed that by promoting economic expansion and encouraging the development of the arts and sciences, the government would enhance Americans' freedom. Among the proponents of an activist federal government was John Quincy Adams, who served as president from 1825 to 1829.

In his first annual message to Congress, in December 1825, he set forth a comprehensive program for government action. He called for legislation promoting agriculture, commerce, and manufacturing, and "the mechanical and elegant arts." His plans included government-financed improvements in transportation, scientific expeditions, and the establishment of a national astronomical observatory. Adams astonished many listeners with his bold statement, "Liberty is power." The United States, the freest nation on earth, he predicted, would also become the mightiest.

Adams's proposals alarmed all believers in strict construction of the Constitution. Few of his ambitious ideas received support in Congress. Not until the twentieth century would the kind of national economic planning and educational and scientific involvement envisioned by Adams be realized.

───────

IN ASSUMING HER station among the civilized nations of the earth it would seem that our country had contracted the engagement to contribute her share of mind, of labor, and of expense to the improvement of those parts of knowledge which lie beyond the reach of individual acquisition, and particularly to geographical and astronomical science. Looking back to the history only of the half century since the declaration of our independence, and observing the generous emulation with which the Governments of France,

Great Britain, and Russia have devoted the genius, the intelligence, the treasures of their respective nations to the common improvement of the species in these branches of science, is it not incumbent upon us to inquire whether we are not bound by obligations of a high and honorable character to contribute our portion of energy and exertion to the common stock? The voyages of discovery prosecuted in the course of that time at the expense of those nations have not only redounded to their glory, but to the improvement of human knowledge. We have been partakers of that improvement and owe for it a sacred debt, not only of gratitude, but of equal or proportional exertion in the same common cause. Of the cost of these undertakings, if the mere expenditures of outfit, equipment, and completion of the expeditions were to be considered the only charges, it would be unworthy of a great and generous nation to take a second thought. One hundred expeditions of circumnavigation ... would not burden the exchequer of the nation fitting them out so much as the ways and means of defraying a single campaign in war. But if we take into the account the lives of those benefactors of mankind of which their services in the cause of their species were the purchase, how shall the cost of those heroic enterprises be estimated, and what compensation can be made to them or to their countries for them? Is it not by bearing them in affectionate remembrance? Is it not still more by imitating their example by enabling countrymen of our own to pursue the same career and to hazard their lives in the same cause?

• • •

In inviting the attention of Congress to the subject of internal improvements upon a view thus enlarged it is not my design to recommend the equipment of an expedition for circumnavigating the globe for purposes of scientific research and inquiry. We have objects of useful investigation nearer home, and to which our cares may be more beneficially applied. The interior of our own territories has yet been very imperfectly explored. Our coasts along many degrees of latitude upon the shores of the Pacific Ocean, though much frequented by our spirited commercial navigators, have been barely visited by our public ships. The River of the West, first fully discovered and navigated by a countryman of our own, still bears the name of the ship in which he ascended its waters, and claims the protection of our armed national flag at its mouth. With the establishment of a military post there or at some other point of that coast, recommended by my predecessor and already matured in the deliberations of the last Congress, I would suggest the expediency of connecting the equipment of a public ship for the exploration of the whole northwest coast of this continent....

• • •

Connected with the establishment of an university, or separate from it, might be undertaken the erection of an astronomical observatory, with provision for the support of an astronomer, to be in constant attendance of observation upon the phenomena of the heavens, and for the periodical publication of his observations. It is with no feeling of pride as an American that the remark may be made that on the comparatively small territorial surface of Europe there are existing upward of 130 of these light-houses of the skies, while throughout the whole American hemisphere there is not one. If we reflect a moment upon the discoveries which in the last four centuries have been made in the physical constitution of the universe by the means of these buildings and of observers stationed in them, shall we doubt of their usefulness to every nation? And while scarcely a year passes over our heads without bringing some new astronomical discovery to light, which we must fain receive at second hand from Europe, are we not cutting ourselves off from the means of returning light for light while we have neither observatory nor observer upon our half of the globe and the earth revolves in perpetual darkness to our unsearching eyes?

The Constitution under which you are assembled is a charter of limited powers. After full and solemn deliberation upon all or any of the objects which, urged by an irresistible sense of my own duty, I have recommended to your attention should you come to the conclusion that, however desirable in themselves, the enactment of laws for effecting them would transcend the powers committed to you by that venerable instrument which we are all bound to support, let no consideration induce you to assume the exercise of powers not granted to you by the people. But if the power to exercise exclusive legislation in all cases whatsoever over the District of Columbia; if the power to lay and collect taxes, duties, imposts, and excises, to pay the debts and provide for the common defense and general welfare of the United States; if the power to regulate commerce with foreign nations and among the several States and with the Indian tribes, to fix the standard of weights and measures, to establish post-offices and post-roads, to declare war, to raise and support armies, to provide and maintain a navy, to dispose of and make all needful rules and regulations respecting the territory or other property belonging to the United States, and to make all laws which shall be necessary and proper for carrying these powers into execution—if these powers and others enumerated in the Constitution may be effectually brought into action by laws promoting the improvement of agriculture, commerce, and manufactures, the cultivation and encouragement of the mechanic and of the elegant arts, the advancement of literature, and the progress of the sciences, ornamental and profound, to refrain from exercising them for the benefit of the people themselves would be to hide in the earth the talent committed to our charge—would be treachery to the most sacred of trusts.

The spirit of improvement is abroad upon the earth. It stimulates the hearts and sharpens the faculties not of our fellow-citizens alone, but of the nations of Europe and of their rulers. While dwelling with pleasing satisfaction upon the superior excellence of our political institutions, let us not be unmindful that liberty is power; that the nation blessed with the largest portion of liberty must in proportion to its numbers be the most powerful nation upon earth, and that the tenure of power by man is, in the moral purposes of his Creator, upon condition that it shall be exercised to ends of beneficence, to improve the condition of himself and his fellowmen. While foreign nations less blessed with that freedom which is power than ourselves are advancing with gigantic strides in the career of public improvement, were we to slumber in indolence or fold up our arms and proclaim to the world that we are palsied by the will of our constituents, would it not be to cast away the bounties of Providence and doom ourselves to perpetual inferiority? In the course of the year now drawing to its close we have beheld, under the auspices and at the expense of one State of this Union, a new university unfolding its portals to the sons of science and holding up the torch of human improvement to eyes that seek the light. We have seen under the persevering and enlightened enterprise of another State the waters of our Western lakes mingle with those of the ocean. If undertakings like these have been accomplished in the compass of a few years by the authority of single members of our Confederation, can we, the representative authorities of the whole Union, fall behind our fellow-servants in the exercise of the trust committed to us for the benefit of our common sovereign by the accomplishment of works important to the whole and to which neither the authority nor the resources of any one State can be adequate?

Questions

1. Why does President Adams believe that the federal government should promote the sciences and arts?

2. What does he mean by the remark "Liberty is power"?

62. Andrew Jackson, Veto of the Bank Bill (1832)

Source: James D. Richardson, ed., A Compilation of the Messages and Papers of the Presidents *(Washington, D.C., 1896–99), vol. 3, pp. 1139–54.*

The central political struggle of the Age of Jackson was the president's war on the Bank of the United States. Many Americans, including Jackson, distrusted bankers as "non-producers" who contributed nothing to the nation's wealth but profited from the labor of others. They especially resented the economic power concentrated in the hands of the Second Bank of the United States, a private corporation that conducted the federal government's financial business and regulated currency issued by state banks. The Bank had been given a twenty-year charter by Congress in 1816. Many Democrats, suspicious of concentrated political and economic power, called it the Monster Bank, an illegitimate union of political authority and entrenched economic privilege.

The issue of the Bank's future came to a head in 1832, when the institution's allies persuaded Congress to approve a bill extending it for another twenty years. Jackson vetoed the bill. His veto message is perhaps the central document of what would come to be called "Jacksonian democracy." The proper role of government, Jackson insisted, was to offer "equal protection" to all citizens. In a democracy, it was unacceptable for Congress to create a source of economic power and privilege unaccountable to the people. Jackson presented himself to "humble" Americans as their defender. His effective appeal to popular sentiments helped him win reelection in 1832, ensuring the death of the Bank of the United States.

———

THE BILL "TO modify and continue" the act entitled "An act to incorporate the subscribers to the Bank of the United States" ... ought not to become a law. The powers and privileges possessed by the existing bank are unauthorized by the Constitution, subversive of the rights of the States, and dangerous to the liberties of the people.... The present corporate body, denominated the president, directors, and company of the Bank of the United States, ... enjoys an exclusive privilege of banking under the authority of the General Government, a monopoly of its favor and support, and, as a necessary consequence, almost a monopoly of the foreign and domestic exchange. The powers, privileges, and favors bestowed upon it in the original charter, by increasing the value of the stock far above its par value, operated as a gratuity of many millions to the stockholders....

Every monopoly and all exclusive privileges are granted at the expense of the public, which ought to receive a fair equivalent. The many millions which this act proposes to bestow on the stockholders of the existing bank must come directly or indirectly out of the earnings of the American people.... It is not conceivable how the present stockholders can have any claim to the special favor of the Government.... Should [the Bank's] influence become concentered, as it may under the operation of such an act as this, in the hands of a self-elected directory ... will there not be cause to tremble for the purity of our elections? ...

It is maintained by the advocates of the bank that its constitutionality in all its features ought to be considered as settled by precedent and by the decision of the Supreme Court. To this conclusion I can not assent.... The Congress, the Executive, and the Court must each for itself be guided by its own opinion of the Constitution. Each public officer who takes an oath to support the Constitution swears that he will support it as he understands it, and not as it is understood by others.... The opinion of the judges has no more authority over Congress than the opinion of Congress has over the judges, and on that point the President is independent of both....

It is to be regretted that the rich and powerful too often bend the acts of government to their selfish purposes. Distinctions in society will always exist under every just government. Equality of talents, of education, or of wealth can not be produced by human institutions. In the full enjoyment of the gifts of Heaven and the fruits of superior industry, economy, and virtue, every man is equally entitled to protection by law; but when the laws undertake to add to these natural and just advantages artificial distinctions, to grant titles, gratuities, and exclusive privileges, to make the rich richer and the potent more powerful, the humble members of society—the farmers, mechanics, and laborers—who have neither the time nor the means of securing like favors to themselves, have a right to complain of the injustice of their Government. There are no necessary evils in government. Its evils exist only in its abuses. If it would confine itself to equal protection, and, as Heaven does its rains, shower its favors alike on the high and the low, the rich and the poor, it would be an unqualified blessing. In the act before me there seems to be a wide and unnecessary departure from these just principles.

Nor is our Government to be maintained or our Union preserved by invasions of the rights and powers of the several States. In thus attempting to make our General Government strong we make it weak. Its true strength consists in leaving individuals and States as much as possible to themselves—in making itself felt, not in its power, but in its beneficence; not in its control, but in its protection; not in binding the States more closely to the center, but leaving each to move unobstructed in its proper orbit.

Experience should teach us wisdom. Most of the difficulties our Government now encounters ... have sprung from an abandonment of the legitimate objects of Government. ... Many of our rich men have not been content with equal protection and equal benefits, but have besought us to make them richer by act of Congress. By attempting to gratify their desires we have ... arrayed section against section, interest against interest, and man against man. We [must] at least take a stand against all new grants of monopolies and exclusive privileges, against any prostitution of our Government to the advancement of the few at the expense of the many.

Questions

1. Why does Jackson distinguish between just and unjust "distinctions in society"?

2. What does Jackson see as the legitimate scope of governmental action?

63. Virginia Petition for the Right to Vote (1829)

Source: **Proceedings and Debates of the Virginia State Convention**
of 1829–1830 *(Richmond, 1830), pp. 25–31.*

The challenge to property qualifications for voting, which began during
the American Revolution, reached its culmination in the first part of the
nineteenth century. No state that entered the Union after the original
thirteen required ownership of property to vote. In the older states, constitutional conventions during the 1820s and 1830s debated once again who
should be able to participate in American democracy.

By the 1820s, only North Carolina, Rhode Island, and Virginia still
retained property qualifications for voting. One of the first actions of
Virginia's constitutional convention of 1829–1830 was to consider a memorial from "non-freeholders" of Richmond—men who did not possess enough
land to enable them to vote. Those who owned property, declared their
statement, did not necessarily possess "moral or intellectual endowments"
superior to those of the poor. "They alone deserve to be called free," they
added, "who participate in the formation of their political institutions."
The large slaveholders who dominated Virginia politics successfully
resisted demands for changes in voting qualifications in 1829, but a
subsequent constitutional convention, in 1850, eliminated the property
requirement.

———

YOUR MEMORIALISTS, AS their designation imports, belong to
that class of citizens, who, not having the good fortune to possess a
certain portion of land, are, for that cause only, debarred from the
enjoyment of the right of suffrage. Experience has but too clearly
evinced, what, indeed, reason had always foretold, by how frail a
tenure they hold every other right, who are denied this, the highest
prerogative of freemen. The want of it has afforded both the pretext
and the means of excluding the entire class, to which your memorialists belong, from all participation in the recent election of the
body, they now respectfully address. Comprising a very large part,

probably a majority of male citizens of mature age, they have been passed by, like aliens or slaves, as if destitute of interest, or unworthy of a voice, in measures involving their future political destiny: whilst the freeholders, sole possessors, under the existing Constitution, of the elective franchise, have, upon the strength of that possession alone, asserted and maintained in themselves, the exclusive power of new-modelling the fundamental laws of the State: in other words, have seized upon the sovereign authority.

It cannot be necessary, in addressing the Convention now assembled, to expatiate on the momentous importance of the right of suffrage, or to enumerate the evils consequent upon its unjust limitation. Were there no other than that your memorialists have brought to your attention, and which has made them feel with full force their degraded condition, well might it justify their best efforts to obtain the great privilege they now seek, as the only effectual method of preventing its recurrence. To that privilege, they respectfully contend, they are entitled equally with its present possessors. Many are bold enough to deny their title. None can show a better. It rests upon no subtle or abstruse reasoning; but upon grounds simple in their character, intelligible to the plainest capacity, and such as appeal to the heart, as well as the understanding, of all who comprehend and duly appreciate the principles of free Government. . . .

How do the principles thus proclaimed, accord with the existing regulation of suffrage? A regulation, which, instead of the equality nature ordains, creates an odious distinction between members of the same community; robs of all share, in the enactment of the laws, a large portion of the citizens, bound by them, and whose blood and treasure are pledged to maintain them, and vests in a favoured class, not in consideration of their public services, but of their private possessions, the highest of all privileges. . . .

Surely it were much to be desired that, every citizen should be qualified for the proper exercise of all his rights, and the due performance of all his duties. But the same qualifications that entitle him to assume the management of his private affairs, and to claim all other privileges of citizenship, equally entitle him, in the judgment of your memorialists, to be entrusted with this, the dearest of all his privileges, the most important of all his concerns. But if otherwise, still they cannot discern in the possession of land any evidence of peculiar merit, or superior title. To ascribe to a landed possession, moral or intellectual endowments, would truly be regarded as ludicrous, were it not for the gravity with which the proposition is maintained, and still more for the grave consequences flowing from it. Such possession no more proves him who has it, wiser or better, than it proves him taller or stronger, than him who has it not. That cannot be a fit criterion for the exercise of any right, the possession of which does not indicate the existence, nor the want of it the absence, of any essential qualification. . . .

Your memorialists do not design to institute a comparison; they fear none that can be fairly made between the privileged and the proscribed classes. They may be permitted, however, without disrespect, to remark, that of the latter, not a few possess land: many, though not proprietors, are yet cultivators of the soil: others are engaged in avocations of a different nature, often as useful, presupposing no less integrity, requiring as much intelligence, and as fixed a residence, as agricultural pursuits. Virtue, intelligence, are not among the products of the soil. Attachment to property, often a sordid sentiment, is not to be confounded with the sacred flame of patriotism. The love of country, like that of parents and offspring, is engrafted in our nature. It exists in all climates, among all classes, under every possible form of Government. Riches oftener impair it than poverty. Who has it not is a monster. . . .

Let us concede that the right of suffrage is a social right; that it must of necessity be regulated by society. Still the question recurs, is the existing limitation proper? For obvious reasons, by almost universal consent, women and children, aliens and slaves, are excluded. It were useless to discuss the propriety of a rule that scarcely admits of diversity of opinion. What is concurred in by those who constitute the society, the body politic, must be taken to be right. But the exclusion of these classes for reasons peculiarly applicable to them, is no argument for excluding others to whom no one of those reasons applies.

It is said to be *expedient*, however, to exclude non-freeholders also. Who shall judge of this expediency? The society: and does that embrace the proprietors of certain portions of land only? Expedient, for whom? for the freeholders. A harsh appellation would he deserve, who, on the plea of expediency, should take from another his property: what, then, should be said of him who, on that plea, takes from another his rights, upon which the security, not of his property only, but of his life and liberty depends? ...

They alone deserve to be called free, or have a guarantee for their rights, who participate in the formation of their political institutions, and in the control of those who make and administer the laws.

Questions

1. What "obvious reasons" exclude women, children, noncitizens, and slaves from the right to vote, and why do the non-freeholders not question them?

2. How do the writers define political freedom?

———

64. Appeal of the Cherokee Nation (1830)

Source: E. C. Tracy, Memoir of the Life of Jeremiah Evarts *(Boston, 1845), pp. 149–58.*

One of the early laws of Andrew Jackson's administration, the Indian Removal Act of 1830, provided for uprooting the Cherokee and four other tribes, with a total population of around 60,000 living in the Southeast. The Cherokee had made great efforts to become citizens, establishing schools, adopting a constitution modeled on that of the United States, and becoming successful farmers, many of whom owned slaves. But in his messages to Congress, Jackson referred to them as "savages" and supported Georgia's effort to seize Cherokee land and nullify the tribe's laws.

Cherokee leaders petitioned Congress, proclaiming their desire to "remain on the land of our fathers," as guaranteed in treaties with the federal government. They also went to court to protect their rights. Chief Justice John Marshall held that Georgia's action in extending its jurisdiction over the Cherokee violated the tribe's treaties with Washington. But presidents Jackson and Van Buren refused to recognize the ruling's validity. Eventually, nearly all the Cherokee, along with the other "civilized tribes," were forced to leave their homes. More than 4,000 Indians perished during the winter of 1838–1839 on the Trail of Tears, as the removal route to present-day Oklahoma came to be called.

━━━━━

WE ARE AWARE that some persons suppose it will be for our advantage to remove beyond the Mississippi. We think otherwise. Our people universally think otherwise. Thinking that it would be fatal to their interests, they have almost to a man sent their memorial to Congress, deprecating the necessity of a removal. This question was distinctly before their minds when they signed their memorial. Not an adult person can be found, who has not an opinion on the subject; and if the people were to understand distinctly, that they could be protected against the laws of the neighboring States, there is probably not an adult person in the nation, who would think it best to remove; though possibly a few might emigrate individually. There are doubtless many who would flee to an unknown country, however beset with dangers, privations and sufferings, rather than be sentenced to spend six years in a Georgia prison for advising one of their neighbors not to betray his country. And there are others who could not think of living as outlaws in their native land, exposed to numberless vexations, and excluded from being parties or witnesses in a court of justice. It is incredible that Georgia should ever have enacted the oppressive laws to which reference is here made, unless she had supposed that something extremely terrific in its character was necessary, in order to make the Cherokees willing to remove. We are not willing to remove; and if we could be brought to this extremity, it would be, not by argument; not because our judgment was satisfied; not because our condition will be improved—but only because we cannot endure to be deprived of our national and individual rights, and subjected to a process of intolerable oppression.

We wish to remain on the land of our fathers. We have a perfect and original right to claim this, without interruption or molestation. The treaties with us, and laws of the United States made in pursuance of treaties, guaranty our residence, and our privileges, and secure us against intruders. Our only request is, that these treaties may be fulfilled, and these laws executed.

But if we are compelled to leave our country, we see nothing but ruin before us. The country west of the Arkansas territory is unknown to us. From what we can learn of it, we have no prepossessions in its favor. All the inviting parts of it, as we believe, are preoccupied by various Indian nations, to which it has been assigned. They would regard us as intruders, and look upon us with an evil eye. The far greater part of that region is, beyond all controversy, badly supplied with wood and water; and no Indian tribe can live as agriculturists without these articles. All our neighbors, in case of our removal, though crowded into our near vicinity, would speak a language totally different from ours, and practice different customs. The original possessors of that region are now wandering savages, lurking for prey in the neighborhood. They have always been at war, and would be easily tempted to turn their arms against peaceful emigrants. Were the country to which we are urged much better than it is represented to be, and were it free from the objections which we have made to it, still it is not the land of our birth, nor of our affections. It contains neither the scenes of our childhood, nor the graves of our fathers.

Questions

1. What reasons do the Cherokee give for rejecting the idea of moving beyond the Mississippi River?

2. How do the Cherokee understand their "national and individual rights"?

---

65. Appeal of Forty Thousand Citizens (1838)

Source: **Appeal of Forty Thousand Citizens Threatened with Disfranchisement, to the People of Pennsylvania** *(Philadelphia, 1838), pp. 3–11.*

The expansion of political democracy for white men went hand in hand with the elimination of democratic participation for blacks. Every state that entered the Union between 1800 and 1860, with the single exception of Maine, limited the right to vote to whites. And several states that had allowed black men to vote, including Connecticut, New York, and Tennessee, either eliminated the right entirely or added such high property qualifications that few could qualify. In 1837, a constitutional convention in Pennsylvania, home to the largest free black community in the North, stripped blacks of the right to vote. (Thaddeus Stevens, later a leading advocate of emancipation and black suffrage in Congress, refused to sign the document because of this provision.) In response, a large gathering in Philadelphia issued a protest to "fellow citizens" of Pennsylvania.

FELLOW CITIZENS:—We appeal to you from the decision of the "Reform Convention," which has stripped us of a right peaceably enjoyed during forty-seven years under the Constitution of this commonwealth. We honor Pennsylvania and her noble institutions too much to part with our birthright as her free citizens without a struggle. To all her citizens the right of suffrage is valuable in proportion as she is free; but surely there are none who can so ill afford to spare it as ourselves.

Was it the intention of the people of this commonwealth that the convention to which the Constitution was committed for revision and amendment, should tear up and cast away its first principles? Was it made the business of the Convention to deny "that all men are born equally free," by making political rights depend upon the skin in which a man is born? Or to divide what our fathers bled to unite, to wit, TAXATION and REPRESENTATION? We will not allow ourselves for one moment to suppose, that the majority of the people of Pennsylvania are not too respectful of the rights and too liberal towards the feelings of others as well as too much enlightened to their own interests, to deprive of the right of suffrage a single individual who may safely be trusted with it. And we cannot believe that you have found among those who bear the burdens of taxation any who have proved, by their abuse of the right, that it is not safe in their hands. This is a question, fellow-citizens, in which we plead *your* cause as well as our own. It is the safeguard of the strongest that he lives under a government which is obliged to respect the voice of the weakest. When you have taken from an individual his right to vote, you have made the government, in regard to him, a mere despotism; and you have taken a step towards making it a despotism to all.—To your women and children, their inability to vote at the polls may be no evil, because they are united by the consanguinity and affection with those who can do it. To foreigners and paupers the want of the right may be tolerable because a little time or labor will make it theirs. They are candidates for the privilege, and hence substantially enjoy its benefits. But when a distinct class of the community, already sufficiently the objects of prejudice, are wholly, and for ever, disfranchised and excluded, to the remotest posterity, from the possibility of a voice in regard to the laws under which they are to live—it is the same thing as if their abode were transferred to the dominions of the Russian Autocrat, or of the Grand Turk. They have lost their check upon oppression, their wherewith to but friends, their panoply of manhood; in short, they are thrown upon the mercy of a despotic majority. Like every other despot, this despot majority, will believe in the mildness of its own sway; but who will the more willingly submit to it for that? . . .

By the careful inquiry of a committee appointed by the "Pennsylvania Society for Promoting the Abolition of Slavery," it has been ascertained that the colored population of Philadelphia and its suburbs, numbering 18,768 souls, possess at the present time, of real and personal estate, not less than $1,350,000. They have paid for taxes during the last year $3,232.83, for house, water, and ground rent, $166,963.50. This committee estimate the income of the holders of real estate occupied by the colored people, to be 7½ per cent on a capital of about $2,000,000. Here is an addition to the wealth of their white brethren. But the rents and taxes are not all; to pay them, the colored people must be employed in labor, and here is another profit to the whites, for no man employs another unless he can make his labor profitable to himself. For a similar reason, a profit is made by all the whites who sell to colored people the necessaries or luxuries of life. Though the aggregate amount of the wealth derived by the whites from our people can only be conjectured, its importance is worthy of consideration by those who would make it less by lessening our motive to accumulate for ourselves. . . .

That we are not neglectful of our religious interests, nor of the education of our children, is shown by the fact that there are among us in Philadelphia, Pittsburg, York, West Chester, and Columbia, 22 churches, 48 clergymen, 26 day schools, 20 Sabbath schools, 125 Sabbath school teachers, 4 literary societies, 2 public libraries, consisting of about 800 volumes, besides 8,333 volumes in private libraries, 2 tract societies, 2 Bible societies, and 7 temperance societies.

In other parts of the State we are confident our condition will compare very favorably with that in Philadelphia, although we are not furnished with accurate statistics.

Our fathers shared with yours the trials and perils of the wilderness. Among the facts which illustrate this, it is well known that the founder of your capital, from whom it bears the name of Harrisburg, was rescued by a *colored man*, from a party of Indians, who had captured, and bound him to the stake for execution. In gratitude for this act, he *invited colored persons* to settle in his town, and offered them land on favorable terms. When our common country has been invaded by a foreign foe, colored men have hazarded their lives in its defence. Our fathers fought by the side of yours in the struggle which made us an independent republic.

Questions

1. What evidence do the free blacks present to establish that they are worthy of the right to vote?

2. How do the protesters link their claims to the legacy of the American Revolution?

CHAPTER 11

The Peculiar Institution

66. Frederick Douglass on the Desire for Freedom (1845)

Source: **Narrative of the Life of Frederick Douglass, an American Slave** *(Boston, 1845), pp. 39–43.*

No American of the nineteenth century spoke more eloquently or effectively against slavery and racial inequality than Frederick Douglass. Born into slavery in 1818, he became a major figure in the crusade for abolition, the drama of emancipation, and the effort during Reconstruction to give meaning to black freedom. He was also active in other reform movements, such as the campaign for women's rights.

Douglass experienced slavery in all its variety, from work as a house servant and as a skilled craftsman in a Baltimore shipyard to labor as a plantation field hand. In 1838, having borrowed the free papers of a black sailor, he escaped to the North. He went on to become perhaps the era's most prominent antislavery orator and editor, and wrote three versions of his autobiography. The first, which appeared in 1845, offered an eloquent, brief account of his experiences in slavery and his escape.

I WAS NOW about twelve years old, and the thought of being *a slave for life* began to bear heavily upon my heart. Just about this time, I got hold of a book entitled "The Columbian Orator." Every opportunity I got, I used to read this book. Among much of other interesting matter, I found in it a dialogue between a master and his slave. The slave was represented as having run away from his master three times. The dialogue represented the conversation which took place between them, when the slave was retaken the third time. In this dialogue, the whole argument in behalf of slavery was brought forward by the master, all of which was disposed of by the slave. The slave was made to say some very smart as well as impressive things in reply to his master—things which had the desired though unexpected effect; for the conversation resulted in the voluntary emancipation of the slave on the part of the master.

In the same book, I met with one of [British politician Richard B.] Sheridan's mighty speeches on and in behalf of Catholic emancipation. These were choice documents to me. I read them over and over again with unabated interest. They gave tongue to interesting thoughts of my own soul, which had frequently flashed through my mind, and died away for want of utterance. The moral which I gained from the dialogue was the power of truth over the conscience of even a slaveholder. What I got from Sheridan was a bold denunciation of slavery, and a powerful vindication of human rights. The reading of these documents enabled me to utter my thoughts, and to meet the arguments brought forward to sustain slavery; but while they relieved me of one difficulty, they brought on another even more painful than the one of which I was relieved. The more I read, the more I was led to abhor and detest my enslavers. I could regard them in no other light than a band of successful robbers, who had left their homes, and gone to Africa, and stolen us from our homes, and in a strange land reduced us to slavery. I loathed them as being the meanest as well as the most wicked of men. As I read and contemplated the subject, behold! that very discontentment which Master Hugh had predicted would follow my learning to read had already come, to torment and sting my soul to unutterable anguish. As I writhed under it, I would at times feel that learning to read had been a curse rather than a blessing. It had given me a view of my wretched condition, without the remedy. It opened my eyes to the horrible pit, but to no ladder upon which to get out. In moments of agony, I envied my fellow-slaves for their stupidity. I have often wished myself a beast. I preferred the condition of the meanest reptile to my own. Any thing, no matter what, to get rid of thinking! It was this everlasting thinking of my condition that tormented me. There was no getting rid of it. It was pressed upon me by every object within sight or hearing, animate or inanimate. The silver trump of freedom had roused my soul to eternal wakefulness. Freedom now appeared, to disappear no more forever. It was heard in every sound, and seen in every thing. It was ever present to torment me with a sense of my wretched condition. I saw nothing without seeing it, I heard nothing without hearing it, and felt nothing without feeling it. It looked from every star, it smiled in every calm, breathed in every wind, and moved in every storm.

I often found myself regretting my own existence, and wishing myself dead; and but for the hope of being free, I have no doubt but that I should have killed myself, or done something for which I should have been killed. While in this state of mind, I was eager to hear any one speak of slavery. I was a ready listener....

• • •

I went one day down on the wharf of Mr. Waters; and seeing two Irishmen unloading a scow of stone, I went, unasked, and helped them. When we had finished, one of them came to me and asked me if I were a slave. I told him I was. He asked, "Are ye a slave for life?" I told him that I was. The good Irishman seemed to be deeply affected by the statement. He said to the other that it was a pity so fine a little fellow as myself should be a slave for life. He said it was a shame to hold me. They both advised me to run away to the north; that I should find friends there, and that I should be free. I pretended not to be interested in what they said, and treated them as if I did not understand them; for I feared they might be treacherous. White men have been known to encourage slaves to escape, and then, to get the reward, catch them and return them to their masters. I was afraid that these seemingly good men might use me so; but I nevertheless remembered their advice, and from that time I resolved to run away. I looked forward to a time at which it would be safe for me to escape. I was too young to think of doing so immediately; besides, I wished to learn how to write, as I might have occasion to write my own pass. I consoled myself with the hope that I should one day find a good chance. Meanwhile, I would learn to write.

Questions

1. To whom is Douglass addressing his book, and how does the intended audience affect his argument?

2. Why does Douglass so strongly link education with freedom?

---

67. The Proslavery Argument (1854)

Source: George Fitzhugh, Sociology for the South, or the Failure of Free Society *(Richmond, 1854), pp. 225–55.*

In the thirty years before the outbreak of the Civil War, proslavery thought came to dominate southern public life. Racism—the belief that blacks were innately inferior to whites and unsuited for life in any condition other than slavery—formed one pillar of the proslavery ideology. Most slaveholders also found legitimation for slavery in biblical passages such as the injunction that servants should obey their masters. Still other defenders of slavery insisted that the institution guaranteed equality for whites. Some proslavery writers began to question the ideals of liberty, equality, and democracy so widely shared elsewhere in the nation. The Virginia writer George Fitzhugh took the argument to its most radical conclusion, explicitly repudiating Jeffersonian ideals of liberty and equality as proper foundations for a good society. Indeed, wrote Fitzhugh, slave owners and slaves shared a community of interest unknown in "free society." All workers, white and black, North and South, according to Fitzhugh, would fare better having individual owners, rather than living as "slaves" of the economic marketplace.

━━━━━━━━━━

TEN YEARS AGO [I] became satisfied that slavery, black or white, was right and necessary. . . . Liberty and equality are new things under the sun. The free states of antiquity abounded with slaves. The feudal system that supplanted Roman institutions changed the form of slavery, but brought with it neither liberty nor equality. France and the Northern States of our Union have alone fully and fairly tried the experiment of a social organization founded upon universal liberty and equality of rights. . . . The experiment has already failed, if we are to form our opinions from the discontent of the masses. . . . Liberty and equality have not conduced to enhance the comfort or the happiness of the people. . . . The struggle to better one's condition, to pull others down or supplant them is the great organic law of free society. All men being equal, all aspire to the highest honors and the largest possessions. . . . None but the selfish virtues are encouraged, because none other aid a man in the race of free competition. . . . The bestowing upon men of equality of rights, is but giving license to the strong to oppress the weak. . . .

There is no rivalry, no competition to get employment among slaves, as among free laborers. Nor is there a war between master and slave. The master's interest prevents his reducing the slave's allowance or wages in infancy or sickness, for he might lose the slave by so doing. His feeling for his slave never permits him to stint him in old age. The slaves are all well fed, well clad, have plenty of fuel, and are happy. They have no dread of the future—no fear of want. A state of dependence is the only condition in which reciprocal affection can exist among human beings—the only situation in which the war of competition ceases, and peace, amity and good will arise. A state of independence always begets more or less of jealous rivalry and hostility. A man loves his children because they are weak, helpless and dependent; he loves his wife for similar reasons. . . .

Questions

1. What are Fitzhugh's main criticisms of "free society"?

2. Why does he present an analogy between the condition of slaves and that of women?

---

68. William Sewall, The Results of British Emancipation (1860)

Source: William G. Sewall, The Ordeal of Free Labor in the British West Indies *(New York, 1861), pp. 311–17.*

By 1850, slavery was on the road to abolition in most of the Western Hemisphere. The British had abolished slavery in their Caribbean colonies in 1833, the French in 1848. The newly independent nations of Spanish America had adopted plans for gradual emancipation. Only in the United States, Brazil, Cuba, and Puerto Rico did slavery survive.

Americans followed carefully the results of emancipation elsewhere in the hemisphere, and its aftermath became part of debate over slavery. Was abolition a success or failure? Defenders of slavery in the American South pointed to the decline in sugar production in the key British island of Jamaica as proof that blacks would not work productively except as slaves. Abolitionists insisted that the planters had failed to adapt to the system of free labor, and that the lives of the former slaves had improved in numerous ways. On the eve of the Civil War, William G. Sewall published a series of articles in the *New York Times* reporting on conditions in the British West Indies and defending the abolition of slavery there. His account appeared as a book the following year.

EMANCIPATION WAS AN isolated experiment in each of the different colonies. Precedents and rules of action for one were no precedents or rules of action for another. Here there were obstacles to overcome and difficulties to surmount which there did not exist, or existed only in a mitigated form. Each colony was a field of battle upon which the banners of free labor and slave labor were flung to the winds; and while in some, where resistance was feeble, all trace of the contest has disappeared, and prosperity has revived, in others, where resistance was strong and determined, the exhaustion that follows a long war and a long reign of oppression weighs heavily upon a dispirited people. Let us not be deceived. Let us not misinterpret the true meaning of Jamaica's desolation at the present time. Let no one be so mad as to believe that it is the work of freedom.... Let no one question the victory, though its choicest fruits are yet to be reaped. Let no one doubt that freedom, when it overturned a despotism and crushed a monopoly, unshackled, at the same time, the commerce, the industry, and the intelligence of the islands, and laid the foundations of permanent prosperity....

If free labor be tested by any other gauge than that of sugar-production, its success in the West Indies is established beyond all cavil and beyond all peradventure. If the people merit any consideration whatever—if their independence, their comfort, their industry, their education, form any part of a country's prosperity—then the West Indies are a hundred-fold more prosperous now than they were in the most flourishing times of slavery. If peace be an element of prosperity—if it be important to enjoy uninterrupted tranquility and be secure from servile war and insurrection—then the West Indies have now an advantage that they never possessed before it was given them by emancipation.

If a largely-extended commerce be an indication of prosperity, then all the West Indies, Jamaica alone excepted, have progressed under a system of free labor, although that system hitherto has been but imperfectly developed....

One of the most natural and legitimate results of emancipation was to allow every man to do what seemed to him best—to achieve independence if he could—to pursue, in any case, the path of industry most agreeable to his tastes, and most conducive to his happiness. When we look at the vast political and social structure that has been demolished—the new and grander edifice that has been erected—the enemies that have been vanquished—the prejudices that have been uprooted—the education that has been sown broadcast, the ignorance that has been removed—the industry that has been trained and fostered—we can not pause to criticize defects, for we are amazed at the progress of so great a revolution within the brief space of twenty-five years. . . .

I have endeavored to show—and I hope successfully—that the experiment of free labor in the West Indies has established its superior economy, as well as its possibility. Not a single island fails to demonstrate that the Creoles of African descent, in all their avocations and in all their pursuits, work, under a free system, for proper remuneration, though their labor is often ignorantly wasted and misdirected. That arises from want of education, want of training, want of good example.

Questions

1. Why does Sewall consider emancipation in the British West Indies a success, despite the decline in sugar production in Jamaica?

2. What lessons do you think Sewall believes Americans should learn from the experience of British emancipation?

69. Rules of Highland Plantation (1838)

Source: Bennet H. Barrow, "Rules of Highland Plantation," from Plantation Life in the Florida Parishes of Louisiana, 1836–1846, as reflected in the Diary of Bennet H. Barrow, *ed. Edwin Adams David. Copyright © 1943, Columbia University Press. Reprinted with permission of the publisher and LSU Libraries, Baton Rouge, La.*

Southern planters published numerous articles on how best to manage slave labor. Many insisted that treating their slaves kindly would result in a more efficient workforce. A wealthy Louisiana slaveholder, Bennet H. Barrow considered himself a model of planter paternalism who, by his own standards, treated his slaves well. An advocate of rigorous plantation discipline, he drew up a series of strict rules, which he recommended that other owners follow. The rules illustrated that even the most well-intended owners claimed complete authority over the lives of their slaves. Inadvertently, the rules also revealed planters' fears about disobedience and resistance among their slaves.

No Negro shall leave the place at any time without my permission.... No Negro shall be allowed to marry out of the plantation.

No Negro shall be allowed to sell anything without my express permission. I have ever maintained the doctrine that my Negroes have no time whatever, that they are always liable to my call without questioning for a moment the propriety, of it. I adhere to this on the grounds of expediency and right. The very security of the plantation requires that a general and uniform control over the people of it should be exercised. Who are to protect the plantation from the intrusions of ill designed persons when everybody is abroad? ... To render this part of the rule justly applicable, however, it would be necessary that such a settled arrangement should exist on the plantation to make it unnecessary for a negro to leave it—or to have a good plea for doing so. You must therefore make him as comfortable at home as possible, affording him what is essentially necessary for his happiness—you must provide for him yourself and by that means create in him a habit of perfect dependence on you. Allow it once to be understood by a Negro that he is to provide for himself, and you that moment give him an undeniable claim on you for a portion of his time to make this provision, and should you from necessity, or any other cause, encroach upon his time, disappointment and discontent are seriously felt.

If I employ a laborer to perform a certain quantum of work per day and I agree to pay him a certain amount for the performance of said work, when he has accomplished it I of course have no further claim on him for his time or services—but how different is it with a slave. . . . If I furnish my negro with every necessary of life, without the least care on his part—if I support him in sickness, however long it may be, and pay all his expenses, though he does nothing—if I maintain him in his old age, . . . am I not entitled to an exclusive right in his time?

No rule that I have stated is of more importance than that relating to Negroes marrying out of the plantation. . . . It creates a feeling of independence, from being, of right, out of the control of the masters for a time.

Never allow any man to talk to your Negroes, nothing more injurious.

Questions

1. Why does Barrow think that slaves have greater obligations to their owners than free laborers do to their employers?

2. Why does Barrow think it so important to prevent "any man" from speaking with his slaves?

70. Slavery and the Bible (1850)

Source: De Bow's Review, *vol. 9 (September 1850), pp. 281–86.*

White southerners developed an elaborate set of arguments defending slavery in the period before the Civil War. They insisted that slaves were better off than free laborers in the North and that blacks were inherently liable to lapse into "barbarism" if freed from the supervision of paternalistic whites. One pillar of proslavery thought was the idea that the institution was sanctioned by the Bible, as in this essay from the influential southern magazine *De Bow's Review.* So common had the biblical defense of slavery become by 1850 that the editor prefaced the essay with the following comment: "This paper has been handed us for publication, and, as it contains a summary of the Bible argument for slavery, we give it place, though the subject is growing hacknied [that is, so familiar as to be lacking in any originality]." Nonetheless, De Bow decided to publish it.

A VERY LARGE PARTY in the United states believe that holding slaves is morally wrong; this party founds its belief upon precepts taught in the Bible, and takes that book as the standard of morality and religion. We, also, look to the same book as our guide in the same matters; yet, we think it right to hold slaves—do hold them, and have held and used them from childhood.

As we come to such opposite conclusions from the same foundation, it may be well to consider, whether the Bible teaches us anything whatever, in regard to slavery; if so, what is it and how is it taught.

The anti-slavery party maintain, that the Bible teaches nothing *directly* upon the subject, but, that it establishes rules and principles of action, from which they infer, that in holding slaves, we are guilty of a moral wrong. This mode of reasoning would be perfectly fair, if the Bible really taught nothing directly upon the subject of slavery; but when that book applies the principles it lays down to the particular subject in controversy, we must take the application to be correct. We think we can show, that the Bible teaches clearly and conclusively that the holding of slaves is right; and if so, no deduction from general principles can make it wrong, if that book is true.

From the earliest period of our time down to the present moment, slavery has existed in some form or under some name, in almost every country of the globe. It existed in every country known, even by name, to any one of the sacred writers, at the time of his writing; yet none of them condemns it in the slightest degree. Would this have been the case had it been wrong in itself? Would not some one of the host of sacred writers have spoken of this alleged crime, in such terms as to show, in a manner not to be misunderstood, that God wished all men to be equal?

Abraham, the chosen servant of God, had his bond servants, whose condition was similar to, or worse than, that of our slaves. He considered them as his property, to be bought and sold as any other property which he owned. In Genesis xvii, 13, 23, 27, we are told that God commanded Abraham to circumcise all his bond-servants, *"bought with his money,"* and that Abraham obeyed God's commandment on this same day. In Genesis xx, 14, we are told that Abimelech took sheep and oxen, and *men servants* and *women servants*, and gave them to Abraham. In chapter xii, verse 14, we are told that Abraham possessed sheep and oxen, and he asses, and men servants and maid servants, and she asses, and camels. Also, in Genesis xxvi, 14, Isaac is said to have had possessions of flocks and herds, and a great store of servants. In other places in Genesis, they are spoken of, but always as property....

Paul wrote an epistle to Philemon, a Christian, a disciple of his, and a slaveholder. He sent it to him by Onesimus, also a convert, a slave of Philemon, who was a fugitive. In it, he prays Philemon to charge the fault of Onesimus to him, saying he would repay it, unless Philemon forgave it for his sake.

Now, had the holding of slaves been a crime, Paul's duty to Philemon would have required him to instruct Philemon, that he had no rights over Onesimus, but that the attempt to hold him in servitude was criminal; and his duty to Onesimus would have been, in such case, to send him to some foreign free country, whereby he might have escaped from oppression. But Paul sent him back. Our northern friends think that they manage these matters better than Paul did.

We find, then, that both the Old and New Testaments speak of slavery—that they do not condemn the relation, but, on the contrary, expressly allow it or create it; and they give commands and exhortations, which are based upon its legality and propriety. It can not, then, be wrong.

What we have written is founded solely upon the Bible, and can have no force, unless it is taken for truth. If that book is of divine origin, the holding of slaves is right: as that which God has permitted, recognized and commanded, cannot be inconsistent with his will.

Questions

1. Why do white southerners feel that it is important to show that the Bible sanctions slavery?

2. How do you think the author's understanding of the relationship of slavery and the Bible differs from that of the slaves, most of whom also considered themselves Christians?

---

71. Letter by a Fugitive Slave (1840)

Source: Joseph Taper, excerpts from "Letter from Joseph Taper to Joseph Long, November 11, 1840," in the Joseph Long Papers located in the Rare Book, Manuscript, and Special Collections Library, Duke University. Reprinted by permission.

No one knows how many slaves succeeded in escaping from bondage before the Civil War. Some who managed to do so settled in northern cities like Boston, Cincinnati, and New York. But because federal law required that fugitives be returned to slavery, many continued northward until they reached Canada.

One successful fugitive was Joseph Taper, a slave in Frederick County, Virginia, who in 1837 ran away to Pennsylvania with his wife and children. Two years later, learning that a "slave catcher" was in the neighborhood, the Tapers fled to Canada. In 1840, Taper wrote to a white acquaintance in Virginia recounting some of his experiences. The biblical passage to which Taper refers reads: "And I will come near to you to judgment; and I will be a swift witness against the sorcerers, and against the adulterers, and against false swearers, and against those that oppress the hireling in his wages, the widow, and the fatherless, and that turn aside the stranger from his right, and fear not me, saith the Lord of hosts."

DEAR SIR,

I now take the opportunity to inform you that I am in a land of liberty, in good health.... I have paid 50 dollars rent this year: next year I expect to build. The Queen of England has granted 50 acres of land to every colored man who will accept of the gift, and become an actual settler. Also a yoke of oxen and plough, for every two families. This is a very great encouragement to those who have come here for the liberty which God had designed for them....

Since I have been in the Queen's dominions I have been well contented, Yes well contented for Sure, man is as God intended he should be. That is, all are born free and equal. This is a wholesome law, not like the Southern laws which puts man made in the image of God, on level with brutes. O, what will become of the people, and where will they stand in the day of Judgment. Would that the 5th verse of the 3d chapter of Malachi were written as with the bar of iron, and the point of a diamond upon every oppressor's heart that they might repent of this evil, and let the oppressed go free....

We have good schools, and all the colored population supplied with schools. My boy Edward who will be six years next January, is now reading, and I intend keeping him at school until he becomes a good scholar.

I have enjoyed more pleasure within one month here than in all my life in the land of bondage.... My wife and self are sitting by a good comfortable fire happy, knowing that there are none to molest [us] or make [us] afraid. God save Queen Victoria. The Lord bless her in this life, and crown her with glory in the world to come is my prayer.

Yours With much respect
most obt, Joseph Taper

Questions

1. How does Taper's letter reverse the rhetoric, common among white Americans, which saw the United States as a land of freedom and the British empire as lacking in liberty?

2. What aspects of life in Canada does Taper emphasize as elements of his new freedom?

---

72. Solomon Northup, The New Orleans Slave Market (1853)

Source: Solomon Northup, Twelve Years a Slave *(Auburn, NY: Derby and Miller, 1853), pp. 78–82.*

The ending of the slave trade from Africa in 1808 stimulated the rapid expansion of the domestic slave trade within the United States. More than two million slaves were sold between 1820 and 1860, a majority to local buyers but hundreds of thousands from older states to "importing" states of the Lower South. The public slave market of New Orleans was one great center of the slave trade, where slaves were sold to man the plantations of the expanding Cotton Kingdom.

A free black resident of New York State, Solomon Northup was kidnapped in 1841 while in Washington, D.C., and sold as a slave. After twelve years, during which he labored on plantations in Louisiana, he managed to contact friends in the North who arranged for his release. His memoir, published in 1853, became one of the most widely read accounts of slavery by someone who had experienced it. In the twenty-first century it became the basis for an Academy Award–winning film. In this passage, Northup describes a sale at the New Orleans slave market.

THE VERY AMIABLE, pious-hearted Mr. Theophilus Freeman, partner or consignee of James H. Burch, and keeper of the slave pen in New-

Orleans, was out among his animals early in the morning. With an occasional kick of the older men and women, and many a sharp crack of the whip about the ears of the younger slaves, it was not long before they were all astir, and wide awake. Mr. Theophilus Freeman bustled about in a very industrious manner, getting his property ready for the sales-room, intending, no doubt, to do that day a rousing business.

In the first place we were required to wash thoroughly, and those with beards, to shave. We were then furnished with a new suit each, cheap, but clean. The men had hat, coat, shirt, pants and shoes; the women frocks of calico, and handkerchiefs to bind about their heads. We were now conducted into a large room in the front part of the building to which the yard was attached, in order to be properly trained, before the admission of customers. The men were arranged on one side of the room, the women on the other. The tallest was placed at the head of the row, then the next tallest, and so on in the order of their respective heights. Emily was at the foot of the line of women. Freeman charged us to remember our places; exhorted us to appear smart and lively,—sometimes threatening, and again, holding out various inducements. During the day he exercised us in the art of "looking smart," and of moving to our places with exact precision. . . .

Next day many customers called to examine Freeman's "new lot." The latter gentleman was very loquacious, dwelling at much length upon our several good points and qualities. He would make us hold up our heads, walk briskly back and forth, while customers would feel of our hands and arms and bodies, turn us about, ask us what we could do, make us open our mouths and show our teeth, precisely as a jockey examines a horse which he is about to barter for or purchase. Sometimes a man or woman was taken back to the small house in the yard, stripped, and inspected more minutely. Scars upon a slave's back were considered evidence of a rebellious or unruly spirit, and hurt his sale.

One old gentleman, who said he wanted a coachman, appeared to take a fancy to me. From his conversation with Burch, I learned he was a resident in the city. I very much desired that he would buy me, because I conceived it would not be difficult to make my escape from

New-Orleans on some northern vessel. Freeman asked him fifteen hundred dollars for me. The old gentleman insisted it was too much, as times were very hard. Freeman, however, declared that I was sound and healthy, of a good constitution, and intelligent. He made it a point to enlarge upon my musical attainments. The old gentleman argued quite adroitly that there was nothing extraordinary about the nigger, and finally, to my regret, went out, saying he would call again. During the day, however, a number of sales were made. David and Caroline were purchased together by a Natchez planter. They left us, grinning broadly, and in the most happy state of mind, caused by the fact of their not being separated. Lethe was sold to a planter of Baton Rouge, her eyes flashing with anger as she was led away.

The same man also purchased Randall. The little fellow was made to jump, and run across the floor, and perform many other feats, exhibiting his activity and condition. All the time the trade was going on, Eliza was crying aloud, and wringing her hands. She besought the man not to buy him, unless he also bought her self and Emily. She promised, in that case, to be the most faithful slave that ever lived. The man answered that he could not afford it, and then Eliza burst into a paroxysm of grief, weeping plaintively. Freeman turned round to her, savagely, with his whip in his uplifted hand, ordering her to stop her noise, or he would flog her. He would not have such work—such snivelling; and unless she ceased that minute, he would take her to the yard and give her a hundred lashes. Yes, he would take the nonsense out of her pretty quick—if he didn't, might he be d—d. Eliza shrunk before him, and tried to wipe away her tears, but it was all in vain. She wanted to be with her children, she said, the little time she had to live. All the frowns and threats of Freeman, could not wholly silence the afflicted mother. She kept on begging and beseeching them, most piteously not to separate the three. Over and over again she told them how she loved her boy. A great many times she repeated her former promises—how very faithful and obedient she would be; how hard she would labor day and night, to the last moment of her life, if he would only buy them all together. But it was of no avail; the man could not afford it. The bargain was agreed upon, and Randall must go alone. Then Eliza ran to him; embraced him passionately; kissed him again and again; told him to remember her—all the while her tears falling in the boy's face like rain.

Freeman damned her, calling her a blubbering, bawling wench, and ordered her to go to her place, and behave herself; and be somebody. He swore he wouldn't stand such stuff but a little longer. He would soon give her something to cry about, if she was not mighty careful, and that she might depend upon.

The planter from Baton Rouge, with his new purchases, was ready to depart.

"Don't cry, mama. I will be a good boy. Don't cry," said Randall, looking back, as they passed out of the door.

What has become of the lad, God knows. It was a mournful scene indeed. I would have cried myself if I had dared.

Questions

1. What aspects of the buying and selling of slaves does Northup single out for condemnation?

2. What light does Northup's account shed on the biblical arguments in defense of slavery in document 70 above?

CHAPTER 12

An Age of Reform, 1820–1840

73. Robert Owen, "The First Discourse on a New System of Society" (1825)

Source: Robert Owen, The First Discourse on a New System of Society, as Delivered in the Hall of Representatives, at Washington, on the 25th of February, 1825 *(London, 1825), pp. 3–15.*

The increasing economic inequality and intense economic competition promoted by the market revolution led some Americans to create their own miniature societies based on equality and harmony. Through their efforts, the words "socialism" and "communism," meaning societies in which productive property is owned by the community rather than private individuals, entered the language of politics.

The most important secular communitarian (meaning a person who plans or lives in a cooperative community) was Robert Owen, a British factory owner. In 1824, he purchased the Harmony community in Indiana originally founded by the Protestant religious leader George Rapp, and renamed it New Harmony. Early in 1825, Owen addressed a gathering of notable Americans in the hall of the House of Representatives—one of the few foreign citizens ever to speak there—and outlined his vision of "a new system of society."

THE RESULT OF ... [my] reading, reflection, experiments, and personal communication, has been to leave an irresistible impression on my mind, that society is in error; that the notions on which all its institutions are founded are not true; that they necessarily generate deception and vice; and that the practices which proceed from them are destructive of the happiness of human life.

The reflections which I am enabled to make upon the facts which the history of our race presented to me, led me to conclude that the great object intended to be attained, by the various institutions of every age and country, was, or ought to be, to secure happiness for the greatest number of human beings. That this object could be obtained only, first, by a proper training and education from birth, of the physical and mental powers of each individual; second, by arrangements to enable each individual to procure in the best manner at all times, a full supply of those things which are necessary and the most beneficial for human nature; and third, that all individuals should be so united and combined in a social system, as to give to each the greatest benefit from society....

• • •

Man, through ignorance, has been, hitherto, the tormentor of man.

He is here, in a nation deeming itself possessed of more privileges than all other nations, and which pretensions, in many respects, must be admitted to be true. Yet, even here, where the laws are the most mild, and consequently the least unjust and irrational, individuals are punished even to death, for actions which are the natural and necessary effects arising from the injurious circumstances which the government and society, to which they belong, unwisely permit to exist; while other individuals are almost as much injured by being as unjustly rewarded for performing actions for which, as soon as they shall become rational beings, they must be conscious they cannot be entitled to a particle of merit....

• • •

My desire now is to introduce into these States, and through them to the world at large, a new social system, formed in practice of an entire new combination of circumstances, all of them having a direct moral, intellectual, and beneficial tendency, fully adequate to effect the most important improvements throughout society. This system has been solely derived from the facts relative to our common nature, which I have previously explained.

In this new social arrangement, a much more perfect system of liberty and equality will be introduced than has yet any where existed, or been deemed attainable in practice. Within it there will be no privileged thoughts or belief; every one will be at full liberty to express the genuine impressions which the circumstances around them have made on their minds as well as all their own undisguised reflections thereon, and then no motive will exist for deception or insincerity of any kind. . . .

The degrading and pernicious practices in which we are now trained, of buying cheap and selling dear, will be rendered wholly unnecessary; for so long as this principle shall govern the transactions of men, nothing really great or noble can be expected from mankind. . . .

• • •

In the new system, union and co-operation will supersede individual interest, and the universal counteraction of each other's objects; and, by the change, the powers of one man will obtain for him the advantages of many, and all will become as rich as they will desire. The very imperfect experiments of the Moravians, Shakers, and Harmonites, give sure proof of the gigantic superiority of union over division, for the creation of wealth. But these associations have been hitherto subject to many disadvantages, and their progress and success have been materially counteracted by many obstacles which will not exist under a system, founded on a correct knowledge of the constitution of our nature. . . .

Under this system, real wealth will be too easily obtained in perpetuity and full security to be much longer valued as it is now by society, for the distinctions which it makes between the poor and rich. For, when the new arrangements shall be regularly organized and completed, a few hours daily, of healthy and desirable employment, chiefly applied to direct modern mechanical and other scientific improvements, will be amply sufficient to create a full supply, at all times, of the best of every thing for every one, and then all things will be valued according to their intrinsic worth, will be used beneficially, and nothing will be wasted or abused. . . .

• • •

This is a revolution from a system in which individual reward and punishment has been the universal practice, to one, in which individual reward and punishment will be unpracticed and unknown, except as a grievous error of a past wretched system. On this account, my belief has long been, that wherever society should be fully prepared to admit of one experiment on the new system, it could not fail to be also prepared to admit the principle from which it has been derived, and to be ready for all the practice which must emanate from the principle; and, in consequence, that the change could not be one of slow progression, but it must take place at once, and make an immediate, and almost instantaneous resolution in the minds and manners of the society in which it shall be introduced—unless we can imagine that there are human beings who prefer sin and misery to virtue and happiness. . . .

It is to effect this change that I am here this night; that, if possible, a mortal blow shall be now given to the fundamental error which, till now, has governed this wretched world, and inflicted unnumbered cruelties and miseries upon its inhabitants. The time has passed, within the present hour, when this subject can be no longer mentioned or hidden from the public mind of this country. It must now be open to the most free discussion, and I well know what will be the result. . . .

Questions

1. What does Owen see as the greatest "errors" of society in the 1820s?

2. How does he plan to increase the enjoyment of "liberty and equality"?

74. Philip Schaff on Freedom as Self-Restraint (1855)

Source: Philip Schaff, America. A Sketch of the Political, Social, and Religious Character of the United States of North America *(New York, 1855), pp. 43–47.*

Numerous reform movements arose in the United States in the decades before the Civil War, promising to liberate Americans from social injustice and from evils like drink, poverty, and slavery. The reformers did not propose that individuals should simply follow their own desires without restraint. Their definition of the free individual was the person who internalized the practice of self-control.

Philip Schaff, a Swiss-German minister who emigrated to Pennsylvania in 1843 to teach at a small college and later wrote a "sketch" of American society for a European audience, offered perceptive comments on reformers' understanding of freedom. "True national freedom, in the American view," Schaff observed, was "anything but an absence of restraint." Rather, it "rests upon a moral groundwork, upon the virtue of self-possession and self-control in individual citizens." As an example, Schaff offered the temperance movement, which sought to convince Americans to renounce intoxicating liquor. The conflict between freedom as following a moral code (imposed, if necessary, by the government) and freedom as choosing without outside interference how to conduct one's life would be repeated in many subsequent eras of American history.

———

THE WHOLE ANGLO-AMERICAN conception of freedom is specifically different from the purely negative notion which prevails amongst the radicals and revolutionists on the continent of Europe. With the American, freedom is anything but a mere absence of restraint, an arbitrary, licentious indulgence, every one following his natural impulse, as the revolutionists would have it. It is a rational, moral self-determination, hand in hand with law, order, and authority. True national freedom, in the American view, rests upon a moral groundwork, upon the virtue of self-possession and self-control in individual citizens. He alone is worthy of this great blessing and capable of enjoying it, who holds his passions in check; is master of his sensual nature; obeys natural laws, not under pressure from without, but from inward impulse, cheerfully and joyfully. But the negative and hollow liberalism, or rather the radicalism, which undermines the authority of law and sets itself against Christianity and the church, necessarily dissolves all social ties, and ends in anarchy; which then passes very easily into the worst and most dangerous form of despotism.

These sound views of freedom, in connection with the moral earnestness and the Christian character of the nation, form the basis of the North American republic, and can alone secure its permanence. We also find there, indeed, beyond all question, utterly unsound and dangerous radical tendencies; in the political elections all wild passions, falsehood, calumny, bribery, and wickedness of all sorts, are let loose; and even the halls of the legislatures and of Congress are frequently disgraced by the misconduct of unprincipled demagogues, so that multitudes of the best citizens, disgusted with the wire-pulling and mean selfishness of self-styled friends of the people, shrink from any active participation in politics, or discharge their duty as citizens by nothing more, at most, than their vote at the ballot-box. But on the whole, there prevails undeniably among the people a sound conservative tone, which exerts a constant influence in favor of right and order; and it is an imposing spectacle, when immediately after the election of a president or governor, a universal calm at once succeeds the furious storm of party strife, and the conquered party patiently submits to the result, never dreaming of such a thing as asserting its real or supposed rights in any violent way. Any dissatisfaction—for such certainly has place there as well as elsewhere—reaches never to the republican form of government, but only to the manner of its exercise, not to the constitution of the land, but only to the measures of the dominant party; and it seeks redress of its wrong always in a lawful, constitutional way. So far as this goes, it may well be asserted, that the North American Union, with all the fluctuation and insecurity of its affairs in particular instances—which is to be expected in so new a country—stands in general more firmly on its feet, and is safer from violent revolutions, than any country on the continent of Europe.

A very characteristic proof of our assertion, that American freedom is different in principle from radicalism and licentiousness, and rests entirely on the basis of self-control and self-restraint, is presented in the really sublime temperance movement, particularly in the "Maine liquor law," as it is called. This law wholly forbids, not directly the drinking—for this would be an infringement of personal liberty,— but the manufacture and sale of all intoxicating drinks, including even wine and beer, except for medicinal, mechanical, and sacramental purposes. This law was first introduced a few years ago in the predominantly Puritanical, New England State of Maine, and has since been extended to several other states by a popular majority; and even in the great States of New York, Pennsylvania, and Ohio, the most zealous efforts are now making by public addresses, by tracts and periodicals, and other means of agitation, to secure the election of legislators favorable to the temperance cause, who will strike at the root of the terrible evil, and remove even the temptation to drunkenness. Even last fall, shortly before the election, I was personal witness of the zeal and earnestness, with which the agents of the temperance society, ministers and laymen, canvassed the counties of Pennsylvania, and spreading their tent under the open heaven, after a solemn introduction by singing and prayer, eloquently described the horrible consequences, temporal and eternal, of intemperance, and demonstrated to the people by the most convincing arguments, the duty of using their elective franchise in a way demanded by the public weal, in the consciousness of their high responsibility to God and the world.

It must be granted that this Maine temperance law, *in itself considered*, goes too far, and is to be ranked with radical legislation. . . .

• • •

Yet, think of the "Maine liquor law" as we may,—and we would here neither advocate nor condemn it,—we must admire the moral energy and self-denial of a free people, which would rather renounce an enjoyment in itself lawful, than see it drive thousands of weak persons to bodily and spiritual ruin.

To those, who see in America only the land of unbridled radicalism and of the wildest fanaticism for freedom, I take the liberty to put the modest question: In what European state would the government have the courage to enact such a prohibition of the traffic in all intoxicating drinks, and the people the self-denial to submit to it?

Questions

1. How does Schaff believe Christianity influences American understandings of freedom?

2. Why does Schaff have reservations about the "Maine law" prohibiting the manufacture and sale of liquor?

———

75. David Walker's Appeal (1829)

Source: Walker's Appeal, in Four Articles, . . . to the Coloured Citizens of the World . . . , *3rd ed. (Boston, 1830), pp. 3–5, 9, 22–24.*

A pioneering document of militant abolitionism, David Walker's *Appeal to the Coloured Citizens of the World* condemned the hypocrisy of a nation that proclaimed its belief in liberty yet every day violated its professed principles. Born free in North Carolina, Walker moved to Boston, where he became a used clothing dealer and an outspoken critic of slavery. At a time when most opponents of slavery called for a peaceful, gradual end to the institution and the "colonization" outside of the country of those who became free, Walker insisted that blacks had as much right to live in the United States as whites and spoke of the possibility of armed struggle against slavery. Walker also challenged racism by invoking the achievements of ancient civilizations in Africa, and he urged black Americans to identify with the black republic of Haiti, an early example of internationalism in African-American thought. When free black sailors were found carrying copies of Walker's pamphlet, southern states issued a reward for his arrest or death. Walker died, apparently of natural causes, in 1830, but his words inspired a generation of black abolitionists.

———————

HAVING TRAVELED OVER a considerable portion of these United States, and having, in the course of my travels, taken the most accurate observations of things as they exist—the result of my observations has warranted the full and unshaken conviction, that we, (coloured people of these United States) are the most degraded, wretched, and abject set of beings that ever lived since the world began; and I pray God that none like us ever may live again until time shall be no more. They tell us of the Israelites in Egypt, the Helots in Sparta, and of the Roman Slaves, which last were made up from almost every nation under heaven, whose sufferings under those ancient and heathen nations, were, in comparison with ours, under this enlightened and Christian nation, no more than a cipher—or, in other words, those heathen nations of antiquity, had but little more among them than the name and form of slavery; while wretchedness and endless miseries were reserved ... to be poured out upon our fathers, ourselves and our children, by Christian Americans! ... I appeal to Heaven for my motive in writing—who knows that my object is, if possible, to awaken in the breasts of my afflicted, degraded and slumbering brethren, a spirit of inquiry and investigation respecting our miseries and wretchedness in this Republican Land of Liberty!!!!!!...

My beloved brethren:—The Indians of North and of South America—the Greeks—the Irish, subjected under the king of Great Britain—the Jews, that ancient people of the Lord—the inhabitants of the islands of the sea—in fine, all the inhabitants of the earth, (except however, the sons of Africa) are called men, and of course are, and ought to be free. But we, (coloured people) and our children are brutes!! and of course are, and ought to be SLAVES to the American people and their children forever!! to dig their mines and work their farms; and thus go on enriching them, from one generation to another with our blood and our tears!!!! ...

When we take a retrospective view of the arts and sciences—the wise legislators—the Pyramids, and other magnificent buildings—the turning of the channel of the river Nile, by the sons of Africa ..., among whom learning originated, and was carried thence into Greece, where it was improved upon and refined. Thence among the Romans, and all over the then enlightened parts of the world, and it has been enlightening the dark and benighted minds of men from then, down to this day. I say, when I view retrospectively, the renown of that once mighty people, the children of our great progenitor I am indeed cheered. Yea further, when I view that mighty son of Africa, Hannibal, one of the greatest generals of antiquity, who defeated and cut off so many thousands of the white Romans or murderers, and who carried his victorious arms, to the very gate of Rome, and I give it as my candid opinion, that had Carthage been well united and had given him good support, he would have carried that cruel and barbarous city by storm. But they were disunited, as the coloured people are now, in the United States of America, the reason our natural enemies are enabled to keep their feet on our throats.

Beloved brethren—here let me tell you, and believe it, that the Lord our God, as true as he sits on his throne in heaven, and as true as our Savior died to redeem the world, will give you a Hannibal, and when the Lord shall have raised him up, and given him to you for your possession, O my suffering brethren! remember the divisions and consequent sufferings of Carthage and of Hayti. ... But what need have I to refer to antiquity, when Hayti, the glory of the blacks and terror of tyrants, is enough to convince the most avaricious and stupid of wretches?

Questions

1. Why does Walker address his pamphlet to "the coloured citizens of the world" and not just the United States?

2. What lessons does Walker think black Americans should learn from the history of the ancient world and that of Haiti?

---

76. Frederick Douglass on the Fourth of July (1852)

Source: Frederick Douglass, My Bondage and My Freedom *(New York, 1855), pp. 441–45.*

The greatest oration on American slavery and American freedom was delivered in Rochester, New York, in 1852 by Frederick Douglass. Speaking just after the annual Independence Day celebration, Douglass posed the question, "What, to the American slave, is your 4th of July?" He answered that July Fourth festivities revealed the hypocrisy of a nation that proclaimed its belief in liberty yet daily committed "practices more shocking and bloody" than any other country on earth. Like other abolitionists, however, Douglass also laid claim to the founders' legacy. The Revolution had proclaimed "the great principles of political freedom and of natural justice, embodied in [the] Declaration of Independence," from which subsequent generations had tragically strayed. Only by abolishing slavery and freeing the ideals of the Declaration from the bounds of race could the United States, he believed, recapture its original mission.

FELLOW-CITIZENS, PARDON me, allow me to ask, why am I called upon to speak here to-day? What have I, or those I represent, to do with your national independence? Are the great principles of political freedom and of natural justice, embodied in that Declaration of

Independence, extended to us? and am I, therefore, called upon to bring our humble offering to the national altar, and to confess the benefits and express devout gratitude for the blessings resulting from your independence to us?

Would to God, both for your sakes and ours, that an affirmative answer could be truthfully returned to these questions! Then would my task be light, and my burden easy and delightful. For *who* is there so cold, that a nation's sympathy could not warm him? Who so obdurate and dead to the claims of gratitude, that would not thankfully acknowledge such priceless benefits? Who so stolid and selfish, that would not give his voice to swell the hallelujahs of a nation's jubilee, when the chains of servitude had been torn from his limbs? I am not that man. In a case like that, the dumb might eloquently speak, and the "lame man leap as an hart."

But, such is not the state of the case. I say it with a sad sense of the disparity between us. I am not included within the pale of this glorious anniversary! Your high independence only reveals the immeasurable distance between us. The blessings in which you, this day, rejoice, are not enjoyed in common. The rich inheritance of justice, liberty, prosperity and independence, bequeathed by your fathers, is shared by you, not by me. The sunlight that brought life and healing to you, has brought stripes and death to me. This Fourth [of] July is *yours*, not *mine*. You may rejoice, *I* must mourn. To drag a man in fetters into the grand illuminated temple of liberty, and call upon him to join you in joyous anthems, were inhuman mockery and sacrilegious irony. Do you mean, citizens, to mock me, by asking me to speak to-day? If so, there is a parallel to your conduct. And let me warn you that it is dangerous to copy the example of a nation whose crimes, towering up to heaven, were thrown down by the breath of the Almighty, burying that nation in irrecoverable ruin! I can to-day take up the plaintive lament of a peeled and woesmitten people!

• • •

Fellow-citizens; above your national, tumultuous joy, I hear the mournful wail of millions whose chains, heavy and grievous yesterday, are, today, rendered more intolerable by the jubilee shouts that reach them. If I do forget, if I do not faithfully remember those bleeding children of sorrow this day, "may my right hand forget her cunning, and may my tongue cleave to the roof of my mouth!" To forget them, to pass lightly over their wrongs, and to chime in with the popular theme, would be treason most scandalous and shocking, and would make me a reproach before God and the world. My subject, then fellow-citizens, is AMERICAN SLAVERY. I shall see, this day, and its popular characteristics, from the slave's point of view. Standing, there, identified with the American bondman, making his wrongs mine, I do not hesitate to declare, with all my soul, that the character and conduct of this nation never looked blacker to me than on this 4th of July! Whether we turn to the declarations of the past, or to the professions of the present, the conduct of the nation seems equally hideous and revolting. America is false to the past, false to the present, and solemnly binds herself to be false to the future. Standing with God and the crushed and bleeding slave on this occasion, I will, in the name of humanity which is outraged, in the name of liberty which is fettered, in the name of the constitution and the Bible, which are disregarded and trampled upon, dare to call in question and to denounce, with all the emphasis I can command, everything that serves to perpetuate slavery—the great sin and shame of America! "I will not equivocate; I will not excuse"; I will use the severest language I can command; and yet not one word shall escape me that any man, whose judgement is not blinded by prejudice, or who is not at heart a slaveholder, shall not confess to be right and just.

For the present, it is enough to affirm the equal manhood of the negro race. Is it not astonishing that, while we are ploughing, planting and reaping, using all kinds of mechanical tools, erecting houses, constructing bridges, building ships, working in metals of brass, iron, copper, silver and gold; that, while we are reading, writing and cyphering, acting as clerks, merchants and secretaries, having among us lawyers, doctors, ministers, poets, authors, editors, orators and teachers; that, while we are engaged in all manner of enterprises common to other men, digging gold in California, capturing the whale in the Pacific, feeding sheep and cattle on the hillside, living, moving, acting, thinking, planning, living in families as husbands, wives and children, and, above all, confessing and worshipping the Christian's God, and looking hopefully for life and immortality beyond the grave, we are called upon to prove that we are men!

Would you have me argue that man is entitled to liberty? that he is the rightful owner of his own body? You have already declared it. Must I argue the wrongfulness of slavery? Is that a question for Republicans? Is it to be settled by the rules of logic and argumentation, as a matter beset with great difficulty, involving a doubtful application of the principle of justice, hard to be understood? How should I look to-day, in the presence of Americans, dividing, and subdividing a discourse, to show that men have a natural right to freedom? speaking of it relatively, and positively, negatively, and affirmatively. To do so, would be to make myself ridiculous, and to offer an insult to your understanding. There is not a man beneath the canopy of heaven, that does not know that slavery is wrong *for him.*

What, am I to argue that it is wrong to make men brutes, to rob them of their liberty, to work them without wages, to keep them ignorant of their relations to their fellow men, to beat them with sticks, to flay their flesh with the lash, to load their limbs with irons, to hunt them with dogs, to sell them at auction, to sunder their families, to knock out their teeth, to burn their flesh, to starve them into obedience and submission to their masters? Must I argue that a system thus marked with blood, and stained with pollution, is *wrong?* No! I will not. I have better employments for my time and strength, than such arguments would imply.

What, then, remains to be argued? Is it that slavery is not divine; that God did not establish it; that our doctors of divinity are mistaken? There is blasphemy in the thought. That which is inhuman, cannot be divine! *Who* can reason on such a proposition? They that can, may; I cannot. The time for such argument is past.

At a time like this, scorching irony, not convincing argument, is needed. O! had I the ability, and could I reach the nation's ear, I would, to-day, pour out a fiery stream of biting ridicule, blasting reproach, withering sarcasm, and stern rebuke. For it is not light that is needed, but fire; it is not the gentle shower, but thunder. We need the storm, the whirlwind, and the earthquake. The feeling of the nation must be quickened; the conscience of the nation must be roused; the propriety of the nation must be startled; the hypocrisy of the nation must be exposed; and its crimes against God and man must be proclaimed and denounced.

What, to the American slave, is your 4th of July? I answer: a day that reveals to him, more than all other days in the year, the gross injustice and cruelty to which he is the constant victim. To him, your celebration is a sham; your boasted liberty, an unholy license; your national greatness, swelling vanity; your sounds of rejoicing are empty and heartless; your denunciations of tyrants, brass fronted impudence; your shouts of liberty and equality, hollow mockery; your prayers and hymns, your sermons and thanksgivings, with all your religious parade, and solemnity, are, to him, mere bombast, fraud, deception, impiety, and hypocrisy—a thin veil to cover up crimes which would disgrace a nation of savages. There is not a nation on the earth guilty of practices, more shocking and bloody, than are the people of these United States, at this very hour.

Go where you may, search where you will, roam through all the monarchies and despotisms of the old world, travel through South America, search out every abuse, and when you have found the last, lay your facts by the side of the everyday practices of this nation, and you will say with me, that, for revolting barbarity and shameless hypocrisy, America reigns without a rival.

Questions

1. What does Douglass hope to accomplish by accusing white Americans of injustice and hypocrisy?

2. What evidence does Douglass present to disprove the idea of black inferiority?

77. Catharine Beecher on the "Duty of American Females" (1837)

Source: Catharine E. Beecher, Essay on Slavery and Abolitionism, with Reference to the Duty of American Females *(Philadelphia, 1837), pp. 5–6, 27, 41, 101–8, 128.*

The abolitionist movement enabled women to carve out a place in the public sphere. Women attended antislavery meetings and circulated petitions to Congress. Most prominent during the 1830s were Angelina and Sarah Grimké, the daughters of a South Carolina slaveowner. The sisters had been converted to Quakerism and abolitionism while visiting Philadelphia. They began to deliver popular lectures that offered a scathing condemnation of slavery from the perspective of those who had witnessed its evils firsthand. In 1836, Angelina Grimké wrote *Appeal to the Christian Women of the South*, urging them to take a stand against slavery.

The sight of women lecturing in public to mixed male-female audiences and taking part in public debate on political questions aroused considerable criticism. The prominent writer Catharine Beecher responded to Grimké's essay by reprimanding her for stepping outside "the domestic and social sphere," urging her to accept the fact that "heaven" had designated man "the superior" and woman "the subordinate."

───────

My DEAR FRIEND:

Your public address to Christian females at the South has reached me, and I have been urged to aid in circulating it at the North. I have also been informed, that you contemplate a tour, during the ensuing year, for the purpose of exerting your influence to form Abolition Societies among ladies of the non-slave-holding States.

Our acquaintance and friendship give me a claim to your private ear; but there are reasons why it seems more desirable to address you, who now stand before the public as an advocate of Abolition measures, in a more public manner.

The object I have in view, is to present some reasons why it seems unwise and inexpedient for ladies of the non-slave-holding States to unite themselves in Abolition Societies; and thus, at the same time, to exhibit the inexpediency of the course you propose to adopt. . . .

Now Abolitionists are before the community, and declare that all slavery is sin, which ought to be immediately forsaken; and that it is their object and intention to promote the *immediate emancipation* of all the slaves in this nation. . . . [R]eproaches, rebukes, and sneers, were employed to convince the whites that their prejudices were sinful. . . .

[T]he severing of the Union by the present mode of agitating the question . . . may be one of the results, and, if so, what are the probabilities for a Southern republic that has torn itself off for the purpose of excluding foreign interference, and for the purpose of perpetuating slavery? . . .

Heaven has appointed to one sex the superior, and to the other the subordinate station, and this without any reference to the character or conduct of either. It is therefore as much for the dignity as it is for the interest of females, in all respects to conform to the duties of this relation. . . . But while woman holds a subordinate relation in society to the other sex, it is not because it was designed that her duties or her influence should be any the less important, or all-pervading. But it was designed that the mode of gaining influence and of exercising power should be altogether different and peculiar. . . .

Woman is to win every thing by peace and love; by making herself so much respected, esteemed and loved, that to yield to her opinions and to gratify her wishes, will be the free-will offering of the heart. But this is to be all accomplished in the domestic and social circle. . . . But the moment woman begins to feel the promptings of ambition, or the thirst for power, her aegis of defence is gone. All the sacred protection of religion, all the generous promptings of chivalry, all the poetry of romantic gallantry, depend upon woman's retaining her place as dependent and defenceless, and making no claims, and maintaining no right but what are the gifts of honour, rectitude and love.

A woman may seek the aid of co-operation and combination among her own sex, to assist her in her appropriate offices of piety, charity, maternal and domestic duty; but whatever, in any measure, throws a woman into the attitude of a combatant either for herself or others—whatever binds her in a party conflict—whatever obliges her in any way to exert coercive influences, throws her out of her appropriate sphere....

If it is asked, "May not woman appropriately come forward as a suppliant for a portion of her sex who are bound in cruel bondage?" It is replied, that, the rectitude and propriety of any such measure, depend entirely on its probable results. If petitions from females will operate to exasperate; if they will be deemed obtrusive, indecorous, and unwise, by those to whom they are addressed; ... if they will be the opening wedge, that will eventually bring females as petitioners and partisans into every political measure that may tend to injure and oppress their sex ... then it is neither appropriate nor wise, nor right, for a woman to petition for the relief of oppressed females....

In this country, petitions to congress, in reference to the official duties of legislators, seem, IN ALL CASES, to fall entirely without the sphere of female duty. Men are the proper persons to make appeals to the rulers whom they appoint, and if their female friends, by arguments and persuasions, can induce them to petition, all the good that can be done by such measures will be secured. But if females cannot influence their nearest friends, to urge forward a public measure in this way, they surely are out of their place, in attempting to do it themselves....

It is allowed by all reflecting minds, that the safety and happiness of this nation depends upon having the *children* educated, and not only intellectually, but morally and religiously. There are now nearly two millions of children and adults in this country who cannot read, and who have no schools of any kind. To give only a small supply of teachers to these destitute children, who are generally where the population is sparse, will demand *thirty thousand teachers* at the moment and an addition of *two thousand every year*. Where is this army of teachers to be found? Is it at all probable that the other sex will afford even a moderate portion of this supply? . . . Men will be educators in the college, in the high school, in some of the most honourable and lucrative common schools, but the *children*, the *little children* of this nation must, to a wide extent, be taught by females, or remain untaught. . . . And as the value of education rises in the public mind . . . women will more and more be furnished with those intellectual advantages which they need to fit them for such duties.

The result will be, that America will be distinguished above all other nations, for well-educated females and for the influence they will exert on the general interests of society. But if females, as they approach the other sex, in intellectual elevation, begin to claim, or to exercise in any manner, the peculiar prerogatives of that sex, education will prove a doubtful and dangerous blessing. But this will never be the result. For the more intelligent a woman becomes, the more she can appreciate the wisdom of that ordinance that appointed her subordinate station.

But it may be asked, is there nothing to be done to bring this national sin of slavery to an end? Must the internal slave-trade, a trade now ranked as piracy among all civilized nations, still prosper in our bounds? Must the very seat of our government stand as one of the chief slave-markets of the land; and must not Christian females open their lips, nor lift a finger, to bring such a shame and sin to an end? To this it may be replied, that Christian females may, and can say and do much to bring these evils to an end; and the present is a time and an occasion when it seems most desirable that they should know, and appreciate, and *exercise* the power which they do possess for so desirable an end. . . .

In the present aspect of affairs among us, when everything seems to be tending to disunion and distraction, it surely has become the duty of every female instantly to relinquish the attitude of a partisan, in every matter of clashing interests, and to assume the office of a mediator, and an advocate of peace. And to do this, it is not necessary that a woman should in any manner relinquish her opinion as to the evils or the benefits, the right or the wrong, of any principle of practice. But, while quietly holding her own opinions, and calmly avowing them, when conscience and integrity make the duty imperative, every female can employ her influence, not for the purpose of exciting or regulating public sentiment, but rather for the purpose of promoting a spirit of candour, forbearance, charity, and peace.

Questions

1. How does Beecher think women should exert power within American society?

2. Why does she believe that the abolitionist movement is dangerous?

---

78. Angelina Grimké on Women's Rights (1837)

Source: The Liberator, *October 13, 1837.*

In response to Catharine Beecher's criticism, Angelina Grimké wrote a series of twelve letters forthrightly defending the right of women to take part in political debate. The final one addressed the question of women's rights directly. "I know nothing," she wrote, "of men's rights and women's rights." "My doctrine," she declared, "is that whatever is morally right for man to do, it is morally right for woman to do." The Grimké sisters soon retired from the fray, after Angelina married the abolitionist Theodore Weld. But their writings helped to spark the movement for women's rights that arose in the 1840s.

SINCE I ENGAGED in the investigation of the rights of the slave, I have necessarily been led to a better understanding of my own; for I have found the Anti-Slavery cause to be the high school of morals in our land—the school in which human rights are more fully investigated, and better understood and taught, than in any other benevolent enterprise. Here one great fundamental principle is disinterred, which, as soon as it is uplifted to public view, leads the mind into a thousand different ramifications, into which the rays of this central light are streaming with brightness and glory. Here we are led to examine why human beings have any rights. It is because they are moral beings; the rights of all men, from the king to the slave, are built upon their moral nature: and as all men have this moral nature, so all men have essentially the same rights. These rights may be plundered from the slave, but they cannot be alienated: his right and title to himself is as perfect now, as is that of Lyman Beecher: they are written in his moral being, and must remain unimpaired as long as that being continues.

Now it naturally occurred to me, that if rights were founded in moral being, then the circumstance of sex could not give to man higher rights and responsibilities, than to woman. To suppose that it did, would be to deny the self-evident truth, "that the physical constitution is the mere instrument of the moral nature." To suppose that it did, would be to break up utterly the relations of the two natures, and to reverse their functions, exalting the animal nature into a monarch, and humbling the moral into a slave; "making the former a proprietor, and the latter its property." When I look at human beings as moral beings, all distinction in sex sinks to insignificance and nothingness; for I believe it regulates rights and responsibilities no more than the color of the skin or the eyes. My doctrine then is, that whatever it is morally right for man to do, it is morally right for woman to do. Our duties are governed, not by difference of sex, but by the diversity of our relative connections in life, and the variety of gifts and talents committed to our care, and the different eras in which we live.

This regulation of duty by the mere circumstance of sex, rather than by the fundamental principle of moral being, has led to all that multifarious train of evils flowing out of the anti-christian doctrine of masculine and feminine virtues. By this doctrine, man has been converted into the warrior, and clothed in sternness, and those other kindred qualities, which, in the eyes of many, belong to his character as a man; whilst woman has been taught to lean upon an arm of flesh, to sit as a soul arrayed "in gold and pearls, and costly array," to be admired for her personal charms, and caressed and humored like a spoiled child, or converted into a mere drudge to suit the convenience of her lord and master. This principle has spread desolation over the whole moral world, and brought into all the diversified relations of life, "confusion and every evil work." It has given to man a charter for the exercise of tyranny and selfishness, pride and arrogance, lust and brutal violence. It has robbed woman of essential rights, the right to think and speak and act on all great moral questions, just as men think and speak and act; the right to share their responsibilities, dangers, and toils; the right to fulfill the great end of her being, as a help meet for man, as a moral, intellectual and immortal creature, and of glorifying God in her body and her spirit which are His. Hitherto, instead of being a help meet to man, in the highest, noblest sense of the term, as a companion, a co-worker, an equal; she has been a mere appendage of his being, and instrument of his convenience and pleasure, the pretty toy, with which he wiled away his leisure moments, or the pet animal whom he humored into playfulness and submission. Woman, instead of being regarded as the equal of man, has uniformly been looked down upon as his inferior, a mere gift to fill up the measure of his happiness. In the poetry of "romantic gallantry," it is true, she has been called the "last best gift of God to man"; but I believe I speak forth the words of truth and soberness when I affirm, that woman never was given to man. She was created, like him, in the image of God, and crowned with glory and honor; created only a little lower than the angels,—not, as is too generally presumed, a little lower than man; on her brow, as well as on his, was placed the "diadem of beauty," and in her hand the scepter of universal dominion....

Measure her rights and duties by the sure, unerring standard of moral being, not by the false rights and measures of a mere circumstance of her human existence, and then will it become a self-evident truth, that whatever it is morally right for a man to do, it is morally right for a woman to do. I recognize no rights but human rights—I know nothing of men's rights and women's rights; for in Christ Jesus, there is neither male nor female; and it is my solemn conviction, that, until this important principle of equality is recognized and carried out into practice, that vain will be the efforts of the church to do anything effectual for the permanent reformation of the world. Woman was the first transgressor, and the first victim of power. In all the heathen nations, she has been the slave of man, and no Christian nation has ever acknowledged her rights. Nay more, no Christian Society has ever done so either, on the broad and solid basis of humanity. I know that in some few denominations, she is permitted to preach the gospel; but this is not done from a conviction of her equality as a human being, but of her equality in spiritual gifts—for we find that woman, even in these Societies, is not allowed to make the Discipline by which she is to be governed. Now, I believe it is her right to be consulted in all the laws and regulations by which she is to be governed, whether in Church or State, and that the present arrangement of Society, on those points, are a violation of human rights, an usurpation of power over her, which is working mischief, great mischief, in the world. If Ecclesiastical and Civil governments are ordained of God, then I contend that woman has just as much right to sit in solemn counsel in Conventions, Conferences, Associations, and General Assemblies, as man—just as much right to sit upon the throne of England, or in the Presidential chair of the United States, as man....

• • •

I believe the discussion of Human Rights at the North has already been of immense advantage to this country. It is producing the happiest influence upon the minds and hearts of those who are engaged in it; ... Indeed, the very agitation of the question, which it involved, has been highly important. Never was the heart of man so expanded; never were its generous sympathies so generally and so perseveringly excited. These sympathies, thus called into existence, have been useful preservatives of national virtue. I therefore do wish very much to promote the Anti-Slavery excitement at the North, because I believe it will prove a useful preservative of national virtue....

The discussion of the wrongs of slavery has opened the way for the discussion of other rights, and the ultimate result will most certainly be "the breaking of every yoke," the letting the oppressed of every grade and description go free—an emancipation far more glorious than any the world has ever yet seen, an introduction into that liberty wherewith Christ hath made his people free....

Questions

1. Why does Angelina Grimké call the abolitionist movement the nation's foremost "school [of] human rights"?

2. What role does she think the difference between the sexes should play in determining a person's rights and obligations?

79. Protest Statement of Lucy Stone and Henry Blackwell (1855)

Source: Elizabeth Cady Stanton et al., History of Woman Suffrage *(New York, 1881), vol. 1, pp. 260–61.*

A graduate of Oberlin College, Lucy Stone was the first woman from Massachusetts to earn a college degree. She became a widely admired lecturer on

abolitionism and feminism, and one of the leading advocates of women's
rights of the pre–Civil War years. In 1855 she married another reformer,
Henry B. Blackwell. Under the prevailing common law principle of cover-
ture, married women surrendered most of their legal rights to their husband, a situation the couple considered unjust. At their wedding they read a
"protest" against laws relating to marriage and women's freedom more generally. They also worked out a private agreement whereby each partner
would retain control of his or her income and property, nor would one determine where they would live without the consent of the other. Very unusually for the time, Lucy Stone also retained her maiden name after marrying.

WHILE WE ACKNOWLEDGE our mutual affection by publicly assuming the relationship of husband and wife, yet in justice to ourselves
and a great principle, we deem it a duty to declare that this act on
our part implies no sanction of, nor promise of voluntary obedience
to such of the present laws of marriage, as refuse to recognize the wife
as an independent, rational being, while they confer upon the husband an injurious and unnatural superiority, investing him with
legal powers which no honorable man would exercise, and which no
man should possess. We protest especially against the laws which
give to the husband:

1. The custody of the wife's person.
2. The exclusive control and guardianship of their children.
3. The sole ownership of her personal, and use of her real estate,
unless previously settled upon her, or placed in the hands of trust-
ees, as in the case of minors, lunatics, and idiots.
4. The absolute right to the product of her industry.
5. Also against laws which give to the widower so much larger and
more permanent interest in the property of his deceased wife, than
they give to the widow in that of the deceased husband.
6. Finally, against the whole system by which "the legal existence
of the wife is suspended during marriage," so that in most States,
she neither has a legal part in the choice of her residence, nor can

she make a will, nor sue or be sued in her own name, nor inherit property.

We believe that personal independence and equal human rights can never be forfeited, except for crime; that marriage should be an equal and permanent partnership, and so recognized by law; that until it is so recognized, married partners should provide against the radical injustice of present laws, by every means in their power.

We believe that where domestic difficulties arise, no appeal should be made to legal tribunals under existing laws, but that all difficulties should be submitted to the equitable adjustment of arbitrators mutually chosen.

Thus reverencing law, we enter our protest against rules and customs which are unworthy of the name, since they violate justice, the essence of law.

Henry B. Blackwell

Lucy Stone

Questions

1. What aspects of the law of marriage seem most objectionable to the couple?

2. What is the "great principle" to which they refer at the beginning of the "Protest"?

CHAPTER 13

A House Divided, 1840–1861

80. John L. O'Sullivan, Manifest Destiny (1845)

Source: John L. O'Sullivan, "Annexation," United States Magazine, and Democratic Review, *vol. 17 (July–August 1845), pp. 5–10.*

The expansionist spirit of the 1840s was captured in the phrase "manifest destiny," coined by John L. O'Sullivan, a New York journalist. O'Sullivan employed it to suggest that the United States had a divinely appointed mission to occupy all of North America. This right to the continent was provided by the nation's mission to extend the area of freedom. In the excerpt that follows, O'Sullivan defends the annexation of Texas, and suggests that California, then a province of Mexico, would be the next area to be absorbed into the United States, linked to the rest of the country by a new transcontinental railroad. O'Sullivan foresees the day when one government will control the entire North American continent. The spirit of manifest destiny would soon help to justify the Mexican War and, half a century later, the annexation of Puerto Rico and the Philippines as a result of the Spanish-American War.

—————

IT IS TIME now for all opposition to annexation of Texas to cease.... Texas is now ours. Already, before these records are written, her convention has undoubtedly ratified the acceptance, by her congress, of our proffered invitation into the Union; and made the requisite changes in her already republican form of constitution to adapt it to its future federal relations. Her star and stripe may already be said to have taken their place in the glorious blazon of our common nationality; and the sweep of our eagle's wing already includes within its circuit the wide extent of her fair and fertile land.

She is no longer to us a mere geographical space—a certain combination of coast, plain, mountain, valley, forest, and stream. She is no longer to us a mere country on the map.... It is time when all should cease to treat her as alien, and even adverse ... and cease ... thwarting our policy and hampering our power, limiting our greatness and checking the fulfillment of our manifest destiny to overspread the continent allotted by Providence for the free development of our yearly multiplying millions.

• • •

It is wholly untrue, and unjust to ourselves, the pretense that the annexation has been a measure of spoliation, unrightful and unrighteous of military conquest under forms of peace and law of territorial aggrandizement at the expense of justice....

The independence of Texas was complete and absolute. It was an independence, not only in fact, but of right.... If Texas became peopled with an American population, it was by no contrivance of our government, but on the express invitation of that of Mexico herself; accompanied with such guaranties of state independence, and the maintenance of a federal system analogous to our own.... She was released, rightfully and absolutely released, from all Mexican allegiance, or duty of cohesion to the Mexican political body, by acts and fault of Mexico herself, and Mexico alone. There was never a clearer case. It was not revolution; it was resistance to revolution: and resistance under such circumstances as left independence the necessary resulting state, caused by the abandonment of those with whom her former federal association had existed.

Nor is there any just foundation for the charge that annexation is a great pro-slavery measure calculated to increase and perpetuate that institution. Slavery had nothing to do with it. Opinions were and are greatly divided, both at the North and South, as to the influence to be exerted by it on slavery and the slave states....

Every new slave state in Texas will make at least one free state from among those in which that institution now exists—to say nothing of those portions of Texas on which slavery cannot spring and grow—to say nothing of the far more rapid growth of new states in the free West and Northwest, as these fine regions are overspread by the emigration fast flowing over them from Europe, as well as from the Northern and Eastern states of the Union as it exists....

California will, probably, next fall away from the loose adhesion which, in such a country as Mexico, holds a remote province in a slight equivocal kind of dependence on the metropolis. Imbecile and distracted, Mexico never can exert any real government authority over such a country....

In the case of California this is now impossible. The Anglo-Saxon foot is already on its borders. Already the advance guard of the irresistible army of Anglo-Saxon emigration has begun to pour down upon it, armed with the plough and the rifle, and marking its trail with schools and colleges, courts and representative halls, mills and meetinghouses. A population will soon be in actual occupation of California, over which it will be idle for Mexico to dream of dominion. They will necessarily become independent. All this without agency of our government, without responsibility of our people....

And they will have a right to independence—to self-government—to the possession of the homes conquered from the wildness of their own labors and dangers, sufferings and sacrifices—a better and a truer right than the artificial title of sovereignty in Mexico, a thousand miles distant, inheriting from Spain a title good only against those who have none better. Their right to independence will be the natural right of self-government belonging to any community strong enough to maintain it.... This will be their title to independence; and by this title, there can be no doubt that the population now fast streaming down upon California will both assert and maintain that independence.

Whether they will attach themselves to our Union or not is not to be predicted with any certainty. Unless the projected railroad across the continent to the Pacific be carried into effect, perhaps they may not; though even in that case, the day when the empires of the Atlantic and Pacific would again flow together into one, as soon as their inland border should approach each other. But that great work, colossal as appears the plan on its first suggestion, cannot remain long unbuilt.

Its [the transcontinental railroad] necessity for this very purpose of binding and holding together in its iron clasp our fast settling Pacific region with that of the Mississippi Valley, the natural facility of the route, the ease with which any amount of labor for the construction can be drawn in from the overcrowded populations of Europe, to be paid in the lands made valuable by the progress of the work itself and its immense utility, to the whole commerce of the world with the whole eastern coast of Asia, alone almost sufficient for the support of such a road—these considerations give assurance that the day cannot be distant which shall witness the conveyance of representatives from Oregon and California to Washington [D.C.] within less time than a few years ago was devoted to a similar journey by those from Ohio; while the magnetic telegraph will enable the editors of the *San Francisco Union*, the *Astoria Evening Post*, or the *Nootka Morning News*, to set up in type the first half of the President's inaugural before the echoes of the latter half shall have died away beneath the lofty porch of the Capitol, as spoken from his lips.

Away, then, with all idle French talk of balances of power on the American continent. There is no growth in Spanish America! Whatever progress of population may be in British Canada, is only for their own early severance of their present colonial relation to the little island 3,000 miles across the Atlantic; soon to be followed by annexation, and destined to swell the still accumulating momentum of our progress.

And whosoever may hold the balance, though they should cast into the opposite scale all the bayonets and cannon, not only of

France and England, but of Europe entire, how would it kick the beam against the simple, solid weight of the 250, or 300 million, and American millions destined to gather beneath the flutter of the stars and stripes, in the fast hastening year of the Lords 1845!

Questions

1. What connection does O'Sullivan see between manifest destiny and the idea of American freedom?

2. What does O'Sullivan mean when he describes America's destiny to rule the entire continent as "manifest"?

81. A Protest against Anti-Chinese Prejudice (1852)

Source: **Daily Alta California** *(San Francisco), May 5, 1852.*

The discovery of gold in California in 1848 unleashed a massive influx of migrants hoping to make their fortunes. The non-Indian population, under 15,000 in 1848, rose to over 360,000 by 1860. Prospectors came to the gold fields from all over the world—the eastern states, Europe, Latin America, and Asia. Nearly 25,000 Chinese landed between 1849 and 1852, most of them young men who had signed long-term labor contracts and went to work for the state's mines and railroads. Anti-Chinese sentiment quickly developed and in 1852 the state's governor, Democrat John Bigler, proposed that the legislature restrict Chinese immigration (even though the Constitution gives power over immigration to the federal government). In response, Norman Asing, a naturalized American citizen and leader of the Chinese community of San Francisco, issued an eloquent appeal for equal rights for the Chinese.

Sir: I am a Chinaman, a republican, and a lover of free institutions; am much attached to the principles of the government of the United States, and therefore take the liberty of addressing you as the chief of the government of this State. Your official position gives you a great opportunity of good and evil. ... The effect of your late message has been thus far to prejudice the public mind against my people, to enable those who wait the opportunity to hunt them down, and rob them of the rewards of their toil. You may not have meant that this should be the case, but you can see what will be the result of your propositions.

I am not much acquainted with your logic, that by excluding population from this State you enhance its wealth. I have always considered that population was wealth; particularly a population of producers, of men who by the labor of their hands or intellect, enrich the warehouses or the granaries of the country with the products of nature and art. You are deeply convinced you say "that to enhance the prosperity and preserve the tranquility of this State, Asiatic immigration must be checked." This, your Excellency, is but one step towards a retrograde movement of the government, which, on reflection, you will discover; and which the citizens of this country ought never to tolerate. It was one of the principal causes of quarrel between you (when colonies) and England; when the latter pressed laws against emigration, you looked for immigration; it came, and immigration made you what you are—your nation what it is. It transferred you at once from childhood to manhood and made you great and respectable throughout the nations of the earth. I am sure your Excellency cannot, if you would, prevent your being called the descendant of an immigrant, for I am sure you do not boast of being a descendant of the red man. But your further logic is more reprehensible. You argue that this is a republic of a particular race—that the Constitution of the United States admits of no asylum to any other than the pale face. This proposition is false in the extreme, and you know it. The declaration of your independence, and all the acts of your government, your people, and your history are all against you. ...

We would beg to remind you that when your nation was a wilderness, and the nation from which you sprung barbarous, we exercised most of the arts and virtues of civilized life; that we are possessed of a language and a literature, and that men skilled in science and the arts are numerous among us; that the productions of our manufactories, our sail, and workshops, form no small share of the commerce of the world; and that for centuries, colleges, schools, charitable institutions, asylums, and hospitals, have been as common as in your own land. That our people cannot be reproved for their idleness, and that your historians have given them due credit for the variety and richness of their works of art, and for their simplicity of manners, and particularly their industry. And we beg to remark, that so far as the history of our race in California goes, it stamps with the test of truth the fact that we are not the degraded race you would make us. We came amongst you as mechanics or traders, and following every honorable business of life. . . .

I am a naturalized citizen, your Excellency, of Charleston, South Carolina, and a Christian, too; and so hope you will stand corrected in your assertion "that none of the Asiatic class" as you are pleased to term them, have applied for benefits under our naturalization act. I could point out to you numbers of citizens, all over the whole continent, who have taken advantage of your hospitality and citizenship, and I defy you to say that our race have ever abused that hospitality or forfeited their claim on this or any of the governments of South America, by an infringement on the laws of the countries into which they pass. You find us peculiarly peaceable and orderly. It does not cost your state much for our criminal prosecution. We apply less to your courts for redress, and so far as I know, there are none who are a charge upon the state, as paupers.

Questions

1. Why does Asing argue that the governor's proposal violates the Constitution and the principles of the Declaration of Independence?

2. How does he invoke the history of China to bolster his criticism of the idea of excluding Chinese immigrants from the United States?

---

82. Resistance to the Fugitive Slave Act (1850)

Source: **Middletown Sentinel and Witness,** *October 29, 1850.*

The passage of the Fugitive Slave Act in 1850 tested in the most direct way the relationship between law and liberty. Numerous northerners announced that they would not obey the new measure, which abrogated local laws that sought to prevent the kidnapping of free blacks. It required individuals to assist in the capture of fugitives if called upon by federal authorities, and did not allow an accused fugitive slave to testify at a hearing that determined his or her status. In the previous year, Henry David Thoreau had published his well-known essay on civil disobedience, which defended the right to violate unjust laws. In 1850, six residents of Middletown, Connecticut, in a similar spirit, wrote a letter to the local newspaper explaining why they would not obey the new law.

THE UNDERSIGNED ARE friends of law. We reverence law. We are of the party of law and order. Law comes from the bosom of God and is sacred. Even an imperfect law we will respect and bear with, till we can obtain its modification or repeal. But all is not law which calls itself law. When iniquity frames itself into law, the sacredness of law is gone. When an enactment, falsely calling itself law, is imposed upon us, which disgraces our country, which invades our conscience, which dishonors our religion, which is an outrage upon our sense of justice, we take our stand against the imposition.

The Fugitive Slave Law commands all good citizens to be slave catchers. Good citizens *cannot* be slave catchers, any more than light can be darkness. You tell us, the Union will be endangered if we oppose this law. We reply, that greater things than the Union will be endangered, if we submit to it: Conscience, Humanity, Self-respect are greater than the Union, and these must be preserved at all hazards. This pretended law commands us to withhold food and raiment and shelter from the most needy—we cannot obey. It commands us to be base and dishonorable—we cannot obey.... When our sense of decency is clean gone forever, we will turn slave catchers; till then, never. You tell us that great men made this law. If great men choose to disgrace themselves, choose to put off all manliness, and plunge all over into meanness and dishonor, it does not follow that small men should do so too. If Beacon Street [a chief commercial street in Boston] and Marshfield [Daniel Webster's estate] choose to turn slave catchers, let them. We farmers and working men choose to stay by our plows and mills.... We are not yet ready to give ourselves over to all manner of villainy. Be the consequence what it may, come fines, come imprisonment, come what will, this thing you call law *we will not obey.*"

Questions

1. Whom do the Connecticut writers seem to blame for the Fugitive Slave Act?

2. How do the writers justify deciding to break the law?

———

83. American Party Platform (1856)

Source: W. S. Tisdale, ed., The True American's Almanac and Politician's Manual for 1857 (New York, 1857).

Hostility to immigrants has been a persistent feature of American life. In 1854, as the Whig Party broke apart over the slavery issue, two new parties made their appearance—the Republicans, devoted to stopping the westward expansion of slavery, and the Native American Party (sometimes called the Know-Nothings because it originated as a secret society whose members were not supposed to reveal information about the organization), dedicated to limiting the political power of immigrants and making it more difficult for them to become naturalized citizens. In the elections of 1854, the Know-Nothings made significant gains in several northern states and the upper tier of slave states. They won support from native-born workers who feared that immigration was exerting downward pressure on wages, and among voters seeking a platform on which northerners and southerners could unite. In 1856, the Native American Party candidate for president, Millard Fillmore, received over 20 percent of the vote. But the party soon fell victim to the sectional divisions that were roiling the political system.

1. An humble acknowledgment to the Supreme Being, for his protecting care vouchsafed to our fathers in their successful Revolutionary struggle, and hitherto manifested to us, their descendants, in the preservation of the liberties, the independence and the union of these States.

2. The perpetuation of the Federal Union and Constitution, as the palladium of our civil and religious liberties, and the only sure bulwarks of American Independence.

3. Americans must rule America, and to this end native-born citizens should be selected for all State, Federal, and municipal offices of government employment, in preference to all others. Nevertheless,

4. Persons born of American parents residing temporarily abroad, should be entitled to all the rights of native-born citizens.

5. No person should be selected for political station (whether of native or foreign birth), who recognizes any allegiance or obligation of any description to any foreign prince, potentate or power, or who refuses to recognize the Federal and State Constitution (each within its sphere) as paramount to all other laws, as rules of political action.

6. The unequaled recognition and maintenance of the reserved rights of the several States, and the cultivation of harmony and fra-

ternal good will between the citizens of the several States, and to this end, non-interference by Congress with questions appertaining solely to the individual States, and non-intervention by each State with the affairs of any other State.

7. The recognition of the right of native-born and naturalized citizens of the United States, permanently residing in any Territory thereof, to frame their constitution and laws, and to regulate their domestic and social affairs in their own mode, subject only to the provisions of the Federal Constitution, with the privilege of admission into the Union whenever they have the requisite population for one Representative in Congress: Provided, always, that none but those who are citizens of the United States, under the Constitution and laws thereof, and who have a fixed residence in any such territory, ought to participate in the formation of the Constitution, or in the enactment of laws for said Territory or State.

8. An enforcement of the principles that no State or Territory ought to admit others than citizens to the right of suffrage, or of holding political offices of the United States.

9. A change in the laws of naturalization, making a continued residence of twenty-one years, of all not heretofore provided for, an indispensable requisite for citizenship hereafter, and excluding all paupers, and persons convicted of crime, from landing upon our shores; but no interference with the vested rights of foreigners.

10. Opposition to any union between Church and State; no interference with religious faith or worship, and no test oaths for office....

13. Opposition to the reckless and unwise policy of the present Administration in the general management of our national affairs, and more especially as shown in removing "Americans" (by designation) and Conservatives in principle, from office, and placing foreigners and Ultraists in their places; as shown in a truckling subserviency to the stronger, and an insolent and cowardly bravado towards the weaker powers; as shown in re-opening sectional agitation; by the repeal of the Missouri Compromise; as shown in granting to unnaturalized foreigners the right of suffrage in Kansas and

Nebraska question; as shown in the corruptions which pervade some of the Departments of the Government; as shown in disgracing meritorious naval officers through prejudice or caprice; and as shown in the blundering mismanagement of our foreign relations.

Questions

1. What aspects of immigration seem to most alarm the American Party?

2. How do they seek to circumvent division over the slavery question?

---

84. Chief Justice Roger B. Taney, The Dred Scott Decision (1857)

Source: Dred Scott v. Sanford, *60 U.S. 393 (156).*

In the Dred Scott decision, the Supreme Court attempted to resolve a divisive question: were free African-American citizens of the United States? Dred Scott, a slave in Missouri, and his wife Harriet had been taken by their owner first to Illinois, where slavery was barred by state law, and then to Wisconsin Territory, where Congress had prohibited it under the Missouri Compromise. On their return to Missouri, Scott sued for their freedom, claiming that residence on free soil had made them free. The case involved several controversial issues, including whether Congress possessed the power to bar slavery from a territory. The Court decided that it did not and that the Missouri Compromise, which had been repealed in 1854, had been constitutional. But first, the Court had to decide whether Scott was a citizen, with standing to sue. For the majority, Chief Justice Roger B. Taney answered no. The nation's founders, he argued, intended to limit American citizenship to white persons alone. Taney's statement that blacks had "no rights which the white man was bound to respect" is remembered today as one of the most infamous in the history of the Supreme Court.

THE QUESTION IS simply this: can a Negro whose ancestors were imported into this country and sold as slaves become a member of the political community formed and brought into existence by the Constitution of the United States, and as such become entitled to all the rights, and privileges, and immunities, guarantied by that instrument to the citizen, one of which rights is the privilege of suing in a court of the United States in the cases specified in the Constitution?

It will be observed that the plea applies to that class of persons only whose ancestors were Negroes of the African race, and imported into this country and sold and held as slaves. The only matter in issue before the court, therefore, is, whether the descendants of such slaves, when they shall be emancipated, or who are born of parents who had become free before their birth, are citizens of a State in the sense in which the word "citizen" is used in the Constitution of the United States. And this being the only matter in dispute on the pleadings, the court must be understood as speaking in this opinion of that class only, that is, of those persons who are the descendants of Africans who were imported into this country and sold as slaves. . . .

The words "people of the United States" and "citizens" are synonymous terms, and mean the same thing. They both describe the political body who, according to our republican institutions, form the sovereignty, and who hold the power and conduct the government through their representatives. They are what we familiarly call the "sovereign people," and every citizen is one of this people and a constituent member of this sovereignty. The question before us is, whether the class of persons described in the plea . . . compose a portion of this people, and are constituent members of this sovereignty? We think they are not, and that they are not included, and were not intended to be included, under the word "citizens" in the Constitution, and can therefore claim none of the rights and privileges which that instrument provides for and secures to citizens of the United States. On the contrary, they were at that time considered as a subordinate and inferior class of beings, who had been subjugated by the dominant race, and, whether emancipated or not, yet remained subject to their authority, and had no rights or privileges but such as those who held the power and the government might choose to grant them....

They had for more than a century before been regarded as beings of an inferior order, and altogether unfit to associate with the white race, either in social or political relations; and so far inferior, that they had no rights which the white man was bound to respect....

The general words [of the Declaration of Independence] would seem to embrace the whole human family ... But it is too clear for dispute, that the enslaved African race were not intended to be included, and formed no part of the people who framed and adopted this declaration; for if the language, as understood in that day, would embrace them, the conduct of the distinguished men who framed the Declaration of Independence would have been utterly and flagrantly inconsistent with the principles they asserted; and instead of the sympathy of mankind to which they so confidently appealed, they would have deserved and received universal rebuke and reprobation.

Yet the men who framed this declaration were great men—high in literary acquirements—high in their sense of honor, and incapable of asserting principles inconsistent with those on which they were acting. They perfectly understood the meaning of the language they used, and how it would be understood by others; and they knew that it would not in any part of the civilized world be supposed to embrace the Negro race, which, by common consent, had been excluded from civilized Governments and the family of nations, and doomed to slavery. They spoke and acted according to the then established doctrines and principles, and in the ordinary language of the day, and no one misunderstood them. The unhappy black race were separated from the white by indelible marks, and laws long before established, and were never thought of or spoken of except as property, and when the claims of the owner or the profit of the trader were supposed to need protection.

Questions

1. What evidence does Taney present that blacks were not considered citizens by the authors of the Declaration of Independence and the Constitution?

2. Why do you think he bases his argument on what he says were the intentions of the founders rather than the situation of free blacks in the 1850s?

———

85. Texas Declaration of Independence (1836)

Source: Texas State Library and Archives Commission.

In the 1820s, some 7,000 emigrants from the United States emigrated to Texas, then part of Mexico, whose government at first welcomed them to the sparsely settled region. But as the number of emigrants grew, the Mexican government became alarmed and sought to discourage newcomers. When the settlers demanded greater autonomy, the Mexican government sent an army to impose central authority. In response, a convention of representatives from American settlements on March 2, 1836, declared Texas an independent nation. Like the revolutionaries of 1776, they issued a Declaration explaining their action. Sixty men signed the Declaration; three had been born in Mexico, the remainder in the United States. Texas would win the war and remain independent until 1845, when it was annexed to the United States.

———

WHEN A GOVERNMENT has ceased to protect the lives, liberty and property of the people, from whom its legitimate powers are derived, and for the advancement of whose happiness it was instituted, and so far from being a guarantee for the enjoyment of those inestimable and inalienable rights, becomes an instrument in the hands of evil rulers for their oppression.

When the Federal Republican Constitution of their country, which they have sworn to support, no longer has a substantial existence, and the whole nature of their government has been forcibly changed, without their consent, from a restricted federative republic, composed of sovereign states, to a consolidated central military despotism, in which every interest is disregarded but that of the army and the priesthood, both the eternal enemies of civil liberty, the everready minions of power, and the usual instruments of tyrants.

When, long after the spirit of the constitution has departed, moderation is at length so far lost by those in power, that even the semblance of freedom is removed, and the forms themselves of the constitution discontinued, and so far from their petitions and remonstrances being regarded, the agents who bear them are thrown into dungeons, and mercenary armies sent forth to force a new government upon them at the point of the bayonet.

When, in consequence of such acts of malfeasance and abdication on the part of the government, anarchy prevails, and civil society is dissolved into its original elements. In such a crisis, the first law of nature, the right of self-preservation, the inherent and inalienable rights of the people to appeal to first principles, and take their political affairs into their own hands in extreme cases, enjoins it as a right towards themselves, and a sacred obligation to their posterity, to abolish such government, and create another in its stead, calculated to rescue them from impending dangers, and to secure their future welfare and happiness.

Nations, as well as individuals, are amenable for their acts to the public opinion of mankind. A statement of a part of our grievances is therefore submitted to an impartial world, in justification of the hazardous but unavoidable step now taken, of severing our political connection with the Mexican people, and assuming an independent attitude among the nations of the earth.

The Mexican government, by its colonization laws, invited and induced the Anglo-American population of Texas to colonize its wilderness under the pledged faith of a written constitution, that they should continue to enjoy that constitutional liberty and republican government to which they had been habituated in the land of their birth, the United States of America.

In this expectation they have been cruelly disappointed, inasmuch as the Mexican nation has acquiesced in the late changes made in the government by General Antonio Lopez de Santa Anna, who having overturned the constitution of his country, now offers us the cruel alternative, either to abandon our homes, acquired by so many privations, or submit to the most intolerable of all tyranny, the combined despotism of the sword and the priesthood. . . .

It has failed to establish any public system of education, although possessed of almost boundless resources, (the public domain), and although it is an axiom in political science, that unless a people are educated and enlightened, it is idle to expect the continuance of civil liberty, or the capacity for self government. . . .

It denies us the right of worshipping the Almighty according to the dictates of our own conscience, by the support of a national religion, calculated to promote the temporal interest of its human functionaries, rather than the glory of the true and living God.

It has demanded us to deliver up our arms, which are essential to our defence, the rightful property of freemen, and formidable only to tyrannical governments.

It has invaded our country both by sea and by land, with intent to lay waste our territory, and drive us from our homes; and has now a large mercenary army advancing, to carry on against us a war of extermination.

It has, through its emissaries, incited the merciless savage, with the tomahawk and scalping knife, to massacre the inhabitants of our defenseless frontiers. . . .

These, and other grievances, were patiently borne by the people of Texas, until they reached that point at which forbearance ceases to be a virtue. We then took up arms in defence of the national constitution. We appealed to our Mexican brethren for assistance. Our appeal has been made in vain. Though months have elapsed, no sympathetic response has yet been heard from the Interior. We are, therefore, forced to the melancholy conclusion, that the Mexican people have acquiesced in the destruction of their liberty, and the substitution therefore of a military government; that they are unfit to be free, and incapable of self government....

We, therefore, the delegates with plenary powers of the people of Texas, in solemn convention assembled, appealing to a candid world for the necessities of our condition, do hereby resolve and declare, that our political connection with the Mexican nation has forever ended, and that the people of Texas do now constitute a free, Sovereign, and independent republic, and are fully invested with all the rights and attributes which properly belong to independent nations; and, conscious of the rectitude of our intentions, we fearlessly and confidently commit the issue to the decision of the Supreme arbiter of the destinies of nations.

Questions

1. In what ways is this Declaration similar to the American Declaration of Independence?

2. What seems to be the attitude of the Texas revolutionaries toward other elements of Texas society (Mexicans, Native Americans, and slaves)?

86. The Lincoln-Douglas Debates (1858)

Source: **Political Debates between Honorable Abraham Lincoln and Honorable Stephen Douglas, in the Celebrated Campaign of 1858** *(Columbus, Ohio, 1860), pp. 71, 75, 178–82, 204, 209, 234, 238.*

Americans' divisions over slavery were brought into sharp focus in 1858 in the election campaign that pitted Illinois senator Stephen A. Douglas, the North's most prominent Democratic leader, against the then little-known Abraham Lincoln.

The Lincoln-Douglas debates, held in seven Illinois towns and attended by tens of thousands of listeners, remain classics of American political oratory. Clashing definitions of freedom lay at their heart. To Lincoln, freedom meant opposition to slavery. Douglas insisted that the essence of freedom lay in local self-government. A large, diverse nation could survive only by respecting the right of each locality to determine its own institutions. He attempted to portray Lincoln as a dangerous radical whose positions threatened to degrade white Americans by reducing them to equality with blacks.

Douglas was reelected. But the campaign created Lincoln's national reputation.

• • •

DOUGLAS: Do you desire to strike out of our state constitution that clause which keeps slaves and free negroes out of the state, and allow the free negroes to flow in, and cover your prairies with black settlements? Do you desire to turn this beautiful state into a free negro colony, in order that when Missouri abolishes slavery she can send one hundred thousand emancipated slaves into Illinois, to become citizens and voters, on an equality with yourselves? If you desire negro citizenship, if you desire to allow them to come into the state and settle with the white man, if you desire them to vote on an equality with yourselves, and to make them eligible to office, to serve on juries, and to adjudge your rights, then support Mr. Lincoln and the Black Republican party, who are in favor of the citizenship of the negro. For one, I am opposed to negro citizenship in any and every form. I believe this government was made on the white basis. I believe it was made by white men, for the benefit of white men and their posterity for ever, and I am in favor of confining citizenship to white men, men of European birth and descent, instead of conferring it upon negroes, Indians and other inferior races.

Mr. Lincoln, following the example and lead of all the little Abolition orators, who go around and lecture in the basements of schools and churches, reads from the Declaration of Independence, that all men were created equal, and then asks how can you deprive a negro of that equality which God and the Declaration of Independence awards to him. He and they maintain that negro equality is guaranteed by the laws of God, and that it is asserted in the Declaration of Independence. If they think so, of course they have a right to say so, and so vote. I do not question Mr. Lincoln's conscientious belief that the negro was made his equal, and hence is his brother, (laughter), but for my own part, I do not regard the negro as my equal, and positively deny that he is my brother or any kin to me whatever.

• • •

LINCOLN: Now gentlemen, I don't want to read at any greater length, but this is the true complexion of all I have ever said in regard to the institution of slavery and the black race. This is the whole of it, and anything that argues me into his idea of perfect social and political equality with the negro, is but a specious and fantastic arrangement of words, by which a man can prove a horse chestnut to be a chestnut horse. I will say here, while upon this subject, that I have no purpose directly or indirectly to interfere with the institution of slavery in the states where it exists. I believe I have no lawful right to do so, and I have no inclination to do so. I have no purpose to introduce political and social equality between the white and the black races. There is a physical difference between the two, which in my judgment will probably forever forbid their living together upon the footing of perfect equality, and inasmuch as it becomes a necessity that there must be a difference, I, as well as Judge Douglas, am in favor of the race to which I belong, having the superior position. I have never said anything to the contrary, but I hold that notwithstanding all this, there is no reason in the world why the negro is not entitled to all the natural rights enumerated in the Declaration of Independence, the right to life, liberty and the pursuit of happiness. I hold that he is as much entitled to these as the white man. I agree with Judge Douglas he is not my equal in many respects— certainly not in color, perhaps not in moral or intellectual endowment. But in the right to eat the bread, without leave of anybody else, which his own hand earns, *he is my equal and the equal of Judge Douglas, and the equal of every living man.*

• • •

DOUGLAS: He tells you that I will not argue the question whether slavery is right or wrong. I tell you why I will not do it. I hold that under the Constitution of the United States, each state of this Union has a right to do as it pleases on the subject of slavery. In Illinois we have exercised that sovereign right by prohibiting slavery within our own limits. I approve of that line of policy. We have performed our whole duty in Illinois. We have gone as far as we have a right to go under the Constitution of our common country. It is none of our business whether slavery exists in Missouri or not. Missouri is a sovereign state of this Union, and has the same right to decide the slavery question for herself that Illinois has to decide it for herself. ("Good.") Hence I do not choose to occupy the time allotted to me discussing a question that we have no right to act upon.

• • •

LINCOLN: The real issue in this controversy—the one pressing upon every mind—is the sentiment on the part of one class that looks upon the institution of slavery *as a wrong*, and of another class that *does not* look upon it as a wrong. The sentiment that contemplates the institution of slavery in this country as a wrong is the sentiment of the Republican party. It is the sentiment around which all their actions—all their arguments circle—from which all their propositions radiate. They look upon it as being a moral, social and political wrong; and while they contemplate it as such, they nevertheless have due regard for its actual existence among us, and the difficulties of getting rid of it in any satisfactory way and to all the constitutional obligations thrown about it. Yet having a due regard for these, they desire a policy in regard to it that looks to its not creating any more danger. They insist that it should as far as may be, *be treated* as a wrong, and one of the methods of treating it as a wrong is to *make provision that it shall grow no larger.* They also desire a policy that looks to a peaceful end of slavery at sometime, as being wrong. . . .

That is the real issue. That is the issue that will continue in this country when these poor tongues of Judge Douglas and myself shall be silent. It is the eternal struggle between these two principles— right and wrong—throughout the world. They are the two principles that have stood face to face from the beginning of time; and will ever continue to struggle. The one is the common right of humanity and the other the divine right of kings. It is the same principle in whatever shape it develops itself. It is the same spirit that says, "You work and toil and earn bread, and I'll eat it." [Loud applause.] No matter in what shape it comes, whether from the mouth of a king who seeks to bestride the people of his own nation and live by the fruit of their labor, or from one race of men as an apology for enslaving another race, it is the same tyrannical principal. I was glad to express my gratitude at Quincy, and I re-express it here to Judge Douglas—*that he looks to no end of the institution of slavery.* That will help the people to see where the struggle really is. It will hereafter place with us all men who really do wish the wrong may have an end. And whenever we can get rid of the fog which obscures the real question—when we can get Judge Douglas and his friends to avow a policy looking to its perpetuation—we can get out from among them that class of men and bring them to the side of those who treat it as a wrong. Then there will soon be an end of it, and that end will be its "ultimate extinction." Whenever the issue can be distinctly made, and all extraneous matter thrown out so that men can fairly see the real difference between the parties, this controversy will soon be settled, and it will be done peaceably too.

• • •

Questions

1. How do Douglas and Lincoln differ in their views on what rights black Americans ought to enjoy?

2. What is Douglas's response to antislavery criticism of slavery in the southern states?

87. South Carolina Ordinance of Secession (1860)

Source: Frank H. Moore, ed., The Rebellion Record *(New York, 1861–68), vol. 1, pp. 3–5.*

In the three months that followed Abraham Lincoln's election as president in November 1860, seven states seceded from the Union. First to act was South Carolina, the state with the highest percentage of slaves in its population and a long history of political radicalism. On December 20, 1860, the legislature unanimously voted to leave the Union. In justifying the right to secede, the legislature issued an *Ordinance of Secession*. It restated the compact theory of the Constitution that had become more and more central to southern political thought during the three decades since the nullification controversy and placed the issue of slavery squarely at the center of the crisis. Rather than accept permanent minority status in a nation governed by their opponents, South Carolina's leaders boldly struck for their region's independence. At stake, they believed, was not a single election but an entire way of life based on slavery.

THE STATE OF South Carolina having resumed her separate and equal place among nations, deems it due to herself, to the remaining United States of America, and to the nations of the world, that she should declare the immediate causes which have led to this act.

In 1787, Deputies were appointed by the States to revise the Articles of Confederation; and on 17th September, 1787, these Deputies recommended, for the adoption of the States, the Articles of Union, known as the Constitution of the United States. . . .

Thus was established by compact between the States, a Government with defined objects and powers, limited to the express words of the grant. . . . We hold that the Government thus established is subject to the two great principles asserted in the Declaration of Independence; and we hold further, that the mode of its formation

subjects it to a third fundamental principle, namely, the law of compact. We maintain that in every compact between two or more parties, the obligation is mutual; that the failure of one of the contracting
parties to perform a material part of the arrangement, entirely
releases the obligation of the other, and that, where no arbiter is provided, each party is remitted to his own judgment to determine the
fact of failure, with all its consequences.

• • •

We affirm that the ends for which this Government was instituted have been defeated, and the Government itself has been made
destructive of them by the action of the non-slaveholding States.
Those States have assumed the right of deciding upon the propriety
of our domestic institutions, and have denied the rights of property
established in fifteen of the States and recognized by the Constitution; they have denounced as sinful the institution of Slavery; they
have permitted the open establishment among them of societies,
whose avowed object is to disturb the peace of and eloin [take away]
the property of the citizens of other States. They have encouraged and
assisted thousands of our slaves to leave their homes; and those who
remain, have been incited by emissaries, books, and pictures, to servile insurrection.

For twenty-five years this agitation has been steadily increasing,
until it has now secured to its aid the power of the common Government. Observing the *forms* of the Constitution, a sectional party has
found within that article establishing the Executive Department,
the means of subverting the Constitution itself. A geographical line
has been drawn across the Union, and all the States north of that
line have united in the election of a man to the high office of President of the United States whose opinions and purposes are hostile
to Slavery. He is to be intrusted with the administration of the common Government, because he has declared that "Government cannot endure permanently half slave, half free," and that the public
mind must rest in the belief that Slavery is in the course of ultimate
extinction.

This sectional combination for the subversion of the Constitution has been aided, in some of the States, by elevating to citizenship persons who, by the supreme law of the land are incapable of becoming citizens; and their votes have been used to inaugurate a new policy, hostile to the South, and destructive of its peace and safety.

On the 4th of March next this party will take possession of the Government. It has announced that the South shall be excluded from the common territory, that the Judicial tribunal shall be made sectional, and that a war must be waged against Slavery until it shall cease throughout the United States.

The guarantees of the Constitution will then no longer exist; the equal rights of the States will be lost. The Slaveholding States will no longer have the power of self-government, or self-protection, and the Federal Government will have become their enemy.

Sectional interest and animosity will deepen the irritation; and all hope of remedy is rendered vain, by the fact that the public opinion at the North has invested a great political error with the sanctions of a more erroneous religious belief.

We, therefore, the people of South Carolina, by our delegates in Convention assembled, appealing to the Supreme Judge of the world for the rectitude of our intentions, have solemnly declared that the Union heretofore existing between this State and the other States of North America is dissolved, and that the State of South Carolina has resumed her position among the nations of the world as a separate and independent state, with full power to levy war, conclude peace, contract alliances, establish commerce, and to do all other acts and things which independent States may of right do.

Questions

1. Why do secessionists place so much emphasis on the growth of antislavery public opinion in the North?

2. What appears to be the main motivation for South Carolina's secession?

CHAPTER 14

A New Birth of Freedom: The Civil War, 1861–1865

88. Alexander H. Stephens, The Cornerstone of the Confederacy (1861)

Source: Frank H. Moore, ed., The Rebellion Record, *vol. 1 (New York: G.P. Putnam, 1861–68), pp. 45–46.*

Alexander H. Stephens, one of Georgia's most prominent political leaders, opposed secession in the winter of 1860–1861, but once his state acted, agreed to serve as the vice president of the Confederacy. In March 1861, he delivered a speech in Savannah that laid out his explanation for the dissolution of the Union and argued that the Confederate Constitution represented a significant improvement over that of the United States. After the war, Stephens would write a long book arguing that the Civil War was caused not by slavery but by a constitutional question—the South's insistence on preserving state sovereignty against an overly powerful national government. In his 1861 speech, however, he forthrightly identified the defense of slavery and of white supremacy as the fundamental motivation of the Confederacy, the "cornerstone" of the new southern nation. Apparently, Stephens's speech embarrassed Confederate president Jefferson Davis, who hoped to gain recognition from European powers by downplaying the role of slavery in the secession movement.

WE ARE PASSING through one of the greatest revolutions in the annals of the world. Seven States have within the last three months thrown off an old government and formed a new. This revolution has been signally marked, up to this time, by the fact of its having been accomplished without the loss of a single drop of blood.

This new constitution. or form of government, constitutes the subject to which your attention will be partly invited. In reference to it, I make this first general remark: it amply secures all our ancient rights, franchises, and liberties. All the great principles of Magna Charta are retained in it. No citizen is deprived of life, liberty, or property, but by the judgment of his peers under the laws of the land. The great principle of religious liberty, which was the honor and pride of the old constitution, is still maintained and secured. All the essentials of the old constitution, which have endeared it to the hearts of the American people, have been preserved and perpetuated.... So, taking the whole new constitution, I have no hesitancy in giving it as my judgment that it is decidedly better than the old.

Allow me briefly to allude to some of these improvements. The question of building up class interests, or fostering one branch of industry to the prejudice of another under the exercise of the revenue power, which gave us so much trouble under the old constitution, is put at rest forever under the new. We allow the imposition of no duty with a view of giving advantage to one class of persons, in any trade or business, over those of another. All, under our system, stand upon the same broad principles of perfect equality. Honest labor and enterprise are left free and unrestricted in whatever pursuit they may be engaged....

But not to be tedious in enumerating the numerous changes for the better, allow me to allude to one other though last, not least. The new constitution has put at rest, forever, all the agitating questions relating to our peculiar institution African slavery as it exists amongst us the proper status of the negro in our form of civilization. This was the immediate cause of the late rupture and present revolution. Jefferson in his forecast, had anticipated this, as the "rock upon which the old Union would split." He was right. What was conjecture with him, is now a realized fact. But whether he fully comprehended the great truth upon which that rock stood and stands, may be doubted. The prevailing ideas entertained by him and most of the leading statesmen at the time of the formation of the old constitution, were that the enslavement of the African was in violation of the laws of nature; that it was wrong in principle, socially, morally, and politically. It was an evil they knew not well how to deal with, but the general opinion of the men of that day was that, somehow or other in the order of Providence, the institution would be evanescent and pass away. This idea, though not incorporated in the constitution, was the prevailing idea at that time. The constitution, it is true, secured every essential guarantee to the institution while it should last, and hence no argument can be justly urged against the constitutional guarantees thus secured, because of the common sentiment of the day. Those ideas, however, were fundamentally wrong. They rested upon the assumption of the equality of races. This was an error. It was a sandy foundation, and the government built upon it fell when the "storm came and the wind blew."

Our new government is founded upon exactly the opposite idea; its foundations are laid, its cornerstone rests, upon the great truth that the negro is not equal to the white man; that slavery, subordination to the superior race, is his natural and normal condition. This, our new government, is the first, in the history of the world, based upon this great physical, philosophical, and moral truth. This truth has been slow in the process of its development, like all other truths in the various departments of science. It has been so even amongst us. Many who hear me, perhaps, can recollect well, that this truth was not generally admitted, even within their day. The errors of the past generation still clung to many as late as twenty years ago. Those at the North, who still cling to these errors, with a zeal above knowledge, we justly denominate fanatics.... They assume that the negro is equal, and hence conclude that he is entitled to equal privileges and rights with the white man. . . . I recollect once of having heard a gentleman from one of the northern States, of great power and ability, announce in the House of Representatives, with imposing effect, that we of the South would be compelled, ultimately, to yield upon this subject of slavery, that it was as impossible to war successfully against a principle in politics, as it was in physics or mechanics. That the principle would ultimately prevail. That we, in maintaining slavery as it exists with us, were warring against a principle, a principle founded in nature, the principle of the equality of men. The reply I made to him was, that upon his own grounds, we should, ultimately, succeed, and that he and his associates, in this crusade against our institutions, would ultimately fail. The truth announced, that it was as impossible to war successfully against a principle in politics as it was in physics and mechanics, I admitted; but told him that it was he, and those acting with him, who were warring against a principle. They were attempting to make things equal which the Creator had made unequal. . . .

As I have stated, the truth of this principle may be slow in development, as all truths are and ever have been, in the various branches of science. It was so with the principles announced by Galileo it was so with Adam Smith and his principles of political economy. . . . Now, they are universally acknowledged. May we not, therefore, look with confidence to the ultimate universal acknowledgment of the truths upon which our system rests? It is the first government ever instituted upon the principles in strict conformity to nature, and the ordination of Providence, in furnishing the materials of human society. Many governments have been founded upon the principle of the subordination and serfdom of certain classes of the same race; such were and are in violation of the laws of nature. Our system commits no such violation of nature's laws. With us, all of the white race, however high or low, rich or poor, are equal in the eye of the law. Not so with the negro. Subordination is his place. He, by nature, or by the curse against Canaan, is fitted for that condition which he occupies in our system. . . . By experience we know that it is best, not only for the superior, but for the inferior race, that it should be so. It is, indeed, in conformity with the ordinance of the Creator. It is not for us to inquire into the wisdom of His ordinances, or to question them. For His own purposes, He has made one race to differ from another, as He has made "one star to differ from another star in glory." The great objects of humanity are best attained when there is conformity to His laws and decrees, in the formation of governments as well as in all things else. Our confederacy is founded upon principles in strict conformity with these laws. This stone which was rejected by the first builders "is become the chief of the corner" the real "corner-stone" in our new edifice.

Questions

1. What argument does Stephens offer for the idea that blacks are innately suited for the condition of slaves?

2. Why does Stephens believe the U.S. Constitution is fundamentally flawed?

89. Marcus M. Spiegel, Letter of a Civil War Soldier (1864)

Source: Marcus M. Spiegel, reproduced from A Jewish Colonel in the Civil War, *edited by Jean Powers Soman and Frank L. Byrne, by permission of the University of Nebraska Press. Copyright 1985 by The Kent State University Press. Copyright 1994 by Jean P. Soman.*

Born into a Jewish family in Germany in 1829, Marcus Spiegel took part in the failed German revolution of 1848. In the following year, he emigrated to Ohio, where he married the daughter of a local farmer. He enlisted in the Union army in 1861. He went to war, he wrote to his brother-in-law, to defend "the flag that was ever ready to protect you and me and every one who sought its protection from oppression." Spiegel rose to the rank of colonel in the 120th Ohio Infantry and saw action in Virginia, Mississippi, and Louisiana. He was an ardent Democrat, who shared the era's racist attitudes and thought Lincoln's Emancipation Proclamation a serious mistake. Yet, as the Union army penetrated the heart of the Deep South, Spiegel became increasingly antislavery. Spiegel died in a minor engagement in Louisiana in May 1864, one of the hundreds of thousands of Americans to perish in the Civil War.

———

PLAQUEMINE LA JAN 22/64

My dear Wife, my sweet Cary!

. . .

... You must not expect any news inasmuch as this [is] as monotonous a place as ever Millersburg can be. We are living here right on the Mississippi River and with exception of three or four Steamboats landing here every day which are called Coast Packets and travel from Baton Rouge to New Orleans and back, we have no news. When I first came here we had four Regiments of Infantry, three Batteries of Artillery and one Company of Cavelery. Since then two Regiments of Infantry, the 22nd and 7th Kentucky and two Batteries have been moved to Baton Rouge where they got up a big scare the other day.

This leaves us the 42nd-Ohio and the 120th Ohio, one Battery and one Company of Cavelery, sufficient to hold this place against all marauding forces they can bring; we are building a very large and formidable Fort here. The weather here is beautiful, just like our June; it is very warm and the air is mild, wholesome and refreshing. I wish to God you could be here. Colonel L. A. Sheldon of the 42nd Ohio is in command here; you know if you remember what I think of him; he commanded our Brigade last year at Chickasaw and Arkansas Post. Yet he is a very clever man and extremely kind to me. He has his wife here; she is from Lorain County; a regular build

Western Reserve Yankee Girl. I do not see her often, though very much pressed to call. I saw her twice in four weeks.

Dr. Stanton, Adjutand, Uncle Josey, Sinsheimer and myself spend most of our time together. There was a report yesterday that there were a lot of Rebels twelve miles from here, so I started out with a Company of Cavelery. Uncle Josey and Doctor Stanton and my friend Lieutenant Miller (whom you saw at home) acted as volunteer Aids, but we found "nary Reb" after a hard ride. I managed to get four dozend Eggs and we came home. We are living in a House all together (i.e. field and Staff); our boy does the cooking for our Mess. Uncle Josey's business does not go very well just now; there are so very few troops here and they have no money and the lines are closed.

I have at present twelve Sergeants in Ohio on the recruiting Service; I do not know how well or whether at all, they succeed. It takes so long somehow to hear from Ohio and the North generally that we do not know what is going on. In New Orleans they have news once a week at least but here it is very irregular.

Captain Moffit sent in his resignation Papers about three months ago and a few days ago they came back accepted. I am very sorry for them indeed. Since I am here I have learned and seen more of what the horrors of Slavery was than I ever knew before and I am glad indeed that the signs of the times show, towards closing out the accursed institution. You know it takes me long to say anything that sounds antidemocratic and it goes hard, but whether I stay in the Army or come home, I am [in] favor of doing away with the institution of Slavery. I am willing for the Planters to hire them and in favor of making the negro work at all events; inasmuch as he is naturally lazy and indolent, but never hereafter will I either speak or vote in favor of Slavery; this is no hasty conclusion but a deep conviction. Yet I never mean hereafter to be a politician, but quietly as a good citizen doing duty to my God, my family, my Country and myself.

Charley has left here about a week ago; I think however he is yet in New Orleans. You must write me a long, long letter and many of them and ask me ten thousand questions in every one and I will take them up one by one and answer them. This is the tirest place I ever was at, during my Soldier life, but the boys are so comfortable and feel so very well that I am not at all anxious to leave here. We had a negro woman cooking for us when Uncle Josey, Charley and Sinsheimer messed with us, but it is so far for them and they left us and we discharged our Cook and have only our boy. One of my men who deserted in Covington and was brought up by the Provost Marshal was tried by a Court Marshal and sentenced to forfeit all his pay and condemned for six months hard labor on Fort Espararox [Esperanza], Texas, with a Ball and Chain on his right leg, a very very hard sentence indeed; I would rather they would have shot him, for death is not so hard as degradation.

I am well and hearty and if I had my dear, dear little family here I would not wish anything better, but as it is my heart is ever yearning for home, home with all its blessings. I hope you are comfortable during this extreme awful cold weather, such as I see by the Papers you must have had; it makes me tremble to think you had to be there without me God grant all was right.

Hamlin must continue to be a good and obedient boy. It is about getting to be a youth and he must endeavor to learn well and make a man so he can aid and assist his father and mother when they get old. I hope soon to be at home when I can teach him and help him along....

Questions

1. What do you think Spiegel means by "the horrors of slavery"?

2. Why does he say that his new antislavery viewpoint "goes hard"?

90. Samuel S. Cox Condemns Emancipation (1862)

Source: Congressional Globe, *37th Congress, 2nd Session, Appendix,* pp. 242–49.

The abolition of slavery seems so inevitable a result of the American Civil War that it is difficult to realize how much controversy it aroused at the time, in both the Union and the Confederacy. In 1862, as the Lincoln administration slowly moved toward ending slavery, most northern Democrats expressed bitter opposition. Some of their arguments are illustrated in this June speech in Congress by Samuel S. Cox of Ohio. Cox supported the war effort but insisted that its goal must be the restoration of the Union "as it was"—that is, with slavery intact. Cox marshaled many arguments against emancipation, including the claims that it would disrupt the nation's economy, violate the Constitution, and alienate many white soldiers. He also invoked racist fears of an influx into the North of emancipated slaves who, he claimed, would lower wages by competing with white laborers and become a drain on public resources. Cox's speech was circulated as a campaign document in the congressional elections of 1862 when, partly because of fear of the consequences of emancipation, Democrats made strong gains in the northern states.

THERE IS SOMETHING needed in making successful civil war besides raising money and armies. You must keep the confidence and spirit of the people. It must not only be animated by a noble passion at the outset, but it must be sustained by confidence in the cause.... Is there a member here who dare say that Ohio troops will fight successfully or fight at all, if the result shall be the flight and movement of the black race by millions northward to their own State? ...

Is it the policy here, as it would seem to be, ... to [convert] the war into a St. Domingo-insurrection, turning the South into one utter desolation? ... We want no more poetry about striking off chains and bidding the oppressed go. Plain people want to know whether the chains will not be put upon white limbs, and *whither* the oppressed are to go. If the industry of the North is to be fettered with their support; if they are to go to Ohio and the North, we want to know it. Nay, we want, if we can, to stop it. . . .

Slavery may be an evil, it may be wrong for southern men to use unpaid labor, but what will be the condition of the people of Ohio when the free jubilee shall have come in its ripe and rotten maturity? If slavery is bad, the condition of the State of Ohio, with an unrestrained black population . . . will be far worse. . . . The free negroes will become equal, or will continue unequal to the whites. Equality is a condition which is self-protective, wanting nothing, asking nothing, able to take care of itself. It is an absurdity to say that two races as dissimilar as black and white, of different origin, of unequal capacity, can succeed in the same society when placed in competition. There is no such example in history of the success of two separate races under such circumstances. . . .

Prejudice, stronger than all principles, though not always stronger than lust, has imperatively separated the whites from the blacks. In the school-house, the church, or the hospital, the black man must not seat himself beside the white; even in death and at the cemetery the line of distinction is drawn. To abolish slavery the North must go still further and forget that fatal prejudice of race which governs it, and which makes emancipation so illusory. To give men their liberty, to open to them the gates of the city, and then say, "there, you shall live among yourself, you shall marry among yourselves, you shall form a separate society in society," is to create a cursed caste, and replace slaves by pariahs.

Questions

1. Why does Cox feel that emancipating slaves endangers the liberties of white northerners?

2. What status does he anticipate for the slaves if they are freed?

91. A Defense of the Confederacy (1861)

Source: Drayton Family Papers, Historical Society of Pennsylvania.

A South Carolina plantation owner and ardent supporter of secession, Thomas F. Drayton explained the reasons for his commitment to the Confederate cause in a letter to his brother Percival, an officer in the U.S. Navy, written from Charleston shortly after the firing on Fort Sumter. The letter insists that other issues than slavery are at stake in the war, yet most of his accusations against the northern states seem to revolve around their hostility to slavery. Thomas F. Drayton went on to serve as a brigadier general in the Confederate army.

My dear Percy

And so Sumter is at last ours, and this too without the loss of a *single* life upon either side.... Before this dispute is over however, I look for abundance of death & blood....

You say I don't yet understand the position you have taken. I do fully, but certainly differ from you when you say that to side with us, would be "battling for slavery against freedom." On the contrary, by siding with us, you likewise defend yourselves at the North against a far greater danger than we are threatened with, which is the enslavement of the *whites*; for the tendency with you is towards consolidation & the abrogation of State rights.... All these evils & horrors will be laid to your doors, because you have encouraged ... in the form of abolition lecturers, fanatical preachers, unscrupulous editors, selfish politicians; ... and by voting for men ... with the *avowed object* of abolishing slavery throughout the Southern States ... who made a merit of John Brown's murderous invasion; set at defiance all fugitive slave laws, ... and whose clergy denounced us indiscriminately as barbarians....

We are fighting for home & liberty. Can the North say as much? Good night. And don't say again, that in siding for us, you would be defending slavery and fighting for what is abhorrent to your feelings & convictions. On the contrary, in fighting on our side, you will be battling for law & order & against abstract fanatical ideas which will certainly bring about vastly greater evils upon our race, than could possibly result from the perpetuation of slavery among us.

Questions

1. Why does Drayton deny that the Confederacy is fighting to defend slavery?

2. How does Drayton appear to define liberty?

92. Frederick Douglass on Black Soldiers (1863)

Source: **Men of Color, to Arms,** *broadside, Rochester, N.Y., March 21, 1863.*

At the beginning of the Civil War, the Union army refused to accept northern black volunteers. But as casualty rolls expanded, pressure mounted to allow blacks to serve. Although preliminary steps to enlist combat troops were taken in a few parts of the South in 1862, only after the Emancipation Proclamation of January 1, 1863, did the recruitment of black soldiers begin in earnest.

Some black units won considerable fame, among them the 54th Massachusetts Volunteers, a company of free blacks from throughout the North commanded by Robert Gould Shaw, a young reformer from a prominent Boston family. In March 1863, Frederick Douglass called on northern blacks to volunteer for this unit. "Liberty won by white men would lose half its luster," he wrote. Douglass realized that by serving in the army, black men would be placing the question of postwar black citizenship on the nation's agenda.

WHEN FIRST THE rebel cannon shattered the walls of Sumter and drove away its starving garrison, I predicted that the war then and there inaugurated would not be fought out entirely by white men. Every month's experience during these dreary years has confirmed that opinion. A war undertaken and brazenly carried on for the perpetual enslavement of colored men, calls logically and loudly for colored men to help suppress it. Only a moderate share of sagacity was needed to see that the arm of the slave was the best defense against the arm of the slaveholder. Hence with every reverse to the national arms, with every exulting shout of victory raised by the slaveholding rebels, I have implored the imperiled nation to unchain against her foes, her powerful black hand. Slowly and reluctantly that appeal is beginning to be heeded. Stop not now to complain that it was not heeded sooner. It may or it may not have been best that it should not. This is not the time to discuss that question. Leave it to the future. When the war is over, the country is saved, peace is established, and the black man's rights are secured, as they will be, history with an impartial hand will dispose of that and sundry other questions. Action! Action! not criticism, is the plain duty of this hour. Words are now useful only as they stimulate to blows. The office of speech now is only to point out when, where, and how to strike to the best advantage. There is no time to delay. The tide is at its flood that leads on to fortune. From East to West, from North to South, the sky is written all over, "Now or never."

Liberty won by white men would lose half its luster. "Who would be free themselves must strike the blow." "Better even die free, than to live slaves." This is the sentiment of every brave colored man amongst us. There are weak and cowardly men in all nations. We have them amongst us. They tell you this is the "white man's war"; that you will be "no better off after than before the war"; that the getting of you into the army is to "sacrifice you on the first opportunity." Believe them not; cowards themselves, they do not wish to have their cowardice shamed by your brave example. Leave them to their timidity, or to whatever motive may hold them back. I have not thought lightly of the words I am now addressing you. The counsel I give comes of close observation of the great struggle now in progress, and of the deep conviction that this is your hour and mine. In good earnest then, and after the best deliberation, I now for the first time during this war feel at liberty to call and counsel you to arms. By every consideration which binds you to your enslaved fellow-countrymen, and the peace and welfare of your country; by every aspiration which you cherish for the freedom and equality of yourselves and your children; by all the ties of blood and identity which make us one with the brave black men now fighting our battles in Louisiana and in South Carolina, I urge you to fly to arms, and smite with death the power that would bury the government and your liberty in the same hopeless grave. I wish I could tell you that the State of New York calls you to this high honor. For the moment her constituted authorities are silent on the subject. They will speak by and by, and doubtless on the right side; but we are not compelled to wait for her. We can get at the throat of treason and slavery through the State of Massachusetts. She was first in the War of Independence; first to break the chains of her slaves; first to make the black man equal before the law; first to admit colored children to her common schools, and she was first to answer with her blood the alarm cry of the nation, when its capital was menaced by rebels. You know her patriotic governor, and you know Charles Sumner. I need not add more.

Massachusetts now welcomes you to arms as soldiers. She has but a small colored population from which to recruit. She has full leave of the general government to send one regiment to the war, and she has undertaken to do it. Go quickly and help fill up the first colored regiment from the North. I am authorized to assure you that you will receive the same wages, the same rations, the same equipments, the same protection, the same treatment, and the same bounty, secured to the white soldiers. You will be led by able and skillful officers, men who will take especial pride in your efficiency and success. They will be quick to accord to you all the honor you shall merit by your valor, and see that your rights and feelings are respected by other soldiers. I have assured myself on these points, and can speak with authority. More than twenty years of unswerving devotion to our common cause may give me some humble claim to be trusted at this momentous crisis. I will not argue. To do so implies hesitation and doubt, and you do not hesitate. You do not doubt. The day dawns; the morning star is bright upon the horizon! The iron gate of our prison stands half open. One gallant rush from the North will fling it wide open, while four millions of our brothers and sisters shall march out into liberty. The chance is now given you to end in a day the bondage of centuries, and to rise in one bound from social degradation to the plane of common equality with all other varieties of men. Remember Denmark Vesey of Charleston; remember Nathaniel Turner of Southampton; remember Shields Green and Copeland, who followed noble John Brown, and fell as glorious martyrs for the cause of the slave. Remember that in a contest with oppression, the Almighty has no attribute which can take sides with oppressors. The case is before you. This is our golden opportunity. Let us accept it, and forever wipe out the dark reproaches unsparingly hurled against us by our enemies. Let us win for ourselves the gratitude of our country, and the best blessings of our posterity through all time. The nucleus of this first regiment is now in camp at Readville, a short distance from Boston. I will undertake to forward to Boston all persons adjudged fit to be mustered into the regiment, who shall apply to me at any time within the next two weeks.

Questions

1. Why does Douglass believe that black service in the Union army will lead to an expansion of blacks' rights in the postwar world?

2. What does Douglass mean when he writes that black soldiers will "wipe out the dark reproaches" directed at blacks "by our enemies"?

93. Letter by the Mother of a Black Soldier (1863)

Source: Ira Berlin et al., eds., Freedom: A Documentary History of Emancipation, 1861–1867, *ser. 2 (New York, 1982), pp. 582–83.*

Within the Union army, black soldiers were anything but equal to white. Serving in segregated units and ineligible, until the end of the war, to rise to the rank of commissioned officers, they were initially paid less than white soldiers. Even more alarming, the Confederacy announced that it would treat captured black soldiers not as prisoners of war but as fugitives who would be remanded to slavery.

One of the more remarkable letters of the Civil War era was written to President Lincoln by Hannah Johnson, the mother of a black soldier. Although, as she notes, she had enjoyed but a "poor education," Mrs. Johnson eloquently advised the president to insist that black prisoners be treated the same as white and resist pressures to rescind the Emancipation Proclamation. The fact that she felt she had a sympathetic recipient in the White House illustrates the enormous changes American society was undergoing as a result of the Civil War. Mrs. Johnson did not know that the day before she wrote the letter, Lincoln had ordered that, for every captured black soldier enslaved, a Confederate prisoner would be put to hard labor for the duration of the war.

———

BUFFALO [NEW YORK] July 31 1863

Excellent Sir

My good friend says I must write to you and she will send it[.] My son went in the 54th regiment. I am a colored woman and my son was strong and able to fight for his country and the colored people have as much to fight for as any. My father was a Slave and escaped from Louisiana before I was born morn forty years agone[.] I have but poor edication but I never went to schol, but I know just as well as any what is right between man and man. Now I know it is right that a colored man should go and fight for his country, and so ought to a white man. I know that a colored man ought to run no greater risques than a white, his pay is no greater his obligation to fight is the same. So why should not our enemies be compelled to treat him the same, Made to do it.

My son fought at Fort Wagoner but thank God he was not taken prisoner, as many were[.] I thought of this thing before I let my boy go but then they said Mr. Lincoln will never let them sell our colored soldiers for slaves, if they do he will get them back quck[.] he will rettallyate and stop it. Now Mr. Lincoln dont you think you oght to stop this thing and make them do the same by the colored men they have lived in idleness all their lives on stolen labor and made savages of the colored people, but they now are so furious because they are proving themselves to be men, such as have come away and got some edication. It must not be so. You must put the rebels to work in State prisons to making shoes and things, if they sell our colored soldiers, till they let them all go. And give their wounded the same treatment. it would seem cruel, but their [is] no other way, and a just man must do hard things sometimes, that shew him to be a great man. They tell me some do you will take back the Proclamation, don't do it. When you are dead and in Heaven, in a thousand years that action of yours will make the Angels sing your praises I know it. Ought one man to own another, law for or not, who made the law, surely the poor slave did not. so it is wicked, and a horrible Outrage, there is no sense in it, because a man has lived by robbing all his life and his father before him, should he complain because the stolen things found on him are taken. Robbing the colored people of their labor is but a small part of the robbery[.] their souls are almost taken, they are made bruits of often. You know all about this[.]

Will you see that the colored men fighting now, are fairly treated. You ought to do this, and do it at once, Not let the thing run along meet it quickly and manfully, and stop this, mean cowardly cruelty. We poor oppressed ones, appeal to you, and ask fair play.

Yours for Christs sake
Hannah Johnson

Questions

1. What is Mrs. Johnson's opinion of slavery and slaveholders?

2. How would you describe the tone Mrs. Johnson adopts in writing to the president?

---

94. Abraham Lincoln, Address at Sanitary Fair, Baltimore (1864)

Source: Abraham Lincoln: Letters and Addresses *(New York, 1903), pp. 295–96.*

Never was freedom's contested nature more evident than during the Civil War. Both sides fought in the name of freedom. "We all declare for liberty," Lincoln observed in a speech in Baltimore in 1864, "but in using the same *word* we do not all mean the same *thing*." He went on to explain the differences between the two sides' understandings of this word. Lincoln noted that Maryland, a slave state before the Civil War, had just adopted a new constitution abolishing slavery. And he announced his intention to investigate reports (later confirmed) that Confederate forces had massacred a number of black Union soldiers after they surrendered at Fort Pillow, Tennessee. The advance of emancipation and the service of black troops, for Lincoln, embodied "the advance of liberty."

THE WORLD HAS never had a good definition of the word liberty, and the American people, just now, are much in want of one. We all declare for liberty; but in using the same word we do not all mean the same thing. With some the word liberty may mean for each man to do as he pleases with himself, and the product of his labor; while with others the same word may mean for some men to do as they please with other men, and the product of other men's labor. Here are two, not only different, but incompatible things, called by the same name, liberty. And it follows that each of the things is, by the respective parties, called by two different and incompatible names—liberty and tyranny.

The shepherd drives the wolf from the sheep's throat, for which the sheep thanks the shepherd as his liberator, while the wolf denounces him for the same act, as the destroyer of liberty, especially as the sheep was a black one. Plainly, the sheep and the wolf are not agreed upon a definition of the word liberty; and precisely the same difference prevails to-day among us human creatures, even in the North, and all professing to love liberty. Hence we behold the process by which thousands are daily passing from under the yoke of bondage hailed by some as the advance of liberty, and bewailed by others as the destruction of all liberty. Recently, as it seems, the people of Maryland have been doing something to define liberty, and thanks to them that, in what they have done, the wolf's dictionary has been repudiated.

It is not very becoming for one in my position to make speeches at great length; but there is another subject upon which I feel that I ought to say a word.

A painful rumor—true, I fear—has reached us of the massacre by the rebel forces at Fort Pillow, in the west end of Tennessee, on the Mississippi River, of some three hundred colored soldiers and white officers, who had just been overpowered by their assailants. There seems to be some anxiety in the public mind whether the government is doing its duty to the colored soldier, and to the service, at this point. At the beginning of the war, and for some time, the use of colored troops was not contemplated; and how the change of purpose was wrought I will not now take time to explain. Upon a clear conviction of duty I resolved to turn that element of strength to account; and I am responsible for it to the American people, to the Christian world, to history, and in my final account to God. Having determined to use the negro as a soldier, there is no way but to give him all the protection given to any other soldier. The difficulty is not in stating the principle, but in practically applying it. It is a mistake to suppose the government is indifferent to this matter, or is not doing the best it can in regard to it. We do not to-day know that a colored soldier, or white officer commanding colored soldiers, has been massacred by the rebels when made a prisoner. We fear it,—believe it, I may say,—but we do not know it. To take the life of one of their prisoners on the assumption that they murder ours, when it is short of certainty that they do murder ours, might be too serious, too cruel, a mistake. We are having the Fort Pillow affair thoroughly investigated; and such investigation will probably show conclusively how the truth is. If after all that has been said it shall turn out that there has been no massacre at Fort Pillow, it will be almost safe to say there has been none, and will be none, elsewhere. If there has been the massacre of three hundred there, or even the tenth part of three hundred, it will be conclusively proved; and being so proved, the retribution shall as surely come. It will be matter of grave consideration in what exact course to apply the retribution; but in the supposed case it must come.

Questions

1. What does Lincoln identify as the essential difference between northern and southern definitions of freedom?

2. What is the purpose of Lincoln's metaphor about the wolf and the sheep and their differing views of liberty?

―――――――

95. Mary Livermore on Women and the War (1883)

Source: Mary A. Livermore, **What Shall We Do with Our Daughters?** *(Boston, 1883), pp. 10–16.*

The Civil War opened new doors of opportunity for northern women. Some took advantage of the wartime labor shortage to move into jobs in factories and into previously largely male professions like nursing. Hundreds of thousands of northern women took part in organizations that gathered money and medical supplies for soldiers and sent books, clothing, and food to the freedmen. Women played a leading role in organizing sanitary fairs—grand bazaars that raised money for soldiers' aid. The suffrage movement suspended operations during the war to devote itself to the Union and emancipation. But from the ranks of this wartime mobilization came many of the leaders of the postwar movement for women's rights. Mary Livermore, the wife of a Chicago minister, toured military hospitals to assess their needs, cared for injured and dying soldiers, and organized two sanitary fairs. She emerged from the war with a deep resentment against women's legal and political subordination and organized her state's first woman suffrage convention. Looking back on her experience two decades later, Livermore concluded that the spirit of the age was emancipating women no less than slaves and creating new opportunities in education, employment, and the law.

THE CONTEMPTUOUS OPINION entertained of woman in the past has found expression, not alone in literature, but also in unjust laws and customs. "In marriage she has been a serf; as a mother she has been robbed of her children; in public instruction she has been ignored; in labor she has been a menial, and then inadequately compensated; civilly she has been a minor, and politically she has had no existence. She has been the equal of man only when punishment, and the payment of taxes, were in question."

Born and bred for generations under such conditions of hindrance, it has not been possible for women to rise much above the arbitrary standards of inferiority persistently set before them. Here and there through the ages some woman endowed with phenomenal force of character has towered above the mediocrity of her sex, hinting at the qualities imprisoned in the feminine nature. It is not strange that these instances have been rare: it is strange, indeed, that women have held their own during these ages of degradation. . . .

• • •

Humanity has moved forward to an era where wrong and slavery are being displaced, and reason and justice are being recognized as the rule of life. Science is extending immeasurably the bounds of knowledge and power; art is refining life, giving to it beauty and grace; literature bears in her hands whole ages of comfort and sympathy; industry, aided by the hundred-handed elements of nature, is increasing the world's wealth; and invention is economizing its labor. The age looks steadily to the redressing of wrong, to the righting of every form of error and injustice; and a tireless and prying philanthropy, which is almost omniscient, is one of the most hopeful characteristics of the time....

• • •

It could not be possible in such an era but that women should share in the justice and kindliness with which the time is fraught. A great wave is lifting them to higher levels. The leadership of the world is being taken from the hands of the brutal and low, and the race is groping its way to a higher ideal than once it knew. It is the evolution of this tendency that is lifting women out of their subject condition, that is emancipating them from the seclusion of the past, and adding to the sum total of the world's worth and wisdom, by giving to them the cultivation human beings need. The demand for their education,—technical and industrial, as well as intellectual,—and for their civil and political rights, is being urged each year by an increasing host, and with more emphatic utterance.

Colleges, professional schools, and universities, closed against them for ages, are opening to them. They are invited to pursue the same course of study as their brothers, and are graduated with the same diplomas. Trades, businesses, remunerative vocations, and learned professions seek them; and even the laws, which are the last to feel the change in public opinion,—usually dragging a whole generation behind,—even these are being annually revised and amended, and then they fail to keep abreast of the advancing civilization.

All this is but prefatory, and prophetic of the time when, for women, law will be synonymous with justice, and no opportunity for knowledge or effort will be denied them on the score of sex. . . .

• • •

It is for our young women that the great changes of the time promise the most: it is for our daughters,—the fair, bright girls, who are the charm of society and the delight of home; the sources of infinite comfort to fathers and mothers, and the sources of great anxiety also. What shall we do with them,—and what shall they do with and for themselves?

"New occasions teach new duties,
Time makes ancient good uncouth,"

and the training of fifty years ago is not sufficient for the girls of today. The changed conditions of life which our young women confront compel greater care and thought on the part of those charged with their education than has herefore been deemed necessary. They are to be weighted with heavy duties, and to assume heavier responsibilities; for the days of tutelage seem to be ended for civilized women, and they are to think and act for themselves.

Questions

1. How does Livermore explain the inequality in status and achievement between men and women?

2. How does Livermore understand freedom for women?

CHAPTER 15

"What Is Freedom?": Reconstruction, 1865–1877

96. Petition of Black Residents of Nashville (1865)

Source: Newspaper clipping enclosed in Col. R. D. Mussey to Capt. C. P. Brown, January 23, 1865, Letters Received, ser. 925, Department of the Cumberland, U.S. Army Continental Commands, National Archives.

At the request of military governor Andrew Johnson, Lincoln exempted Tennessee from the Emancipation Proclamation of 1863 (although many slaves in the state gained their freedom by serving in the Union army). In January 1865, a state convention was held to complete the work of abolition. A group of free blacks of Nashville sent a petition to the delegates, asking for immediate action to end slavery and granting black men the right to vote (which free blacks had enjoyed in the state until 1835). The document emphasized their loyalty to the Union, their natural right to freedom, and their willingness to take on the responsibilities of citizenship. The document offers a revealing snapshot of black consciousness at the dawn of Reconstruction.

To the Union Convention of Tennessee Assembled in the Capitol at Nashville, January 9th, 1865:

We the undersigned petitioners, American citizens of African descent, natives and residents of Tennessee, and devoted friends of the great National cause, do most respectfully ask a patient hearing of your honorable body in regard to matters deeply affecting the future condition of our unfortunate and long suffering race.

First of all, however, we would say that words are too weak to tell how profoundly grateful we are to the Federal Government for the good work of freedom which it is gradually carrying forward; and for the Emancipation Proclamation which has set free all the slaves in some of the rebellious States, as well as many of the slaves in Tennessee.

After two hundred years of bondage and suffering a returning sense of justice has awakened the great body of the American people to make amends for the unprovoked wrongs committed against us for over two hundred years.

Your petitioners would ask you to complete the work begun by the nation at large, and abolish the last vestige of slavery by the express words of your organic law.

Many masters in Tennessee whose slaves have left them, will certainly make every effort to bring them back to bondage after the reorganization of the State government, unless slavery be expressly abolished by the Constitution.

We hold that freedom is the natural right of all men, which they themselves have no more right to give or barter away, than they have to sell their honor, their wives, or their children.

We claim to be men belonging to the great human family, descended from one great God, who is the common Father of all, and who bestowed on all races and tribes the priceless right of freedom. Of this right, for no offence of ours, we have long been cruelly deprived, and the common voice of the wise and good of all countries, has remonstrated against our enslavement, as one of the greatest crimes in all history.

We claim freedom, as our natural right, and ask that in harmony and co-operation with the nation at large, you should cut up by the roots the system of slavery, which is not only a wrong to us, but the source of all the evil which at present afflicts the State. For slavery, corrupt itself, corrupted nearly all, also, around it, so that it has influenced nearly all the slave States to rebel against the Federal Government, in order to set up a government of pirates under which slavery might be perpetrated.

In the contest between the nation and slavery, our unfortunate people have sided, by instinct, with the former. We have little fortune to devote to the national cause, for a hard fate has hitherto forced us to live in poverty, but we do devote to its success, our hopes, our toils, our whole heart, our sacred honor, and our lives. We will work, pray, live, and, if need be, die for the Union, as cheerfully as ever a white patriot died for his country. The color of our skin does not lessen in the least degree, our love either for God or for the land of our birth.

We are proud to point your honorable body to the fact, that so far as our knowledge extends, not a negro traitor has made his appearance since the begining of this wicked rebellion. . . .

Devoted as we are to the principles of justice, of love to all men, and of equal rights on which our Government is based, and which make it the hope of the world. We know the burdens of citizenship, and are ready to bear them. We know the duties of the good citizen, and are ready to perform them cheerfully, and would ask to be put in a position in which we can discharge them more effectually. We do not ask for the privilege of citizenship, wishing to shun the obligations imposed by it.

Near 200,000 of our brethren are to-day performing military duty in the ranks of the Union army. Thousands of them have already died in battle, or perished by a cruel martyrdom for the sake of the Union, and we are ready and willing to sacrifice more. But what higher order of citizen is there than the soldier? or who has a greater trust confided to his hands? If we are called on to do military duty against the rebel armies in the field, why should we be denied the privilege of voting against rebel citizens at the ballot-box? The latter is as necessary to save the Government as the former. . . .

This is not a Democratic Government if a numerous, law-abiding, industrious, and useful class of citizens, born and bred on the soil, are to be treated as aliens and enemies, as an inferior degraded class, who must have no voice in the Government which they support, protect and defend, with all their heart, soul, mind, and body, both in peace and war.

Questions

1. Why do the petitioners place so much emphasis on their loyalty to the Union cause during the war?

2. What understanding of American history and the nation's future do the petitioners convey?

---

97. Petition of Committee on Behalf of the Freedmen to Andrew Johnson (1865)

Source: Henry Bram et al. to the President of the United States, October 28, 1865, P-27, 1865, Letters Received, ser. 15, Washington Headquarters, Freedmen's Bureau Papers, National Archives.

By June 1865, some 40,000 freedpeople had been settled on "Sherman land" in South Carolina and Georgia, in accordance with Special Field Order 15. That summer, however, President Andrew Johnson, who had succeeded Lincoln, ordered nearly all land in federal hands returned to its former owners. In October, O. O. Howard, head of the Freedmen's Bureau, traveled to the Sea Islands to inform blacks of the new policy.

Howard was greeted with disbelief and protest. A committee drew up petitions to Howard and President Johnson. Their petition to the president pointed out that the government had encouraged them to occupy the land and affirmed that they were ready to purchase it if given the opportunity. Johnson rejected the former slaves' plea. And, throughout the South, because no land distribution took place, the vast majority of rural freedpeople remained poor and without property during Reconstruction.

EDISTO ISLAND S.C. Oct 28th, 1865.

To the President of these United States. We the freedmen of Edisto Island South Carolina have learned From you through Major General O O Howard commissioner of the Freedmans Bureau. with deep sorrow and Painful hearts of the possibility of government restoring These lands to the former owners. We are well aware Of the many perplexing and trying questions that burden Your mind and do therefore pray to god (the preserver of all and who has through our Late and beloved President (Lincoln) proclamation and the war made Us A free people) that he may guide you in making Your decisions and give you that wisdom that Cometh from above to settle these great and Important Questions for the best interests of the country and the Colored race: Here is where secession was born and Nurtured Here is were we have toiled nearly all Our lives as slaves and were treated like dumb Driven cattle, This is our home, we have made These lands what they are were the only true and Loyal people that were found in posession of these Lands we have been always ready to strike for Liberty and humanity yea to fight if needs be To preserve this glorious union. Shall not we who Are freedman and have been always true to this Union have the same rights as are enjoyed by Others? Have we broken any Law of these United States? Have we forfieted our rights of property In Land?—If not then! are not our rights as A free people and good citizens of these United States To be considered before the rights of those who were Found in rebellion against this good and just Government (and now being conquered) come (as they Seem) with penitent hearts and beg forgiveness For past offences and also ask if their lands Cannot be restored to them are these rebellious Spirits to be reinstated in their *possessions* And we who have been abused and oppressed For many long years not to be allowed the Privilege of purchasing land But be subject To the will of these large Land owners? God forbid, Land monopoly is injurious to the advancement of the course of freedom, and if Government Does not make some provision by which we as Freedmen can obtain A Homestead, we have Not bettered our condition.

We have been encouraged by Government to take Up these lands in small tracts, receiving Certificates of the same—we have thus far Taken Sixteen thousand (16000) acres of Land here on This Island. We are ready to pay for this land When Government calls for it and now after What has been done will the good and just government take from us all this right and make us Subject to the will of those who have cheated and Oppressed us for many years God Forbid!

We the freedmen of this Island and of the State of South Carolina— Do therefore petition to you as the President of these United States, that some provisions be made by which Every colored man can purchase land and Hold it as his own. We wish to have A home if It be but A few acres without some provision is Made our future is sad to look upon yess our Situation is dangerous we therefore look to you In this trying hour as A true friend of the poor and Neglected race for protection and Equal Rights with the privilege of purchasing A Homestead—A Homestead right here in the Heart of South Carolina.

We pray that God will direct your heart in Making such provision for us as freedmen which Will tend to united these states together stronger Than ever before—May God bless you in the Administration of your duties as the President Of these United States is the humble prayer Of us all.—

In behalf of the Freedmen
        Henry Bram
Committee   Ishmael Moultrie.
        yates. Sampson

Questions

1. How important is it for the petitioners to obtain land on Edisto Island, as opposed to land elsewhere in the country?

2. What do they think is the relationship between owning land and freedom?

98. The Mississippi Black Code (1865)

Source: Walter L. Fleming, ed., **Documentary History of Reconstruction** *(Cleveland, 1906–07), vol. 1, pp. 281–90.*

During 1865, Andrew Johnson put into effect his own plan of Reconstruction, establishing procedures whereby new governments, elected by white voters only, would be created in the South. Among the first laws passed by the new governments were the Black Codes, which attempted to regulate the lives of the former slaves. These laws granted the freedpeople certain rights, such as legalized marriage, ownership of property, and limited access to the courts. But they denied them the right to testify in court in cases that only involved whites, serve on juries or in state militias, or to vote. And in response to planters' demands that the freedpeople be required to work on the plantations, the Black Codes declared that those who failed to sign yearly labor contracts could be arrested and hired out to white landowners. The Black Codes indicated how the white South would regulate black freedom if given a free hand by the federal government. But they so completely violated free labor principles that they discredited Johnson's Reconstruction policy among northern Republicans.

Vagrant Law

Sec. 2.... All freedmen, free negroes and mulattoes in this State, over the age of eighteen years, found on the second Monday in January, 1866, or thereafter, with no lawful employment or business, or found unlawfully assembling themselves together, either in the day or night time, and all white persons so assembling themselves with freedmen, free negroes or mulattoes, or usually associating with freedmen, free negroes or mulattoes, on terms of equality, or living in adultery or fornication with a freed woman, free negro or mulatto, shall be deemed vagrants, and on conviction thereof shall be fined in a sum not exceeding, in the case of a freedman, free negro, or mulatto, fifty dollars, and a white man two hundred dollars, and imprisoned at the discretion of the court, the free negro not exceeding ten days, and the white man not exceeding six months....

Sec. 7.... If any freedman, free negro, or mulatto shall fail or refuse to pay any tax levied according to the provisions of the sixth section of this act, it shall be *prima facie* evidence of vagrancy, and it shall be the duty of the sheriff to arrest such freedman, free negro, or mulatto or such person refusing or neglecting to pay such tax, and proceed at once to hire for the shortest time such delinquent tax-payer to any one who will pay the said tax, with accruing costs, giving preference to the employer, if there be one.

CIVIL RIGHTS OF FREEDMEN

Sec. 1.... That all freedmen, free negroes, and mulattoes may sue and be sued, implead and be impleaded, in all the courts of law and equity of this State, and may acquire personal property, and choses in action, by descent or purchase, and may dispose of the same in the same manner and to the same extent that white persons may: *Provided*, That the provisions of this section shall not be so construed as to allow any freedman, free negro, or mulatto to rent or lease any lands or tenements except in incorporated cities or towns....

Sec. 2.... All freedmen, free negroes, and mulattoes may intermarry with each other, in the same manner and under the same regulations that are provided by law for white persons: *Provided*, That the clerk of probate shall keep separate records of the same.

Sec. 3.... All freedmen, free negroes, or mulattoes who do now and have herebefore lived and cohabited together as husband and wife shall be taken and held in law as legally married, and the issue shall be taken and held as legitimate for all purposes; that it shall not be lawful for any freedman, free negro, or mulatto to intermarry with any white person; nor for any white person to intermarry with any freedman, free negro, or mulatto; and any person who shall so intermarry, shall be deemed guilty of felony, and on conviction thereof shall be confined in the State penitentiary for life; and those shall be deemed freedmen, free negroes, and mulattoes who are of pure negro blood, and those descended from a negro to the third generation, inclusive, though one ancestor in each generation may have been a white person.

Sec. 4.... In addition to cases in which freedmen, free negroes, and mulattoes are now by law competent witnesses, freedmen, free negroes, or mulattoes shall be competent in civil cases, when a party or parties to the suit, either plaintiff or plaintiffs, defendant or defendants; also in cases where freedmen, free negroes, and mulattoes is or are either plaintiff or plaintiffs, defendant or defendants, and a white person or white persons, is or are the opposing party or parties, plaintiff or plaintiffs, defendant or defendants. They shall also be competent witnesses in all criminal prosecutions where the crime charged is alleged to have been committed by a white person upon or against the person or property of a freedman, free negro, or mulatto: *Provided*, that in all cases said witnesses shall be examined in open court, on the stand; except, however, they may be examined before the grand jury, and shall in all cases be subject to the rules and tests of the common law as to competency and credibility.

Sec. 5.... Every freedman, free negro, and mulatto shall, on the second Monday of January, one thousand eight hundred and sixty-six and annually thereafter, have a lawful home or employment, and shall have written evidence thereof....

Sec. 6.... All contracts for labor made with freedmen, free negroes, and mulattoes for a longer period than one month shall be in writing, and in duplicate, attested and read to said freedman, free negro, or mulatto by a beat, city or county officer, or two disinterested white persons of the county in which the labor is to be performed, of which each party shall have one; and said contracts shall be taken and held as entire contracts, and if the laborer shall quit the service of the employer before the expiration of his term of service, without good cause, he shall forfeit his wages for that year up to the time of quitting.

Sec. 7.... Every civil officer shall, and every person may, arrest and carry back to his or her legal employer any freedman, free negro, or mulatto who shall have quit the service of his or her employer before the expiration of his or her term of service without good cause.... *Provided*, that said arrested party, after being so returned, may appeal to the justice of the peace or member of the board of police of the county, who, on notice to the alleged employer, shall try summarily whether said appellant is legally employed by the alleged employer, and has good cause to quit said employer; either party shall have the right of appeal to the county court, pending which the alleged deserter shall be remanded to the alleged employer or otherwise disposed of, as shall be right and just; and the decision of the county court shall be final.

CERTAIN OFFENSES OF FREEDMEN

Sec. 1.... That no freedman, free negro or mulatto, not in the military service of the United States government, and not licensed so to do by the board of police of his or her county, shall keep or carry firearms of any kind, or any ammunition, dirk or bowie knife, and on conviction thereof in the county court shall be punished by fine, not exceeding ten dollars, and pay the costs of such proceedings, and all such arms or ammunition shall be forfeited to the informer....

Sec. 2.... Any freedman, free negro, or mulatto committing riots, routs, affrays, trespasses, malicious mischief, cruel treatment to animals, seditious speeches, insulting gestures, language, or acts, or assaults on any person, disturbance of the peace, exercising the function of a minister of the Gospel without a license from some regularly organized church, vending spirituous or intoxicating liquors, or committing any other misdemeanor, the punishment of which is not specifically provided for by law, shall, upon conviction thereof in the county court, be fined not less than ten dollars, and not more than one hundred dollars, and may be imprisoned at the discretion of the court, not exceeding thirty days.

Sec. 3.... If any white person shall sell, lend, or give to any freedman, free negro, or mulatto any fire-arms, dirk or bowie knife, or ammunition, or any spirituous or intoxicating liquors, such person or persons so offending, upon conviction thereof in the county court of his or her county, shall be fined not exceeding fifty dollars, and may be imprisoned, at the discretion of the court, not exceeding thirty days. . . .

Sec. 5. . . . If any freedman, free negro, or mulatto, convicted of any of the misdemeanors provided against in this act, shall fail or refuse for the space of five days, after conviction, to pay the fine and costs imposed, such person shall be hired out by the sheriff or other officer, at public outcry, to any white person who will pay said fine and all costs, and take said convict for the shortest time.

Questions

1. Why do you think the state of Mississippi required all black persons to sign yearly labor contracts but not white citizens?

2. What basic rights are granted to the former slaves and which are denied to them by the Black Code?

---

99. A Sharecropping Contract (1866)

Source: Records of the Assistant Commissioner for the State of Tennessee, Bureau of Refugees, Freedmen, and Abandoned Lands, National Archives.

Despite the widespread desire for land, few former slaves were able to acquire farms of their own in the post–Civil War South. Most ended up as sharecroppers, working on white-owned land for a share of the crop at the end of the growing season. Sharecropping was a kind of compromise between blacks' desire for independence from white control and planters' desire for a disciplined labor force. This contract, typical of thousands, originated in Shelby County, Tennessee. The laborers signed with an X, as they were illiterate. Typical of early postwar contracts, it gave the planter the right to supervise the labor of his employees. Later, sharecropping contracts afforded former slaves greater autonomy. Families would rent parcels of land, work it under their own direction, and divide the crop with the owner at the end of the year. But as the price of cotton fell continuously after the Civil War, workers found it difficult to profit from the sharecropping system.

THOMAS J. ROSS agrees to employ the Freedmen to plant and raise a crop on his Rosstown Plantation.... On the following Rules, Regulations and Remunerations.

The said Ross agrees to furnish the land to cultivate, and a sufficient number of mules & horses and feed them to make and house said crop and all necessary farming utensils to carry on the same and to give unto said Freedmen whose names appear below one half of all the cotton, corn and wheat that is raised on said place for the year 1866 after all the necessary expenses are deducted out that accrues on said crop. Outside of the Freedmen's labor in harvesting, carrying to market and selling the same and the said Freedmen whose names appear below covenant and agrees to and with said Thomas J. Ross that for and in consideration of one half of the crop before mentioned that they will plant, cultivate, and raise under the management control and Superintendence of said Ross, in good faith, a cotton, corn and oat crop under his management for the year 1866. And we the said Freedmen agrees to furnish ourselves & families in provisions, clothing, medicine and medical bills and all, and every kind of other expenses that we may incur on said plantation for the year 1866 free of charge to said Ross. Should the said Ross furnish us any of the above supplies or any other kind of expenses, during said year, are to settle and pay him out of the net proceeds of our part of the crop the retail price of the county at time of sale or any price we may agree upon. The said Ross shall keep a regular book account, against each and every one or the head of every family to be adjusted and settled at the end of the year.

We furthermore bind ourselves to and with said Ross that we will do good work and labor ten hours a day on an average, winter and summer. The time to run from the time we commence to the time we quit.... We further agree that we will lose all lost time, or pay at the rate of one dollar per day, rainy days excepted. In sickness and women lying in childbed are to lose the time and account for it to the other hands out of his or her part of the crop at the same rates that she or they may receive per annum.

We furthermore bind ourselves that we will obey the orders of said Ross in all things in carrying out and managing said crop for said year and be docked for disobedience. All is responsible for all farming utensils that is on hand or may be placed in care of said Freedmen for the year 1866 to said Ross and are also responsible to said Ross if we carelessly, maliciously maltreat any of his stock for said year to said Ross for damages to be assessed out of our wages for said year.

Samuel (X) Johnson, Thomas (X) Richard, Tinny (X) Fitch, Jessie (X) Simmons, Sophe (X) Pruden, Henry (X) Pruden, Frances (X) Pruden, Elijah (X) Smith

Questions

1. In what ways does the contract limit the freedom of the laborers?

2. What kinds of benefits and risks for the freedpeople are associated with a sharecropping arrangement?

---

100. Elizabeth Cady Stanton, "Home Life" (ca. 1875)

Source: "Home Life," manuscript, ca. 1875, Elizabeth Cady Stanton Papers, Library of Congress.

Women activists saw Reconstruction as the moment for women to claim their own emancipation. With blacks guaranteed equality before the law by the Fourteenth Amendment and black men given the right to vote by the Fifteenth, women demanded that the boundaries of American democracy be expanded to include them as well. Other feminists debated how to achieve "liberty for married women." In 1875, Elizabeth Cady Stanton drafted an essay that demanded that the idea of equality, which had "revolutionized" American politics, be extended into private life. Genuine liberty for women, she insisted, required an overhaul of divorce laws (which generally required evidence of adultery, desertion, or extreme abuse to terminate a marriage) and an end to the authority men exercised over their wives.

Women's demand for the right to vote found few sympathetic male listeners. Even fewer supported liberalized divorce laws. But Stanton's extension of the idea of "liberty for women" into the most intimate areas of private life identified a question that would become a central concern of later generations of feminists.

WE ARE IN the midst of a social revolution, greater than any political or religious revolution, that the world has ever seen, because it goes deep down to the very foundations of society.... A question of magnitude presses on our consideration, whether man and woman are equal, joint heirs to all the richness and joy of earth and Heaven, or whether they were eternally ordained, one to be sovereign, the other slave.... Here is a question with half the human family, and that the stronger half, on one side, who are in possession of the citadel, hold the key to the treasury and make the laws and public sentiment to suit their own purposes. Can all this be made to change base without prolonged discussion, upheavings, heartburnings, violence and war? Will man yield what he considers to be his legitimate authority over woman with less struggle than have Popes and Kings their supposed rights over their subjects, or slaveholders over their slaves? No, no. John Stuart Mill says the generality of the male sex cannot yet tolerate the idea of living with an equal at the fireside; and here is the secret of the opposition to woman's equality in the state and the church—men are not ready to recognize it in the home. This is the real danger apprehended in giving woman the ballot, for as long as man makes, interprets, and executes the laws for himself, he holds the power under any system. Hence when he expresses the fear that liberty for woman would upset the family relation, he acknowledges that her present condition of subjection is not of her own choosing, and that if she had the power the whole relation would be essentially changed. And this is just what is coming to pass, the kernel of the struggle we witness to day.

This is woman's transition period from slavery to freedom and all these social upheavings, before which the wisest and bravest stand appalled, are but necessary incidents in her progress to equality. Conservatism cries out we are going to destroy the family. Timid reformers answer, the political equality of woman will not change it. They are both wrong. It will entirely revolutionize it. When woman is man's equal the marriage relation cannot stand on the basis it is to day. But this change will not destroy it; as state constitutions and statute laws did not create conjugal and maternal love, they cannot annual them. . . . We shall have the family, that great conservator of national strength and morals, after the present idea of man's headship is repudiated and woman set free. To establish a republican form of government [and] the right of individual judgment in the family must of necessity involve discussion, dissension, division, but the purer, higher, holier marriage will be evolved by the very evils we now see and deplore. This same law of equality that has revolutionized the state and the church is now knocking at the door of our homes and sooner or later there too it must do its work. Let us one and all wisely bring ourselves into line with this great law for man will gain as much as woman by an equal companionship in the nearest and holiest relations of life. . . . So long as people marry from considerations of policy, from every possible motive but the true one, discord and division must be the result. So long as the State provides no education for youth on the questions and throws no safeguards around the formation of marriage ties, it is in honor bound to open wide the door of escape. From a woman's standpoint, I see that marriage as an indissoluble tie is slavery for woman, because law, religion and public sentiment all combine under this idea to hold her true to this relation, whatever it may be and there is no other human slavery that knows such depths of degradations as a wife chained to a man whom she neither loves nor respects, no other slavery so disastrous in its consequences on the race, or to individual respect, growth and development....

• • •

By the laws of several states in this republic made by Christian representatives of the people divorces are granted to day for... seventeen reasons.... By this kind of legislation in the several states we have practically decided two important points: 1st That marriage is a dissoluble tie that may be sundered by a decree of the courts. 2nd That it is a civil contract and not a sacrament of the church, and the one involves the other....

A legal contract for a section of land requires that the parties be of age, of sound mind, [and] that there be no flaw in the title.... But a legal marriage in many states in the Union may be contracted between a boy of fourteen and a girl of twelve without the consent of parents or guardians, without publication of banns.... Now what person of common sense, or conscience, can endorse laws as wise or prudent that sanction acts such as these. Let the state be logical: if marriage is a civil contract, it should be subject to the laws of all other contracts, carefully made, the parties of age, and all agreements faithfully observed....

Let us now glance at a few of the popular objections to liberal divorce laws. It is said that to make divorce respectable by law, gospel and public sentiment is to break up all family relations. Which is to say that human affections are the result and not the foundation of the canons of the church and statutes of the state.... To open the doors of escape to those who dwell in continual antagonism, to the unhappy wives of drunkards, libertines, knaves, lunatics and tyrants, need not necessarily embitter the relations of those who *are* contented and happy, but on the contrary the very fact of freedom strengthens and purifies the bond of union. When husbands and wives do not own each other as property, but are bound together only by affection, marriage will be a life long friendship and not a heavy yoke, from which both may sometimes long for deliverance. The freer the relations are between human beings, the happier....

• • •

Home life to the best of us has its shadows and sorrows, and because of our ignorance this must needs be.... The day is breaking. It is something to know that life's ills are not showered upon us by the Good Father from a kind of Pandora's box, but are the results of causes that we have the power to control. By a knowledge and observance of law the road to health and happiness opens before [us]: a joy and peace that passeth all understanding shall yet be ours and Paradise regained on earth. When marriage results from a true union of intellect and spirit and when Mothers and Fathers give to their holy offices even that preparation of soul and body that the artist gives to the conception of his poem, statue or landscape, then will marriage, maternity and paternity acquire a new sacredness and dignity and a nobler type of manhood and womanhood will glorify the race!!

Questions

1. How does Stanton define the "social revolution" the United States underwent after the Civil War?

2. How does Stanton believe that individual freedom within the family can be established?

---

101. Frederick Douglass, "The Composite Nation" (1869)

Source: Philip S. Foner and Daniel Rosenberg, eds., Racism, Dissent, and Asian Americans from 1850 to the Present *(Westport, Conn., 1993), pp. 217–30.*

Another group that did not share fully in the expansion of rights inspired by the Civil War and Reconstruction was Asian-Americans. Prejudices against Asians were deeply entrenched, especially on the West Coast, where most immigrants from Asia lived. When the radical Republican Charles Sumner, senator from Massachusetts, moved to allow Asians to become naturalized citizens (a right that had been barred to them since 1790), senators from California and Oregon objected vociferously, and the proposal was defeated.

Another advocate of equal rights for Asian-Americans was Frederick Douglass. In his remarkable "Composite Nation" speech, delivered in Boston in 1869, Douglass condemned anti-Asian discrimination and called for giving them all the rights of other Americans, including the right to vote. Douglass's comprehensive vision of a country made up of people of all races and national origins and enjoying equal rights was too radical for the time, but it would win greater and greater acceptance during the twentieth century.

———

THERE WAS A time when even brave men might look fearfully at the destiny of the Republic. When our country was involved in a tangled network of contradictions; when vast and irreconcilable social forces fiercely disputed for ascendancy and control; when a heavy curse rested upon our very soil, defying alike the wisdom and the virtue of the people to remove it; when our professions were loudly mocked by our practice and our name was a reproach and a by word to a mocking earth; when our good ship of state, freighted with the best hopes of the oppressed of all nations, was furiously hurled against the hard and flinty rocks of derision, and every cord, bolt, beam and bend in her body quivered beneath the shock, there was some apology for doubt and despair. But that day has happily passed away. The storm has been weathered, and the portents are nearly all in our favor.

There are clouds, wind, smoke and dust and noise, over head and around, and there will always be; but no genuine thunder, with destructive bolt, menaces from any quarter of the sky.

The real trouble with us was never our system or form of Government, or the principles under lying it; but the peculiar composition of our people; the relations existing between them and the compromising spirit which controlled the ruling power of the country.

We have for a long time hesitated to adopt and may yet refuse to adopt, and carry out, the only principle which can solve that difficulty and give peace, strength and security to the Republic, *and that is* the principle of absolute *equality*.

We are a country of all extremes, ends and opposites; the most conspicuous example of composite nationality in the world. Our people defy all the ethnological and logical classifications. In races we range all the way from black to white, with intermediate shades which, as in the apocalyptic vision, no man can name a number.

In regard to creeds and faiths, the condition is no better, and no worse. Differences both as to race and to religion are evidently more likely to increase than to diminish.

We stand between the populous shores of two great oceans. Our land is capable of supporting one fifth of all the globe. Here labor is abundant and here labor is better remunerated than any where else. All moral, social and geographical causes, conspire to bring to us the peoples of all other over populated countries.

Europe and Africa are already here, and the Indian was here before either. He stands to-day between the two extremes of black and white, too proud to claim fraternity with either, and yet too weak to with stand the power of either. Heretofore the policy of our government has been governed by race pride, rather than by wisdom. Until recently, neither the Indian nor the negro has been treated as a part of the body politic. No attempt has been made to inspire either with a sentiment of patriotism, but the hearts of both races have been diligently sown with the dangerous seeds of discontent and hatred.

The policy of keeping the Indians to themselves, has kept the tomahawk and scalping knife busy upon our borders, and has cost us largely in blood and treasure. Our treatment of the negro has slacked humanity, and filled the country with agitation and ill-feeling and brought the nation to the verge of ruin.

Before the relations of these two races are satisfactorily settled, and in spite of all opposition, a new race is making its appearance within our borders, and claiming attention. It is estimated that not less than one-hundred thousand Chinamen are now within the limits of the United States. Several years ago every vessel, large or small, of steam or sail, bound to our Pacific coast and hailing from the Flowery kingdom, added to the number and strength of this element of our population.

Men differ widely as to the magnitude of this potential Chinese immigration. The fact that by the late treaty with China, we bind ourselves to receive immigrants from that country only as the subjects of the Emperor, and by the construction, at least, are bound not to naturalize them, and the further fact that Chinamen themselves have a superstitious devotion to their country and an aversion to permanent location in any other, contracting even to have their bones carried back should they die abroad, and from the fact that many have returned to China, and the still more stubborn that resistance to their coming has increased rather than diminished, it is inferred that we shall never have a large Chinese population in America. This however is not my opinion.

It may be admitted that these reasons, and others, may check and moderate the tide of immigration; but it is absurd to think that they will do more than this. Counting their number now, by the thousands, the time is not remote when they will count them by the millions. The Emperor's hold upon the Chinaman may be strong, but the Chinaman's hold upon himself is stronger.

Treaties against naturalization, like all other treaties, are limited by circumstances. As to the superstitious attachment of the Chinese to China, that, like all other superstitions, will dissolve in the light and heat of truth and experience. The Chinaman may be a bigot, but it does not follow that he will continue to be one, tomorrow. He is a man, and will be very likely to act like a man. He will not be long in finding out that a country which is good enough to live in, is good enough to die in; and that a soil that was good enough to hold his body while alive, will be good enough to hold his bones when he is dead.

Those who doubt a large immigration, should remember that the past furnishes no criterion as a basis of calculation. We live under new and improved conditions of migration, and these conditions are constantly improving. America is no longer an obscure and inaccessible country. Our ships are in every sea, our commerce in every port, our language is heard all around the globe, steam and lightning have revolutionized the whole domain of human thought, changed all geographical relations, make a day of the present seem equal to a thousand years of the past, and the continent that Columbus only conjectured four centuries ago is now the center of the world.

• • •

I have said that the Chinese will come, and have given some reasons why we may expect them in very large numbers in no very distant future. Do you ask, if I favor such immigration, I answer *I would*. Would you have them naturalized, and have them invested with all the rights of American citizenship? *I would*. Would you allow them to vote? *I would*. Would you allow them to hold office? *I would*.

But are there not reasons against all this? Is there not such a law or principle as that of self preservation? Does not every race owe something to itself? Should it not attend to the dictates of common sense? Should not a superior race protect itself from contact with inferior ones? Are not the white people the owners of this continent? Have they not the right to say what kind of people shall be allowed to come here and settle? Is there not such a thing as being more generous than wise? In the effort to promote civilization may we not corrupt and destroy what we have? Is it best to take on board more passengers than the ship will carry?

To all this and more I have one among many answers, altogether satisfactory to me, though I cannot promise that it will be so to you.

I submit that this question of Chinese immigration should be settled upon higher principles than those of a cold and selfish expediency. There are such things in the world as human rights. They rest upon no conventional foundation, but are external, universal, and indestructible. Among these, is the right of locomotion; the right of migration; the right which belongs to no particular race, but belongs alike to all and to all alike. It is the right you assert by staying here, and your fathers asserted by coming here. It is this great right that I assert for the Chinese and the Japanese, and for all other varieties of men equally with yourselves, now and forever. I know of no rights of race superior to the rights of humanity, and when there is a supposed conflict between human and national rights, it is safe to go to the side of humanity. I have great respect for the blue eyes and light haired races of America. They are a mighty people. In any struggle for the good things of this world they need have no fear. They have no need to doubt that they will get their full share.

But I reject the arrogant and scornful theory by which they would limit migratory rights, or any other essential human rights to themselves, and which would make them the owners of this great continent to the exclusion of all other races of men.

I want a home here not only for the negro, the mulatto and the Latin races; but I want the Asiatic to find a home here in the United States, and feel at home here, both for his sake and for ours. Right wrongs no man. If respect is had to majorities, the fact that only one fifth of the population of the globe is white, the other four fifths are colored, ought to have some weight and influence in disposing of this and similar questions. It would be a sad reflection upon the laws of nature and upon the idea of justice, to say nothing of a common Creator, if four-fifths of mankind were deprived of the rights of migration to make room for the one fifth. If the white race may exclude all other races from this continent, it may rightfully do the same in respect to all other lands, islands, capes and continents, and thus have all the world to itself. Thus what would seem to belong to the whole, would become the property only of a part. So much for what is right, now let us see what is wise.

And here I hold that a liberal and brotherly welcome to all who are likely to come to the United States is the only wise policy which this nation can adopt.

• • •

I close these remarks as I began. If our action shall be in accordance with the principles of justice, liberty, and perfect human equality, no eloquence can adequately portray the greatness and grandeur of the future of the Republic.

We shall spread the network of our science and civilization over all who seek their shelter whether from Asia, Africa, or the Isles of the sea. We shall mold them all, each after his kind, into Americans; Indian and Celt, negro and Saxon, Latin and Teuton, Mongolian and Caucasian, Jew and Gentile, all shall here bow to the same law, speak the same language, support the same government, enjoy the same liberty, vibrate with the same national enthusiasm, and seek the same national ends.

Questions

1. What does Douglass mean by the term "composite nationality"?

2. Why does he believe that people should be allowed to move freely from one country to another?

---

102. Robert B. Elliott on Civil Rights (1874)

Source: Civil Rights. Speech of Hon. Robert B. Elliott, of South Carolina, in the House of Representatives, January 6, 1874 *(Washington, D.C., 1874), pp. 1–8.*

One of the South's most prominent black politicians during Reconstruction, Robert B. Elliott appears to have been born in England and arrived in Boston shortly before the Civil War. He came to South Carolina in 1867, where he established a law office and was elected as a delegate to the state's constitutional convention of 1868. During the 1870s, he served in the legislature and was twice elected to the U.S. House of Representatives.

In January 1874, Elliott delivered a celebrated speech in Congress in support of the bill that became the Civil Rights Act of 1875. The measure outlawed racial discrimination in transportation and places of public accommodation like theaters and hotels. Thanks to the Civil War and Reconstruction, Elliott proclaimed, "equality before the law" regardless of race had been written into the laws and Constitution and had become an essential element of American freedom. Reconstruction, he announced, had "settled forever the political status of my race."

Elliott proved to be wrong. By the turn of the century, many of the rights blacks had gained after the Civil War had been taken away. It would be left to future generations to breathe new life into Elliott's dream of "equal, impartial, and universal liberty."

———————

SIR, IT IS scarcely twelve years since that gentleman [Alexander H. Stephens] shocked the civilized world by announcing the birth of a government which rested on human slavery as its corner-stone. The progress of events has swept away that *pseudo*-government which rested on greed, pride, and tyranny; and the race whom he then ruthlessly spurned and trampled on are here to meet him in debate, and to demand that the rights which are enjoyed by their former oppressors—who vainly sought to overthrow a Government which they could not prostitute to the base uses of slavery—shall be accorded to those who even in the darkness of slavery kept their allegiance true to freedom and the Union: Sir, the gentleman from Georgia has learned much since 1861; but he is still a laggard. Let him put away entirely the false and fatal theories which have so greatly marred an otherwise enviable record. Let him accept, in its fullness and beneficence, the great doctrine that American citizenship carries with it every civil and political right which manhood can confer. Let him lend his influence, with all his masterly ability, to complete the proud structure of legislation which makes this nation worthy of the great declaration which heralded its birth, and he will have done that which will most nearly redeem his reputation in the eyes of the world, and best vindicate the wisdom of that policy which has permitted him to regain his seat upon this floor. . . .

• • •

Sir, equality before the law is now the broad, universal, glorious rule and mandate of the Republic. No State can violate that. Kentucky and Georgia may crowd their statute-books with retrograde and barbarous legislation; they may rejoice in the odious eminence of their consistent hostility to all the great steps of human progress which have marked our national history since slavery tore down the stars and stripes on Fort Sumter; but, if Congress shall do its duty, if Congress shall enforce the great guarantees which the Supreme Court has declared to be the one pervading purpose of all the recent amendments, then their unwise and unenlightened conduct will fall with the same weight upon the gentlemen from those States who now lend their influence to defeat this bill, as upon the poorest slave who once had no rights which the honorable gentlemen were bound to respect. . . .

No language could convey a more complete assertion of the power of Congress over the subject embraced in the present bill than is expressed [in the Fourteenth Amendment]. If the States do not conform to the requirements of this clause, if they continue to deny to any person within their jurisdiction the equal protection of the laws, or as the Supreme Court had said, "deny equal justice in its courts," then Congress is here said to have power to enforce the constitutional guarantee by appropriate legislation. That is the power which this bill now seeks to put in exercise. It proposes to enforce the constitutional guarantee against inequality and discrimination by appropriate legislation. It does not seek to confer new rights, nor to place rights conferred by State citizenship under the protection of the United States, but simply to prevent and forbid inequality and discrimination on account of race, color, or previous condition of servitude. Never was there a bill more completely within the constitutional power of Congress. Never was there a bill which appealed for support more strongly to that sense of justice and fair-play which has been said, and in the main with justice, to be a characteristic of the Anglo-Saxon race. The Constitution warrants it; the Supreme Court sanctions it; justice demands it.

Sir, I have replied to the extent of my ability to the arguments which have been presented by the opponents of this measure. I have replied also to some of the legal propositions advanced by gentlemen on the other side; and now that I am about to conclude, I am deeply sensible of the imperfect manner in which I have performed the task. Technically, this bill is to decide upon the civil status of the colored American citizen; a point disputed at the very formation of our present Government, when by a short-sighted policy, a policy repugnant to true republican government, one negro counted as three-fifths of a man. The logical result of this mistake of the framers of the Constitution strengthened the cancer of slavery, which finally spread its poisonous tentacles over the southern portion of the body-politic. To arrest its growth and save the nation we have passed through the harrowing operation of intestine war, dreaded at all times, resorted to at the last extremity, like the surgeon's knife, but absolutely necessary to extirpate the disease which threatened with the life of the nation the overthrow of civil and political liberty on this continent. In that dire extremity the members of the race which I have the honor in part to represent—the race which pleads for justice at your hands to-day, forgetful of their inhuman and brutalizing servitude at the South, their degradation and ostracism at the North—flew willingly and gallantly to the support of the national Government. Their sufferings, assistance, privations, and trials in the swamps and in the rice-fields, their valor on the land and on the sea, is a part of the ever-glorious record which makes up the history of a nation preserved, and might, should I urge the claim, incline you to respect and guarantee their rights and privileges as citizens of our common Republic. But I remember that valor, devotion, and loyalty are not always rewarded according to their just deserts, and that after the battle some who have borne the brunt of the fray may, through neglect or contempt, be assigned to a subordinate place, while the enemies in war may be preferred to the sufferers.

The results of the war, as seen in reconstruction, have settled forever the political status of my race. The passage of this bill will determine the civil status, not only of the negro, but of any other class of citizens who may feel themselves discriminated against. It will form the cap-stone of that temple of liberty, begun on this continent under discouraging circumstances, carried on in spite of the sneers of monarchists and the cavils of pretended friends of freedom, until at last it stands in all its beautiful symmetry and proportions, a building the grandest which the world has ever seen, realizing the most sanguine expectations and the highest hopes of those who, in the name of equal, impartial, and universal liberty, laid the foundation stones.

Questions

1. How does Elliott defend the constitutionality of the Civil Rights Bill?

2. Why does Elliott refer to the "cornerstone speech" of Alexander H. Stephens in making his argument?